History of the Zionist Movement and the Impact Upon Jewish Church Relations Today

Dr. Mark A. Anderson

Faithful Life Publishers
North Fort Myers, FL
FaithfulLifePublishers.com

The History of the Zionist Movement and the Impact Upon Jewish Church Relations Today

Copyright © 2014   Mark Alan Anderson

ISBN: 978-1-63073-037-6

Published and printed by:
Faithful Life Publishers • North Fort Myers, FL 33903
888.720.0950 • info@FaithfulLifePublishers.com
www.FaithfulLifePublishers.com

All Rights Reserved. Trinity Theological Seminary has permission to reproduce and disseminate this document in any form by any means for purposes chosen by the Seminary, including, without limitation, preservation and instruction.

Printed in the United States of America

18 17 16 15 14   1 2 3 4 5

TRINITY COLLEGE OF THE BIBLE
THEOLOGICAL SEMINARY

THE HISTORY OF THE ZIONIST MOVEMENT
AND THE
IMPACT UPON JEWISH CHURCH RELATIONS TODAY

A DISSERTATION SUBMITTED TO
THE FACULTY OF THE DIVISION OF
PHILOSOPHY & APOLOGETICS

IN CANDIDACY FOR THE DEGREE OF
DOCTOR OF PHILOSOPHY & APOLOGETICS

DEPARTMENT OF PHILOSOPHY & THEOLOGY

BY
DR. MARK A. ANDERSON

OTTUMWA, IOWA
FEBRUARY 2014

ABSTRACT

THE HISTORY OF THE ZIONIST MOVEMENT AND THE IMPACT UPON JEWISH CHURCH RELATIONS TODAY

Mark Alan Anderson, PHD

Trinity College of the Bible Theological Seminary

Chair: Dr. Ronald T. Clutter, Dr. Dennis McDonald

Keywords: (Zionist, Zionism, Israel, Palestine, Jew, Middle East, Conflict, Christian)

The purpose of this study is to explore the history of the Zionist movement and its impact upon Jewish Church relationships today. The conflicts between the Jews and the Christian Church have existed from the first century. This conflict reflected a competing religious perspective on the nature and work of God in the world. This relationship has changed over the past three centuries through the growth and development of the Zionist movement formally called Restorationism, culminating with the establishment of the Israeli State in Palestine.

The historical method will be used to examine how the Jewish Church conflict began. The Zionist movement arose beginning from the Puritans through the Enlightenment up to the Holocaust. Different forms of Zionism will be examined along with how the Christian community contributed to the successful beginnings of the Jewish state. A biblical context will be referenced to determine if the success of Zionism is supported by Old Testament warnings.

The significance of the book will be determined by whether Jewish Church conflicts are better understood in light of our understanding of Zionism. In conclusion, various Christian traditions will be compared to determine their impact on Jewish Church relationships overall. It is hopeful that this book would also clarify our understanding of the events in the Middle East.

Mark Anderson

ACKNOWLEDGEMENTS

Dr. Leona Mae Anderson (Honorary PhD of Education)
My Mother and foremost Prayer Warrior, and grammar Editor

Mrs. Zelda Mae Anderson RN MPH
My wife, encourager, prayer partner and Editor

Dr. Ronald T. Clutter
Supervisory Professor

Mrs. Pat Essick
Ottumwa, Iowa Public Library: Reference Librarian & Staff

Dr. Harold F. Hunter
President of Trinity College of the Bible &Theological Seminary
and secretarial, administrative, and financial staff

Mr. Brett Patton
Examination Proctor

Dr. Craig Payne
Dissertation Editor

Mr. Steve Williams
Seminary Dissertation Advisor

Dr. Dennis McDonald
Supervisory Professor

A special thanks also goes out to my children Michael and Jin Hee Anderson, and all my family who prayed and encouraged me on this journey; Sandra & Marcia Anderson, Connie & Merrill McClatchey, Andrea & Craig Cline, Richard & Shirley Merrihew, Sara & Zbig Piekielny, Anna Murphy and Phillip Norton and many friends from Ottumwa Iowa, as well as friends from around the world.

REVIEWS

Dr. Anderson's work traces the struggle Jews have had over the centuries to establish a home land, as well as shedding light on the Palestine issues. Most importantly, it shows the different ways Christians and Jews have interrelated over time. I found this a very interesting and fascinating read. From a layman's view, this book gives me a much better understanding of the many complexities surrounding the Middle East.

> Dr. Ted Haas,
> Medical Doctor at Ottumwa Regional Health Center,
> Ottumwa Iowa, for Women's Health

Dr. Anderson addresses the origin and nature of Zionism as it has been considered through the centuries. It explores the history and components of Zionism as various cultural and national groups have been impacted by it. This work is a sound treatise on the subject which can be a benefit to laypersons and scholars as a sound research source concerning the pro and con of Zionism in the world. Dr. Anderson has done a tremendous job on the subject.

> Dr. Dennis McDonald B.B.A., Th.M., Ph.D.,
> Dallas Theological Seminary

CONTENTS

Abstract iv

Acknowledgements v

Reviews vi

Terminology xi

CHAPTER ONE
INTRODUCTION 1-32
    Purpose 1
    Statement by the Author 4
    What is Zionism? Who is a Jew? 5
    Biblical Mandate for Zionism 8
    Source of Jewish Christian Conflict 12
    A Christian Perspective 20
    The Restoration of the Jews in Holland and the Reformed Church ... 21
    Puritanism and Zionism 23
    Cabalist Judaism and the Connection to Zionism 25
    Moses Mendelssohn: Father of Modern Jewish Enlightenment 29

CHAPTER TWO
MODERN BEGINNINGS OF THE ZIONIST MOVEMENT
AND ITS CAUSES 33-75
    Introduction 33
    French Revolution 35
    Assimilation of Jews into Christian Europe 39
    Assimilation and the Development of Reformed Judaism 43
    Restorationists Try Again 49
    Years of Favor for Zionist Activities: The First Aliyah 52
    Social and Nationalistic Zionism 55
    Eastern Europe and the Pogroms 61
    Christian Zionism Before Herzl 67
    Condition of Jewish-Christian Relationships
        at the End of the Nineteenth Century 73

CHAPTER THREE
FROM HERZL TO INDEPENDENCE:
THE GROWTH OF THE ZIONIST MOVEMENT 76-123
- Early Root of Modern Zionism 76
- Theodor Herzl 78
- William Henry Hechler 81
- Uganda Plan 84
- World War I 85
- Wiseman and Balfour 88
- British Commitments 91
- Arab Jewish Conflict 92
- Churchill White Papers 93
- Revisionist Zionism and Haganah (Jewish Military) 94
- Spiritual Zionism 1930 97
- Passfield White Papers 97
- Jewish Entrepreneurship 98
- The MacDonald White Papers of 1939 99
- Christian Zionists Influence and Jewish Military 100
- Arab Leadership Supports the Nazis 104
- Jewish Terrorism 105
- End of the British Mandate 106
- The Holocaust and the German Church 109
- The Liberal Church 110
- Confessing Church 112
- Christian Support During World War II 113
- Biltmore Conference 114
- Immigration Policies of the West 115
- Truman and the UN Mandate 116
- UN Mandate 119
- Battle for Independence 120
- Independence 122

CHAPTER FOUR
JEWISH-CHRISTIAN RELATIONS TODAY.................................. 124-161
- Reflection 124
- A Christian Defense 125
- Gaining and Maintaining the Jewish State 126
- The Arab Refugee Problem and Zionism 128
- Jewish Immigration 133
- Early Jewish Leadership 134
- Jewish Injustices 136
- Survival 137
- Jewish Renewal 138
- Six-Day War and Yom Kippur 139
- The Palestine Liberation Organization (PLO) 140
- Failed Treaties - Camp David Accords 141
- The Oslo Accords 142
- Palestinian Christians..143
- Review of Spiritual, Political/Practical, and Revisionist Zionism 144
- Zionism Today 145
- Secular Zionism 146
- Spiritual Zionism 147
- Zionism in Israel Today 150
- Jewish-Christian Relations and Theology - Jewish Christian Thawing 151
- Messianic Judaism and the Rise of the Messianic Church 155
- Jewish-Christian Relations Today 157
- Mount Zion and the Land 161

CHAPTER FIVE
THE EFFECTS OF ZIONISM 162-199
- Predictions Come True 162
- Israel and Modern Zionism 162
- Secular Israel 165
- Zionism and the Arab-Jewish Problem 166
- Spiritual Renewal 169

Mainline Protestant Christianity and Israel 170
Catholic Christianity and Israel 171
Evangelical Christianity and Israel..172
Orthodox Versus Secular 174
Messianic Judaism 175
A Revised Biblical Perspective..179
Jewish Ethnicity...183
Preservation of the Jews 186
A Revised Biblical Perspective: Old Testament Tanakh Perspective 187
Issues Today Between Jews and Christians 191
Jewish Success 193
Jewish Successes and Intolerance...194
Jewish-Christian Relationships Today...195
Jewish-Christian Relationships and Zionism...198

CONCLUSION...200

BIBLIOGRAPHY...211

SOURCES CONSULTED 220

ABOUT THE AUTHOR..225

TERMINOLOGY:

Aliyah: Immigration of Jews into Palestine.

Al-Nakba: Arabic for 'the catastrophe' in reference to the Jews reclaiming the land of Palestine as the new State of Israel (1948).

Diaspora: The dispersion of the Jews from Israel to the nations.

Judaism: Form of Jewish worship surrounding the Torah and the keeping of the commandments, Jewish sacrifices and in celebrating the Jewish Festivals. In later years it involved the keeping of the Talmudic laws.

Marranos: Jews converted to Catholicism during the Spanish Inquisition during the 15th and 16th centuries.

Messianic: Jews who have accepted Jesus as the Messiah (Jewish Christians)

Mischling: A German term referring to someone who is part Jewish, used during the Nazi control of Germany to seek out and destroy anyone with Jewish ancestry.

Pale: An enclosing or confining barrier. This term is used in reference to whole Jewish communities being confined to a region within Russia much like Native American Indians were restricted to reservations.

Pogroms: Referring to the persecution and displacement of Jews in Russian and Eastern Europe during the late 1800's and early 1900's.

Torah: The first 5 books of the Bible; the Old Testament Pentateuch.

Tanakh: The cannon of the Jewish Bible including the prophets and writings (The Old Testament)

Ukase: A Russian word for legal ruling or order from the Tsar.

White Papers: Document presented by the British prior to World War II restricting Jewish immigration to Palestine.

Yeshua: Jewish name for Messiah Jesus (Hebrew).

Yishuv: Jewish settlements before the Jewish state of Israel.

Zionism:

    a. Jews simply returning to the land of Palestine

    b. Jews returning to Israel an autonomous Jewish state.

    c. Zionist is a person who advocates the reunification of Jews to the land of Palestine as a Jewish state

CHAPTER ONE

INTRODUCTION

Purpose

The purpose of this book is to examine Zionism and the strong connection between the nation of Israel and Jewish-Church relationships. The Jewish synagogue and the Christian Church have had a competing ideology causing conflict for over 2,000 years. Zionism cannot be clearly understood or defined without first examining the root causes of the Jewish-Christian Church conflict. Throughout history, most faith-based ideologies showed very little tolerance for competing faiths; for example, India split along faith-based differences of Hinduism and Islam, creating Pakistan. Pakistan gained its independence August 14, 1947, as a result of conflicts between Hindus and Muslims. Another example is Northern Ireland, which was awash with the same bloody conflict throughout the United Kingdom between Catholics and Protestants for centuries. They competed over what each considered truth along religious or faith based-ideas. The Christian Church and the Jews have fared no better with a much longer competing history.

What makes the Jewish-Christian conflict unique is that in many respects they agree on the bare essentials of what each considers truth; that truth revolves around a people and a promise or prediction made nearly 4,000 years ago through the patriarch Abraham. Both faiths consider Abraham a true historic figure along with the promises made to him and his posterity, the Jews. One of those promises was that the Jews or the posterity of Abraham would inherit a land including current-day Palestine along with parts of Egypt, Jordan, and the major part of Iraq. " . . . lift up your eyes and look out from the place where you are, northward and southward and eastward and westward; for all the land which you see, I will give it to you and to your descendants forever."[1]

---

1 (Genesis 13:14-15 [New American Standard Bible, 1995]).

The culmination of the Jewish state in 1948 raises the expectation of a hope that embraces both Orthodox Jews and many Christians into a common bond, a Messianic return. Though the Messianic hope is rejected by the great majority of Jews and Gentiles alike, it does raise expectations of an eschatological future, perhaps more so for Christians than Jews. The return of the Jewish state brings front and center some rationale to the predictive abilities of the biblical accounts. The state of Israel has become a lightning rod of conflict among many nations as the Jews seek security amidst the conflict.

The promise given to Abraham and his seed in Genesis and the Torah appears to be an eternal promise to the land of Palestine; "I will give to you and to your descendants after you, the land of your sojournings, all the land of Canaan, for an everlasting possession; and I will be their God."[2] This land is now the state of Israel. The promise carries more than just possession of the land; it also carries some severe warnings that if the Jews fail to keep their promises, they (Jews) will be scattered across the globe. " The Lord will scatter you among the peoples, . . ."[3] This is in fact the case, as we now see Jewish communities in every country on Earth. The promises and warnings are not limited to the Pentateuch, but to several books found in the Old Testament (Jewish Tanakh), as well as in the New Testament.[4] We are told that the Jews will be gathered back to their land of promise for a renewal of the state of Israel; good news for the Jews, but bad news for the Palestinians living in the land. In fact most of the tensions in the world, such as terrorism and the oil crisis, stem from this Arab-Israeli conflict. The connection between the Jewish persecution over the centuries and the rise of the Zionist movement can be understood more clearly from the perspective of the Jewish-Christian conflict.

The Jewish people constitute one of the most perplexing people groups in the world. They are the recipients of a promise that affects

2 (Genesis 17:8)
3 (Deuteronomy 4:27)
4 Some references include the following: (Genesis 12:7; Deuteronomy 30:3-5; Isaiah 11:12; Jeremiah 23:3; 29:14; Ezekiel 20:42)

Introduction

not only themselves but every nation and people on the face of the earth. Several facts are evident concerning the survival of the Jewish people:[5] They have been driven from their land and their homes countless times throughout history, yet they have been able to maintain their identity and purpose. Through the aftermath of World War II, the world witnessed the reincarnation of the Jewish state of Israel. The Jews are here today, they are back in their promised land (Palestine), possessing their language, their culture, and their religion. By fulfilling their ancestral dream of reclaiming the Land of Palestine for a Jewish state,[6] they returned to their place among the nations as a distinct nation after 2,500 years.[7] With that dream came many conflicts in the Middle East that remain the focus of headlines in our papers today.

One primary assumption accompanies this book, one which most Jews and Christians would agree to: The first five books of the Bible are a revelation from God (Yahweh). The books were most likely a compilation of oral and written form prior to Moses in that Genesis states: "This is the book of the generations of Adam."[8] The Bible appears to suggest that Moses is the author of the final 4 books of the Pentateuch,[9] with the addition of the final days of Moses inserted at the end of Deuteronomy. "This section is obviously post-Mosaic, and was probably the work of either Eleazar or Joshua himself."[10] The entire Old Testament known as the Jewish Tanakh is accepted by many Jews and Christians as being a revelation of God. Many within the rabbinic

---

5 The ethnicity of the Jewish race will be discussed in brief later.
6 (Deuteronomy 30:15) The conditions of obedience and faithfulness seem to precede the promise of the land. Some of those conditions have not been fulfilled and could be used to explain the continued conflicts. These issues will be discussed in Chapter 4.
7 This does not take into account a brief 130 years period of the Hasmonean Kingdom between 167-37 BC.
8 (Genesis 5:1)
9 (Deuteronomy 31:24) The Documentary Hypotheses and other such theories will not be discussed in this book.
10 The New Bible Commentary: Revised Edition by D. Guthrie, J.Motyer, A.M. Stibbs, D.J. Wiseman, 229.

tradition will hold primarily to the Torah, rejecting the histories and prophets of the Old Testament. The commitment to the Torah and its oral traditions, as documented in the Jewish Talmud, are one of the greatest dividing points between Jews and Christians today,[11] yet their foundations are the same.[12] Jews and Christians alike generally hold to the authority of the Pentateuch and the predictions that accompany those texts.

Statement by the Author

The initial objective concerning this book was to demonstrate that Zionism and its contribution to the return of the Jews to the land of Palestine, along with the reemergence of Jewish nationhood in Israel, would bring about a thawing in Jewish-Christian relationships. The research suggests this did not happen. Though in some corners of society, where the Christian community interacts with supporters of Israel and where both sides hold to a Zionist philosophy, better communication and cooperation have occurred. These groups have indeed drawn closer at least in the area of dialogue. However, my primary hypothesis that Zionism has opened the door to closer Jewish-Christian relations on a larger scale has failed to materialize. It will be my objective to communicate how and where this relationship has been affected that the reader may better understand what barriers still exist, why they remain, what can be done to close the gaps between two very similar faiths (Judaism and Christianity), and what role Zionism plays in the ongoing conflict between Jews and Christians.

---

11 According to Rabbi Ted Falcon, the Talmud is the combination of the Mishnah, the codification of the Torah, and the commentaries called the Gemara. In Matthew 22:40 Jesus states that the commandments rest on " . . . the whole Law and the Prophets."

12 Both Jews and Christians believe the Pentateuch or the Torah to be written by Moses which holds the basis of each faith system along with the promises concerning the descendants of Abraham and the Land of Palestine.

Introduction

What is Zionism? Who is a Jew?

Before we identify Zionism, it is critical to understand what distinguishes a Jew. What is it to be a Jew, Jewish, or to practice Judaism? "These terms refer initially to people who have been born of Hebrew (Abraham, descendants) ethnicity or who have, by a religious act been admitted to the same status as those who have been born of such parents."[13] Ethnicity is only one factor in designating who is Jewish. Those who would argue that Jews do not exist today or have assimilated into the population carry only a degree of truth. The fact remains there are many ethnic Jews, but ethnicity is only one factor. The other constitutes a religious commitment to the principles of Judaism which is derived from the first five books of the Old Testament Bible (The Torah). In this case, those who practice Judaism are Jewish: "The designations are inclusive of religious and non-religious, observant and non-observant, believing and non-believing. They include the whole spectrum of Jewish religious expression, in its broadest definition, fundamentalist and non-fundamentalist. They include the particular elitist dimensions: Ultra-Orthodoxy, Orthodoxy, conservatism er constructionism, and Reform [sic]."[14] From this perspective, a Jew is one that is either an ethnic Jew or a religious Jew. The culture of Judaism may be passed down through ethnic blood and through religious and cultural adherence to Biblical principles in the Torah and Hebrew Bible. Jews therefore are such through heredity and or conversion by the practice of Judaism.

Zionism is a catch-word often used today as a reference to the Jews as a people and as a philosophical belief system. Zionism was coined by Nathan Birnbaum, " . . . at a discussion meeting in Vienna in 1892 and is a reference to Mount Zion in Jerusalem where the Temple or the Dome of the rock now sits." " . . . Jerusalem was the beginning and the end of Zionism, that Israel could not exist without having full sovereignty

---

13 Anthony J. Kenny, *Catholics, Jews and the State of Israel* (New York: Routledge Taylor & Francis Group, 2008), 6.
14 Kenny, *Catholics, Jews and the State of Israel*, 6.

over the entire city . . . ."[15] It is perhaps the most controversial place on the planet, which three world religions hold as sacred. Thus the temple mount in Jerusalem or Mount Zion is the epicenter of a world religious conflict involving the three great monotheistic faiths: Judaism, Christianity, and Islam.

The primary purpose of this book is to define Zionism in accordance with the people who are primarily responsible for its implementation. Jews and Christians alike have worked toward the Zionist dream of a Jewish state in Palestine. It will be examined in the context of Jewish nationalism as it moved toward security of their own land and state in Palestine. We cannot understand the full impact of this word, Zionism, without its historic roots and how it has developed over the past four centuries. Prior to that, the Jews existed only in what is referred to as the Diaspora, the dispersion among the Gentile nations. This has removed the Jewish people from the foundations of their ancient faith: the land of Palestine and the Temple on Mount Zion in Jerusalem from which we derive the term Zionism.

Zionism fosters emotional responses across the spectrum as people from all backgrounds hold to vastly differing views as to what Zionism means or how it is viewed. Walter Laqueur used Theodor Herzl's response to the fanaticism concerning Jerusalem and Mount Zion during his first visit to Jerusalem: " . . . he saw only the musty deposits of two thousand years of inhumanity, intolerance, and impurity; he perceived superstition and fanaticism on all sides."[16]

In addition to this tension spot, the entire Palestinian region is regarded as a hot spot of tension to which the terrorists of the world allude. For the Palestinian Arab, Zionism is designated as, "the Great

---

15 Walter Laqueur, *A History of Zionism, From the French Revolution to the Establishment of the State of Israel,* (New York: Schocken Books Inc., 1971 Reprint 2003), xxiii.

16 Laqueur, *A History of Zionism, From the French Revolution to the Establishment of the State of Israel,* xxii.

Introduction

Disaster."[17] The Palestinian refugee problem that now exists is a direct result of Zionism. "When it comes to people like the Palestinians they feel dispossessed, deprived and discriminated against. They lost their homeland to Israel and their lands and homes to the Jews. A large number of them cannot find employment while they remain scattered all over the Middle East where the rulers are wary of them. "[18] Though corruption abounds in the Middle East, Israel is often a scapegoat to blame for the world's terrorism and the basis for the Middle East wars in Afghanistan and Iraq. The victims of prolonged injustice around the world also think those who support the countries or groups who inflict miseries on them should also be treated like the perpetrators of such injustice or inhumanity. "That is how many young Arabs have come to see the United States because of its unlimited support for Israel."[19]

The term Zionist is not restricted to or limited to Jewish people wanting to return to Palestine. There are many Christian Zionists who are equally committed to the Zionist ideals held by many Zionist Jews. This development is closely connected to the Christian church who contributed a very active part in the realization of the Zionist dream. The Christian community in the United State wields great influence in regard to undivided support for Israel and the Zionist cause through government policies. It is from this context that we can examine the ongoing relationship or conflict that exists between the Jewish community and the Christian Church today and how the Zionist ideal has contributed to that relationship.

We will examine Zionism from several different perspectives as we seek to understand the implications of this term for the realization of the Israeli state. Many other forms of Zionism were proposed that we will

17 A phrase coined following the successful war of Independence by the Jews against the Arabs in 1948.
18 Ahmed, Sultan. *"The Roots of Terrorism."* (Arab perspective). *Defence Journal* (October 2004). www.defencejournal.com/2001/october/roots.html. (accessed Sept. 25, 2013).
19 Ahmed, Sultan. *"The Roots of Terrorism."* (Arab perspective). *Defence Journal* (October 2004). www.defencejournal.com/2001/october/roots.html. (accessed Sept. 25, 2013).

deal with in later chapters. The primary issue is to see the connection of Zionism to the Jewish-Christian relationships and how this is affecting those relationships in today's environment.

Biblical Mandate for Zionism

Zionism gets its substance from the biblical mandates that Israel will again possess the land of Palestine forever as an eternal inheritance.[20] "Over the past thirty years a belief has gained ground among the right wing (Orthodox Jews) that the entire historical Palestine is 'ours by divine right.'"[21] Walter Laqueur first wrote this reference in 1972, twenty-five years after Israel gained statehood. This would constitute the foundation for the Jewish claim to the land of Israel today. Without this biblical mandate, the Jews would have little claim or right to take the land as their own possession. Whether one agrees or not, the Bible does give some Jewish claim to the land of Palestine.

Modern scholarship tends to place biblical history in the realm of myth from the outset. The problem with this approach is to dismiss, a priori, the historical record of those making such claims as seeming too incredible to be true. This would be true for the Jewish Exodus from Egypt, as well as claims concerning the resurrection of Jesus Christ some 2,000 years ago. This has lead some people to assume that there is no God who acts in history to bring about events in time. " . . . anti-supernaturalism is prevalent among the radical critics of both the Documentary Hypothesis and Form Criticism schools."[22] This approach may have some merit if not for the problem of finding pieces to this puzzle of history that actually fit all the facts to the events we know to be true within history. Alternate accounts of the above mentioned

20 (Genesis 13:15) The implication from this passage is that the land of Palestine (Israel) will be forever.
21 Laqueur, *A History of Zionism, From the French Revolution to the Establishment of the State of Israel,* xxvii.
22 Josh McDowell, *More Evidence that Demands a Verdict* (San Bernadino, CA: Campus Crusade for Christ International, 1977 Fourteenth Edition), 5.

Introduction

examples leave a lot to be desired in explanation: The Jews appearing out of nowhere as a nomadic tribe possessing the land of Canaan as presented by modern scholarship or the resurrection of Jesus as legend, with no explanation how the early disciples could have translated a known lie into the greatest hoax of all time deceiving millions, make up some of these accounts. It is also important to note that Aristotle's dictum regarding "benefit of the doubt," should still apply to Biblical historical evidence.[23] If the data fits the events, some consideration should be given to the source, in this case biblical history.

The history of the Jewish people is replete with examples of extraordinary events. We cannot easily prove many such events or how history unfolded to produce a people that refuse to conform to the norms that cultures around the world have attempted to squeeze them into. The Jews are resilient to such pressures, which only serves to push them farther away from what we call conventional society. Their culture is unique and filled with symbols of purpose and meaning. They know who they are [people of God], why they are here [living example of God's Law], and where they are going [Kingdom of God]. The Bible is just one example of their extraordinary calling to communicate to the world God's calling and purpose for all mankind. It must be understood that both the Old and New Testaments of the Bible were inspired and written primarily by the Jews (Luke being an exception). Jesus was a Jew, who lived under the Law (Torah). The conflict between Jesus and the Jews rested primarily with the interpretation of the Law known as their oral traditions.

The first eleven chapters of Genesis are not germane to this study and will not be referenced in this study. Genesis 12 and following brings into focus the life of Abraham (Father of the Jews), along with the promises of God to Abraham, his descendents, Israel, and the nations. The Pentateuch claims to be a revelation as stated, whether through

---

23 A statement regarding the historical method and John Warwick Montgomery "historical and literary scholarship continues to follow Aristotle's dictum that the benefit of the doubt is to be given to the document itself, not arrogated by the critic to himself. De Arte Poetica, 14606-14616 page 47.

written records, oral tradition or direct communication from God; there is no reason to believe these promises were not real. Again, this cannot be proven one way of another based upon any empirical evidence, but the survival of the Jewish people and the restoration of Israel as a nation gives some merit to the claims and suggests some foundation for the reliability of the text. This assumption carries several responses that justify biblical inspiration; however, this book will focus on the promises directly related to Zionism, Israel, the Jews and the Christian Church.

To gain a biblical perspective, five primary Old Testament passages illustrate the promise of the land. The primary claims include Deuteronomy 31:7 "Be strong and courageous, for you shall go with this people into the land which the Lord has sworn to their fathers to give them, and you shall give it to them as an inheritance." This is worded in the form of a promise or even a prediction. The suggestion from this passage gives the land to the Jews as an inheritance from God. The other primary passage is Ezekiel 37, which speaks of Israel as dead dry bones coming back to life;[24] this carries with it not only the promise of the Jews return to the land of Palestine but that they would be a nation again having a national identity. This event has happened twice, once under King Cyrus of Persia, who decreed the return of the Jews in B.C.E. 538. The second is the UN mandate of 1947 and the Declaration of Independence on May 14, 1948. These two events reflect on the promise to the Jews that they would return to the land of Israel (Palestine). Much of Old Testament Judaism revolves around this promise of "the land" to the Jewish people.

Specific promises given to the Jews concerning the land (Zion):

1. Genesis 12:7 God calls out Abraham from his own country to a new land. This land of Canaan was inhabited by the Canaanites but was promised to Abraham's descendants, the Jews.

2. Genesis 15:18 The promise of land and the promise that Abraham's descendants will inhabit a special land. Abraham's descendents would be called out of slavery to this land that

24 (Ezekiel 37:1-14) gives the illustration of national restoration.

Introduction

will encompass territories between the Nile and the Euphrates. This would include Eastern Egypt, what is current day-Jordan and Western Iraqi nations not friendly to Israel. This goes well beyond the borders of ancient Israel.

3. Genesis 17:8 All the land of Canaan would be given as a everlasting covenant. This suggests that the land will be given to the descendents of Abraham forever. God's promise also includes the prediction that Abraham would be the Father of many nations. Ironically, if one follows the generally accepted line of descendents, those would include the Arab nations through Ishmael and his descendents.

4. Deuteronomy 30:1-5 The blessings and the curses that accompany the promise. The land will carry with it conditions that must be followed; failure to comply will result in banishment to the ends of the earth. The promise is not so good as to anticipate; it assumes the nation will fail to some degree. The anticipation that punishment and persecution will follow seems to indicate troubles down through history. It does not take long to realize this point when one examines the history of the Jews. The good news is that the people would in the end arrive at peace within their promised land.

5. Jeremiah 31:31 The promise that the Jews would not go extinct but continue as a people. This prediction makes a claim that the farthest reaches of history will have a people called Jews that can tie their ancestry back to Abraham.

The promises made to Israel are traced to the patriarch Abraham living in the beginning of the second millennium B.C.E. The Pentateuch, also known as the Torah, is the heart of Rabbinic Judaism, consisting of the first five books of the Bible. The identity of the Jewish people is tied firmly to the promises made to the Jews and the nation of Israel given first to Abraham some 1800 years BCE. First the promise is of a seed that would come from Abraham through his wife Sarah who was well past child-bearing age. "Indeed, I will greatly bless you, and I will greatly multiply your seed . . . ."[25] The blessings of Abraham's seed would extend that promise to everyone. "In your seed all the nations of the earth shall be blessed, . . ."[26] The promises are directed first at the Jewish people and their posterity then through them to the nations. The Jews were selected to be a blessing to the Gentile nations and they should be honored and respected as a people of God. It is through the Jews that the Gentiles were able to come to God.

This promise to the Gentile nations is established in the Mosaic covenant with some qualifications: the faithful observance of the commandments of God. These requirements however, were not kept to God's satisfaction, it would appear. The consequence of this failure is the scattering of the Jews across the face of the Earth.[27] This appears to have happened in several stages: The Assyrian captivity, Babylonian captivity and Greek conquest. Though Persia allowed a remnant of Jews to return to the land and to rebuild the temple, the majority of Jews remained in Babylon and the Jewish presence continued there. The Greeks pushed many Jews into Egypt, Alexandria and Northern Africa. The most prominent dispersions were after the Revolt of 70 CE and the Ben Cochba revolt in 132-135 CE. Though there were many other situations that scattered the Jewish people, the most notable being the Spanish Inquisition, the Diaspora of the Jews stretched to the farthest reaches of the Earth in apparent fulfillment of Isaiah 11:12.28

Source of Jewish Christian Conflict

This section brings some interesting points into focus concerning the conflict between Jews and Gentile believers today. To a large extent, the Jews have been scattered across many nations long before the Christian church came into existence. The history of the Jews

25 (Genesis 22:17)
26 (Genesis 22:18)
27 (Deuteronomy 30:3,4)
28 This reference clearly states that the four corners represent the farthest places on the Earth.

Introduction

provides a significant reason in that the Jews have not been treated well by the Gentile nations over the past 3,500 years, though most of these dispersions were not the fault of the Christian Church. The Christian Church stands out, not as an ally of Judaism or the Jews, but as a foe to be fought and resisted. The barriers between Jews and Christians can be traced back to the New Testament itself, reflecting an ongoing conflict between these two faiths with common roots.

For many Jews today, the Bible is not relevant to their lives. According to some Jewish scholars, both the Old and New Testaments are clouded histories. "The Bible can serve as a very useful historical document if it is kept in mind that its editors have recast tribal traditions and reinterpreted them from a national standpoint that the story is the idealized product of prophetic and priestly imagination, written down many centuries after the events supposedly occurred."[29] This position would fit that of most secular Jews. The relevance of the Old Testament histories serves primarily for culture and tradition rather than any spiritual relevance.

According to the New Testament, Jewish-Christian relationships existed in conflict from the first century onward. Jesus confronted Jewish leadership in respect to their oral traditions which were held in highest respect by the Jews. "Why do you yourselves transgress the commandment of God for the sake of your tradition?"[30] In addition, Jesus continually broke the Sabbath from the Jewish perspective, and the Jewish leaders saw Jesus as a renegade and uneducated Rabbi. The confrontation continued on through the Acts of the early church and into the ministry of Paul, who suffered greatly at the hands of the first-century Jews. These conflicts and others were not between Jews and Gentiles but rather Pharisaic Jews and Christian Jews who claimed to possess the New Covenant spoken of in Jeremiah 31:31-34.

Little is said of the New Testament or of Jesus Christ among Jews except in the negative. The evidence against the New Testament from

---

29 Abram Leon Sachar, *A History of the Jews* (New York: Alfred A. Knopf Publishing, 1967), 12.

30 (Matthew 15:3)

the Talmud is not always clear. Jocz suggests two methods that are employed to discredit the New Testament from Talmudic sources. "The one method is to ridicule, the other is to ignore the adversary altogether."[31] As a result of this division, according to Jocz, the Synagogue generally tried to avoid the Church whenever possible. This is unfortunate, but as one reads through Matthew 23, Jesus the Messiah confronts the works of the Scribes and Pharisees in the Synagogues, which sheds light to that perspective; helping one understand at least in part why the New Testament is so abhorrent to many Jews.[32]

Another barrier rests in the fact that the Church has been one of the great obstacles preventing the Jews from returning to the Land of Zion (Palestine), or for the reoccupation of Jerusalem. Since the fall of Jerusalem in 70 CE under Titus and again in 135 CE after the Bar Cochba revolt against the Romans, Jews were banned from Jerusalem. "In Rome Italian Jews and Jewish displaced persons sojourning in Italy marched in a jubilant procession beneath the famous Arch of Titus." "The Arch is the monument which the ancient Romans erected to celebrate the downfall of Judea and perpetuate the glory of her conqueror."[33] The symbol of Rome is then extended into the Diaspora as the home of the Christian Church. This only adds to the symbolic irony of the Jewish-Christian conflict and removes any connection between Judaism and Christianity as having anything in common.

From the second century on, the Church pulled back from its Jewish roots. Jews were required to give up traditional observances. "Come all the way with us or go back to Judaism. There is no middle ground."[34] This ever-present persistence on the part of the Church to

31 Jakob Jocz, *The Jewish People and Jesus Christ; The Relationship between Church and Synagogue* (Grand Rapids, MI: Baker Book House, 1979), 58.
32 (Matthew 23:1-38)
33 Rufus Learsi, *Fulfillment, The Epic Story of Zionist* (New York: World Publishing, 1951), 3.
34 Stan Telchin, *Betrayed!*, (Grand Rapids, MI.: Baker Publishing Group, Chosen Books, 2007), 88. This reference is from the Council of Antioch concerning changing the date of the Passover.

Introduction

corral the Jews into the Christian community has met with resistance and conflict from its inception and continues in some form to this day. "All of my secular Jewish identity said; "Don't answer them! (Christian questions concerning Messiah) Remember the Crusades. Remember the Inquisition. Remember the Pogroms. Remember the things which have been done to the Jewish people in the name of Christ for the last 2,000 years."[35]

The end result of this New Covenant is a drastic split in Judaism. Even though most may not see the connection between the New Testament (Christianity) and the direction of Judaism following the destruction of Jerusalem and the Temple, the two faiths having the same source become competing ideologies rather than the unity intended in Galatians 2. We have been given division and animosity. The Christian community was caught in a difficult position of trying to figure out what the role of Jews was as they rebelled against the New Covenant, trying to reestablish their own form of Judaism. Rabbinic Judaism rose out of the ashes of this destruction requiring rabbinic Jews to reevaluate their faith. From the council of Jamnia the Jews began the process of establishing the Old Testament Canon and the new direction for Judaism; this left the two faiths in a state of competition with no harmony or peace.

Even though the early Apostolic Christians who were all practicing Jews gave Gentiles grace in respect to the Law and allowed Gentiles to be Gentiles,[36] culture was not the defining issue in becoming a Christian. However, when the tables were reversed, the Gentile church did not allow the Jews to remain within Jewish culture but demanded a complete separation. "The professions of faith required by Jewish converts to Christianity in the ancient and medieval periods indicated a total separation from Judaism required by the church."[37] "I do here now renounce every rite and observance of the Jewish religion,

---

35 Telchin, *Betrayed!*, 65.
36 The Council in Jerusalem found in Acts 15:19-29 gave Gentiles the right of fellowship without circumcision or the Law.
37 David A Rausch, *Legacy of Hatred: Why Christians must Not Forget the Holocaust* (Grand Rapids, MI: Baker Publishing Group, 1990), 25.

detesting all its most solemn ceremonies and tenets that in former days I kept and held."[38] In this case, culture became very strategic and the extraction of all Jewish symbols becomes priority even though the Jewish symbols of Passover, Baptism, and first fruits, among others, all have a definite Christian application that broadens and expands upon Jewish interpretations. In addition, Jesus Christ still adhered to the first covenant law and made clear, the first covenant was still in effect.[39]

The New Testament brings to us some very interesting paradoxes that both unify and divide. While the New Testament is an historical account of a Jewish preacher (Jesus) and his followers, their impact on history goes well beyond the environment in which these events played out. Few if any people in history are more debated, vilified, worshiped, and ignored. Jesus is discussed perhaps more than any other person in history and is understood less. Mainline scholarship seems to agree that Jesus existed, "I do not know any recognized scholar who still holds these views (that Jesus did not exist)."[40] Jesus' life has had a profound impact on Western culture, a condition Jewish scholars have addressed in recent years.

Faith issues have a way of dividing people as sides are drawn quickly and decisively on the person of Jesus. What is even more interesting is the paradox of unity and division mentioned earlier. Even though Jesus is called the Prince of Peace, he said he did not come to bring peace but the sword.[41] This paradoxical statement seems to have come true as we look down the corridors of history between Jews and Christians. Though the early Christians (Jews) continued to practice their Judaism, there was enormous conflict with the idea of Jesus being anything other than a false messiah among Jewish leadership.

---

38 Rausch, *Legacy of Hatred: Why Christians must Not Forget the Holocaust*, 25.
39 (Matthew 5:17,18)
40 Will and Ariel Durant, *Heroes of History: A Brief History of Civilization from Ancient Times to the Dawn of the Modern Age* (New York: Simon Schuster Publishing, 2001), 158.
41 (Matthew 10:34)

Introduction

According to some scholars, Rabbinic Judaism, which arose from the ashes of the first Jewish revolt from 66 to 70 CE, had as one of its objectives to sever or separate the Pharisaic Jews or the Jews of the Law from the new Christian Jews that were spreading their message among the Gentiles during the first century. Jocz writes: "The whole stress of the Synagogue since that time was upon those features of Judaism which emphasized its difference from the new faith."[42] First century Jews split cleanly over the issue of Jesus Christ, seeing him as a false messiah having died and being cursed upon the cross. With a few exceptions in history, little dialogue is made between the Synagogue and the Church.[43] Most Jews preferred to ignore the church whenever possible.

Perception takes front seat for both Jews and Christians in their respective attitudes towards each other through history. Jacob Jocz references the Yosippon in stating, "In the Middle Ages and even up to our own days the (Toledot Yeshu) served as a popular handbook and was almost the only source left to the Jewish people from which to draw their knowledge concerning Jesus Christ."[44] What is unfortunate is this knowledge concerning Jesus Christ and the history surrounding him paints a very sour picture. This attitude through the Middle Ages was the only understanding many Jews had of Jesus. Sachar presents the same scenario: "Jews have known little of him and have wished to know less. Through their long history he was not, to them, the Prince of Peace, the harbinger of goodwill. In his name every conceivable outrage was perpetrated on the despised and cursed race that gave him life."[45] While the Jews were raised to reject the Christ of Christianity, they gave

---

42 Jocz, *The Jewish People and Jesus Christ; The Relationship between Church and Synagogue.* 58.

43 One of the more notable debates between early Christians and Jews is *Dialogue with Trypho*, between Justin Martyr and a Jewish scholar, Trypho, in the mid-second century.

44 Jocz, *The Jewish People and Jesus Christ: The Relationship between Church and Synagogue*, 63. The *Sepher Yosippon* is a first century Jewish historical document with commentary.

45 Sachar, *A History of the Jews*, 124.

no thought to his purpose or value. He was rejected completely and absolutely.

For the Christian community the perception of the Jews was also very destructive. "Most Christians were products of their culture, imbued with the anti-Jewish propaganda passed down from the early church Fathers."[46] This does not include all the church fathers, but enough to set in motion a series of misconceptions that placed enmity between Christians and Jews from the beginning.

It must also be understood that through the majority of Jewish-Christian history, there has been little conflict. Jews and Christians have lived in peace for periods of time. "Even though through the majority of Jewish-Christian history there has been little conflict, the conflicts that did arise were severe."[47] In spite of those quiet periods, most Jews will remember two periods of time where the Christian Jewish relationships reached their most appalling low: First were the Crusades and the events of the Rhineland where many Jews were needlessly murdered. Though the atrocities conducted during the Crusades were not sanctioned by the Church, "It was originally intended that the crusaders should concern themselves solely with the success of their expedition overseas, without intervening in the affairs of the Christian countries of Europe."[48] The atrocities against the Jews were committed by people who made confessions of Christian faith or were sold indulgences that most likely had no connection with true Christian faith. The fact remains that in the name of Christ, people mistreated the Jews for no rational reason.

The second event was the Spanish Inquisitions which forced Christian conversion or expulsion from Spain and Portugal. "Torquemada (A Spanish Dominican Friar) burnt thousands of wretched Marranos at public auto-da-fé in every Spanish city and capped his career by driving

---

46 Rausch, *Legacy of Hatred*, 27.
47 Learsi, *Fulfillment, The Epic Story of Zionism*, 4.
48 Schwarzfuchs, Simon."Crusades: Crusades," *Encyclopaedia Judaica* (2008) http://www.jewishvirtuallibrary.org/jsource/judaica/ejud_0002_0005_0_04737.html (accessed Sept. 24, 2013).

Introduction

two hundred thousand peaceful Jews out of the country."[49] Inquisitions were sanctioned by Popes such as Innocent III and reflected the position of the Medieval Church that they alone were possessors of truth and it was their responsibility to eliminate Christian heresies. "Innocent honestly believed that the Jews were an accursed people, suffering for rejecting Christi and never to be given rest and peace."[50] Christians came to Spain and Portugal forcing Jews to abandon Jewish culture in favor of Christian culture. The bottom line was that Christians were involved in hurting Jews.

In CE 1492, "a proud and noble Jewish community enriched the land (Spain) that harbored it and left a remarkable deposit of spiritual, intellectual, and artistic culture."[51] Moorish Spain gives us an example of a high culture, the result of people working together. "Scholars like Yehudah Halevi, Ibn Gabirol, Ibn Pakuda, the Ibn Ezra and Maimonides, still shed their brilliance."[52] This enlightened society came to an end with the entry of Christianity. "This remnant was driven from Spain fled to Italy and the Turkish dominions, including Palestine, where it continued to bear fruit. The center of the Dispersion came to rest in Poland." [53] Many of those Sephardic Jews moved into Western Europe, beginning a string of events that would eventually lead to the Zionist dream. "Every pinch of the Spanish Inquisition brought new Sephardic families to Holland."[54] It was through Holland that the Zionist movement had its fragile beginnings.

During this period, the Church was extremely cruel to Jews and Christians alike who did not conform to doctrines of the day. "Torquemada [Dominican Friar] burnt thousands of wretched Marranos (Jewish Christians) . . . , it was in the name of the gentle Savior who preached the message of brotherly love."[55] Sachar continues: "all because

---

49 Sachar, *A History of the Jews*, 125.
50 Sachar, *A History of the Jews*, 193.
51 Learsi, *Fulfillment, The Epic Story of Zionism*, 5.
52 Learsi, *Fulfillment, The Epic Story of Zionism*, 5.
53 Learsi, *Fulfillment, The Epic Story of Zionism*, 5.
54 Sachar, *A History of the Jews*, 230.
55 Sachar, *A History of the Jews*, 125.

of Christian bigotry, it was impossible for Jews to regard the Prophet of Nazareth as other than the scourge of God, a fiend unmentionable."[56] As noted, the result of this mistreatment was the Jewish presentation of Jesus in the most vulgar ways, further alienating Jews from the Christian community. It was not until the 19th and 20th century with scholars such as Claude Montefiore and Joseph Klausner that many Jewish scholars would take a more objective view of Jesus and what he represented as a Jewish teacher. "Jesus is held with the very highest respect by many Jewish scholars."[57] Through the effects of the enlightenment and a more open reflection on the New Testament, Jews who have examined the documents have gained a more positive perspective on the person of Jesus than generally existed within the Jewish community.

A Christian Perspective

The Jewish people are unique among the nations; they have been given a special responsibility according to both the Old and New Testaments. They were set apart for a special reason. This separation set up numerous future events that we will discuss later in this book. The Jews carried a special privilege that according to the biblical accounts allowed God to demonstrate His character and purpose. The Jews serve as an object lesson for the world. It seems tragic that the Jews have had to suffer through history, but their suffering was a benefit to the world, in the lessons it teaches us of the severity and graciousness of God.

A second benefit of the Jewish people was the construction of the Old Testament text and its oral traditions. The foundations for God's purposes are clearly stated as His plan for the restoration of the human race is given. "And I (God) will bless those who bless you, And the one who curses you I will curse. And in you [Abraham] all the families of the earth shall be blessed." [58] Without the Jewish people to preserve that

---

56 Sachar, *A History of the Jews*, 125.
57 Claude Montefiore, *The Old Testament and After* (London: Macmillan & Co., 1923), 188.
58 (Genesis 12:3)

Introduction

work (scriptures), we would never know any of the mysteries of God or of life. Many of these mysteries were revealed in the Old Testament texts and are critical to the development of the New Testament.

Jewish people will reject the New Testament as authoritative, based upon their rejection of Jesus as the Messiah, but the Old Testament is critical to the development of who the Messiah would be and what situations would govern His coming and eventual death. Isaiah 53 gives an example of that insight into the necessity of messianic suffering. "All of us like sheep have gone astray, . . . but the LORD had caused the iniquity of us all to fall on Him."[59] The Jewish people were entrusted with that message and they faithfully fulfilled that task. The Tanakh is a testimony to their faithfulness that made the beginning of Christianity possible.

Whether one agrees or not that Jesus is the Messiah, it would seem that through the course of history this messianic movement [Christianity] is responsible for bringing Gentiles from every nation to a faith in the God of the Jews and the patriarchs. Though many Jews may accept Jesus as their Messiah, they do so only at the risk of alienation of their own people. This is understandable in light of the Jewish position on Jesus.

The Restoration of the Jews in Holland and the Reformed Church

If one examines the annals of world and Church history, little is found in regards to the Jewish impact upon the Netherlands, yet the direction of world history was influenced greatly by the events in Holland during the late sixteenth and early seventeenth centuries. Jewish families seeking refuge from the Spanish Inquisition found acceptance within Amsterdam and the Dutch community. "Every pinch of the Spanish Inquisition brought new Sephardic families to Holland."[60] In the beginning, the Jews, who were in fact Marranos, tried to conceal the continuing practice of their Jewish faith. "In 1593 a little group of

---

59 (Isaiah 53:6)
60 Sachar, *A History of the Jews*, 230.

Marranos landed in Amsterdam and worshipped secretly in a private home."[61] It is apparent the Jewish worshipers took no chance that their actions would cause another exile. This fear was a reflection of the harsh realities of being a Jew in the sixteenth century.

The Netherlands declared their Independence from Spain in 1581.[62] Though they declared their Independence, the Dutch were still in the midst of their battle for religious freedom and autonomy. During one of the Jew's Yom Kippur services, they were attacked by suspicious Dutch citizens who suspected the Jews of being Catholics. "When the worshippers explained that they were secret Jews, the council granted them permission to remain, and in 1598 a synagogue was publicly dedicated with almost extravagant joy."[63] The Dutch had no bone to pick with the Jews as their battle was with Spain as well. It most likely proved to be a relief that the Jews represented an ally in their battle for Independence from Spain.

This alliance became an advantage to both the Dutch and the Jews. "The Jews became interested in the carrying trade, and their capital helped to build up the Dutch East and West India companies; which as if in retribution, were the chief instruments in the destruction of Spanish and Portuguese commercial supremacy."[64] The Jews, in a sense, had their revenge on Spain and through the Dutch were able to expand their influence to the new world. The Dutch East and West India companies became the most powerful trading enterprises at that time. Jewish investment helped build up Dutch shipping and the Jewish community thrived in Amsterdam. "Amsterdam became known as 'Dutch Jerusalem'".[65]

---

61 Sachar, *A History of the Jews*, 230.
62 The seven provinces of the Netherlands announced their independence but did not gain Spanish recognition until 1648. Louis Snyder, *The Making of Modern Man: From the Renaissance to the Present* (New York: Van Nostrand Co., 1967), 130-131.
63 Sachar, *A History of the Jews*, 230.
64 Sachar, *A History of the Jews*, 230.
65 Sachar, *A History of the Jews*, 230.

Introduction

The church in Holland had gone through many cycles of change the previous 100 years following the Reformation from Catholicism to Lutheranism, then to Calvinism. Calvinism found a home in the Netherlands, thus creating a tension with Catholic Spain and Rome. The history between the Reformed Church and Judaism was not mired by the same ill-placed statements made by Martin Luther in his *Jews and their Lies*. Luther was at first a strong advocate for the Jews, which may have in time reaped fruit for the Reformed Movement. As history stands, Calvin made few if any negative remarks concerning the Jews except those concerning differences in theology. The Reformed Church thus became a channel for a much closer Jewish-Church relationship going back 300 years.

Puritanism and Zionism

To understand the Christian roots of modern Zionism, one must go back to the Puritans who lived amongst the Dutch in Holland during the mid-seventeenth century. In that day, Zionism was called Restorationism, which implied the need for the Jews to be restored to the land of Palestine. According to Lawrence Epstein, the Puritans had developed a strong evangelical spirit that emphasized personal conversion and the authority of scripture. "The evangelical spirit grew in England after being imported from its original home in Holland."[66] This biblically-based theology carried with it the promises and predictions that the Jews would be restored to the land of Palestine. The implications of that truth became apparent to many groups in addition to the Puritans. "This spirit was evident not only in the official Anglican Church, but in many other sects, especially Methodism."[67] Many within the growing evangelical community of that day began promoting the necessity of the Jew's return to the Promised Land, with "the emergence of thinkers who saw the restoration of Jews as vital to God's plan for the redemption of the

---

66 Lawrence J. Epstein, *Zion's Call* (Lanham, MD: University Press of America, Inc., 1984), 7.
67 Epstein, *Zion's Call*, 7.

world."[68] In simple terms, the Restoration Movement had begun within the confines of Puritanism and would eventually branch out into the greater church.

Many individuals promoted Restorationism as a necessary mission of the church. The most prominent among the church was Sir Henry Finch, Finch was a legal scholar and a Member of Parliament who also had strong connections with King James. Others included Thomas Brightman, called by some "the true founder of Christian Zionism."[69] Brightman adds his emphasis: "There is nothing more certain: the prophets do everywhere confirm it."[70] The Christian community in England through the influence of the Puritans was being influenced toward a Restorationist position that would later bear fruit.

Even though the hope for a return to Palestine was always present among the Jews prior to 1900, very little was done to actively pursue a Zionist dream among the Jews. Active Zionism, among the Jews, was initiated through the efforts of Manasseh Ben Israel, a Dutch Jew. "In 1650 he (Manasseh Ben Israel) petitioned Oliver Cromwell, now virtually dictator of England, to allow the Jews to return."[71] The Jews were banned from England when they were still connected to the Catholic Church back in the twelfth century. Since the Jews were so successful in building up the Dutch East India Company, Cromwell no doubt thought that with the help of the Jews they could benefit England as well. "Cromwell perceived that England needed the commercial expertise that the re-admission of Jews would provide, . . . the Puritans, were urging such a return."[72] Obviously capital along with expertise was a critical motive among the British leaders in addition to theological concerns.

---

68 Epstein, *Zion's Call*, 7.
69 Epstein, *Zion's Call*, 8.
70 Epstein, *Zion's Call* 8; Quote from Brightman's, *A Revelation of Mr. Brightman's Revelation*, 1641.
71 Sachar, *A History of the Jews*, 321.
72 Epstein, *Zion's Call*, 12.

Introduction

Through the work of Manasseh and others in the growing Restoration Movement, closer ties were made possible between Jews and Christians. The idea of a Jewish-Christian alliance during the Middle Ages would have seemed impossible. "An alliance was forged between English Christians and Jews. A movement to hasten the Messiah through eventual restoration of the Jews to their ancient homeland . . . ."[73] These theological connections were made possible because of a warming relationship between Christians and Jews who put their differences to the side in order to work toward a common goal. "Restorationism originated in the rise of the pietistic Protestants in the sixteenth century England, and the eventual emergence of the Puritans' power in England in the seventeenth century."[74] The Puritans represented the early Evangelical Christian Church taking the Bible as the Word of God along with the claims given for the restoration of the Jews to Palestine.

Cabalist Judaism and the Connection to Zionism

With the rise of Restorationism within the Jewish community, made possible in part by the support of the church, including both the Anglican and Reformed communities, many Jews ventured into an imaginative dream world of messianic expectations. The Cabalist Movement may well have been spurred on by such thoughts and brought many within Judaism into that mystical world of empty hopes. "Cabalistic Judaism moved the structures of Judaism with its emphasis on Torah intellect and hard work into a world of spiritualistic fantasy. The harried Jewish masses were credulously sinking more and more deeply into the bogs of a hocus-pocus."[75] The Cabalist movement demonstrates in part the messianic hopes of many Jews that were lying dormant.

Talmudic Judaism now had a competitor as Cabalistic Judaism threatened to gain ascendancy in Jewish life. Few could escape its appeal in an era of dreadful persecution. Cabalism, " . . . fast degenerated into a

73 Epstein, *Zion's Call*, 13.
74 Epstein, *Zion's Call*, 7.
75 Sachar, *A History of the Jews*, 236.

miracle-mongering, weirdly superstitious affair, in which demonology, necromancy, spiritism, and all forms of magic played the chief roles."[76] The Jews were seeking a Savior with hopes that the return of the Messiah was near. The question must have crossed the minds of many Jews: was this man the Messiah? One such messianic hopeful was Reubeni who was astute enough to make no claims. ". . . but men and women dogged his shadow, beseeching his blessing as he rode in state through the streets of Rome."[77] "Meanwhile the Jews of Rome, astonished by the reception accorded to a Jewish emissary of a lost tribe, gave themselves over to the wildest hopes. Was he the forerunner of the Messiah?"[78] Such hopes bent the rational perspectives of many Jews leading them toward disappointment.

With the idea of the return to Palestine, messianic dreamers came upon the scene in the late sixteenth and early seventeenth centuries steering many people's imaginations, the movement grew and drew into it a large portion of the Jewish community. What makes this movement so interesting is that it is so un-characteristic of the practical-mindedness of Jewish history since the time of Jesus Christ. The idea of a miracle worker within the Talmud was presented as the work of a sorcerer, not a spiritual redeemer. "He is going forth to be stoned because he has practiced sorcery. . . ."[79] Yet this movement picked up momentum at a rapid pace. The expectations, it would seem, outpaced the practical realities.

While many other messianic figures entered the scene allowing Cabalism to make a major impact within Judaism, the more prominent of messianic hopefuls were Abraham Abulafia, Shabbathai Zevi and Reubeni. It was Shabbathai Zevi who raised messianic expectation to a frenzy. "Shabbathai became convinced that he was the destined Messiah, and in 1648, a miracle year by Cabalist calculations, he proclaimed

---

76 Sachar, *A History of the Jews*, 230.
77 Sachar, *A History of the Jews*, 230.
78 Sachar, *A History of the Jews*, 238.
79 Talmud, Sanhedrin 43a. This reference is often attributed to Jesus of Nazareth.

Introduction

himself by pronouncing the Ineffable Name."[80] What makes Zevi so difficult for Jews is that not only was he another messianic fraud, but in order to save his own life, Zevi converted to Islam leaving the Cabalism movement flat, empty of hope.

The Church could only stand on the sidelines and watch as these Messianic hopefuls continued to rise and fall. Had the Jews considered with any reliability the New Testament warning to not follow anyone claiming to be the Messiah or a prophet of God? "For false Christs and false prophets will arise and will show great signs and wonders, so as to mislead, if possible, even the elect."[81] Little thought was given to the New Testament by the Jews at any time in history.

The Cabalist movement pushed many Jews to question the reliability and trustworthiness of the Jewish faith. At a time, when according to Sachar many within the intellectual community were moving quickly away from the spiritualist and mystical, the Jews were being carried away by their emotional frenzy. Unfortunately for many within the Jewish community, it created disillusionment when those hopeful expectations proved to be false. It is very likely that this movement and the generations that followed opened wide the door to rationalism as the Jews entered the age of European enlightenment with diminished hopes of any Messianic fulfillment. According to Scholem, "Sabbateanism (followers of Sabbatai Zevi) destroyed Jewish tradition from within a century before the Enlightenment, and may have even brought the latter into existence."[82]

When the Cabalist movement was at its height, enlightenment thinking was gaining ground by another prominent Jew, Baruch Spinoza. Propelled greatly by the shifting tide of reason coming through the birth pangs of the enlightenment, Spinoza was to have a profound

---

80 Sachar, *A History of the Jews*, 242.
81 (Matthew 24:24)
82 Scholem, Gershom. "Sabbatei Zevi: Mystical Messiah and the Centrality of Messianism." *Stanford Encyclopedia of Philosophy*, (April, 10.2008). www.plato.stanford,edu/entries/scholem/. (accessed Sept. 24, 2013).

effect on the Jewish community entering a new age of reason. "Baruch Spinoza showed the way to the emancipation of the Jew under freedom, decency and enlightenment."[83] The contrast between Spinoza and Zevi is stark, as Menuhin demonstrates the extreme positions from within Judaism. "The Eastern Jew Sabbetai Zevi showed the way to decadence, degeneration and nationalistic Messianism which could only originate in hopelessly dark and segregated ghettos."[84] The stark contrast between Spinoza and Zevi translates into reality as many Jews rejected their traditional faith in favor of the new rationalism that left little room for a spiritual reality. The new faith leads to a so-called enlightenment and freedom while the other leads to bondage and confinement within the old system, Cabalist or Orthodox Judaism. This contrast would result in a split within the Jewish community as many elected to embrace a secular life style, rejecting their old faith.

The effects of the Enlightenment brought major changes to the Jewish community. The most prominent individual opening the way to the enlightenment was Moses Mendelssohn. He brought the Jews into contact with the currents of the European world both socially and religiously. "Thousands of keen minds were lifted out of the narrow environment which had stultified Jewish life for centuries and were brought into contact with the stimulating currents of the European world."[85] Times were changing for the Jews and Christians alike as biblical foundations were being questioned by an increasingly secular and skeptical society. "There was little scientific Biblical criticism (Prior to the enlightenment). The Bible was still regarded as a verbally inspired document, . . . part of the old World."[86] Biblical foundations were beginning to dissolve into the quicksand of biblical criticism. Both the Jewish and Christian Bibles were losing some of their prestige.

---

83 Moshe Menuhin, *Decadence of Judaism in Our Time* (Beirut, Lebanon: Institute for Palestinian Studies, 1969), 278.
84 Menuhin, *Decadence of Judaism in Our Time,* 278.
85 Sachar, *A History of the Jews, 328.*
86 Sachar, *A History of the Jews*, 328.

Introduction

Moses Mendelssohn: Father of Modern Jewish Enlightenment

Mendelssohn became a lightning rod for change within Germany and Europe as many Jews were divided concerning the necessity and impact of the cultural changes taking place within Judaism. Walter Laqueur articulates, "Admired by many, bitterly denounced by others, Moses Mendelssohn became a landmark in modern Jewish history, not so much because of what he did, as for what he was: the very symbol of Jewish emancipation."[87] This emancipation was both cultural and religious. All but one of Mendelssohn's children converted to Christianity. "Of Mendelssohn's children all but one changed their faith, and many of his pupils, too, converted."[88] Others switched to the more liberal Reformed Judaism, reflecting a more modernistic approach to worship. These changes, though not significant in themselves, at least in part removed some of the barriers existing between the Jewish and Christian communities.

Unfortunately, many Christian conversions did not necessitate a true heart for God. Some Jews, less scrupulous, discarded their reservations and embraced Christianity. For baptism, as Heine said, ". . . was the entrance ticket to European civilization."[89] Mendelssohn was a major influence on his generation of Jews, moving many into German culture and away from the Jewish ghetto. The very idea according to some Rabbis would result in the abandonment of their Jewish faith. "A leading orthodox rabbi wrote in 1848 about the young Jews of his time, that nine-tenths of them were ashamed of their faith."[90] Orthodox

---

87 Laqueur, *A History of Zionism, From the French Revolution to the Establishment of the State of Israel*, 7- 8.

88 Laqueur, *A History of Zionism, From the French Revolution to the Establishment of the State of Israel*, 9.

89 Laqueur, *A History of Zionism, From the French Revolution to the Establishment of the State of Israel*, 9. Quote from *Sammons Heinrich Heine: A Modern Biography* Heinrich Heine, Heine was a Christian convert but had little interest in religion.

90 Laqueur, *A History of Zionism, From the French Revolution to the Establishment of the State of Israel*, 9. Quote from *Sammons Heinrich Heine: A Modern Biography* Heinrich Heine, Heine was a Christian convert but had little interest in religion.

Judaism's hold on the Jewish people had weakened considerably as a result. This demonstrates much of the separation existing between the Jewish and Christian communities was self-imposed by the Jews themselves. This mistrust, though still present, was beginning to weaken among the Jewish community concerning Christians during the nineteenth century.

The fact Jews wanted to convert to Christianity or another faith reflected the profound influence Mendelssohn had on the Jewish community of his time. "Many Jews became Christian to retain those rights."[91] Through his translations of the Hebrew Bible into German and his assimilation into German culture, Jews were assimilated into the culture. Most German Jews remained within Judaism as Reformed Jews, while others dropped all religious ties altogether, becoming secular Jews. This trend opened wide the opportunities for Jews and Christians to interact. The impact upon the Christian community was the opportunity to befriend a Jew as a neighbor or a friend.

While throughout most of the middle ages, Jews maintained a closed community, those barriers were beginning to fracture. "Jews penned together like cattle in dark overcrowded ghettoes, elsewhere they were not confined to special living quarters and social intercourse with their Christian neighbors was not uncommon."[92] Germany had taken some strides forward in Christian-Jewish relationships as Jews mixed with Christians and vice-versa. The ghetto mentality was losing its grip on the Jewish community and the results were a closer relationship between Jews and Christians. Old Jewish-Christian stereotypes were beginning to crumble, at least within the secular Jewish community.

Mendelssohn's work was not limited to or confined to the Jewish community, but reached out to the secular community as well. "His effort

---

91 Tannenbaum, Andrew. "The Origins of Reform Judaism."*Shamash.org/trb/judaism.* http://www.jewishvirtuallibrary.org/jsource/Judaism/ The_Origins_of_Reform_Judaism.html. (accessed Sept. 24,2013).

92 Laqueur, *A History of Zionism, From the French Revolution to the Establishment of the State of Israel*, 6.

Introduction

to educate himself attracted the attention of non-Jewish well-wishers; within a few years he had published weighty studies on Leibniz's philosophy and the problem of evidence in the metaphysic sciences."[93] Mendelssohn became friends with the German writer Lessing, ("the first free-thinking man in Germany"[94]); "he learned to live with and become integrated into the German community of intellectuals long before he was granted free and full citizenship."[95] Mendelssohn's contributions to science and philosophy were moderate at best, but they did help open some doors to acceptance by the secular community.

It must be remembered at this time Orthodox Judaism was very anti-Zionism. Their belief from the second century on, was that God only could bring the Jews back to the land. "Divine Providence, not human intervention, should determine when and how the Jews will be redeemed from exile and return to Zion."[96] It was felt necessary that the Jews remained close to their religious roots in order to foster such an event, though the belief in the return to Zion never disappeared from the Jewish mind, "next year in Jerusalem."[97] Jews up through the nineteenth century rarely pursued Zionism with any sense of need or urgency.

The barriers separating the Christian community from Jewish Orthodoxy had been maintained for nearly seventeen centuries from the fall of Jerusalem in 136 CE. A small Jewish community has always been a part of the church since the first century, but in part through the efforts of Moses Mendelssohn and the effects of the Enlightenment, Jews became a part of the Church in increasing numbers. Mendelssohn had little impact on Zionism (Restorationism) directly, but through his influence many within Judaism wrestled away from the confines of rigid Jewish Orthodoxy, while others converted to Christianity.

93 Laqueur, *A History of Zionism, From the French Revolution to the Establishment of the State of Israel*, 7.
94 Menuhin, *Decadence of Judaism in Our Time*, 293.
95 Menuhin, *Decadence of Judaism* in Our Time, 293.
96 Shlomo Avineri, *The Making of Modern Zionism: The Intellectual Origins of the Jewish State* (New York: Basic Books Inc., 1981), 5.
97 Reference made at the end of the Passover celebration as a reminder to the Jews of their ultimate hope.

Through the conduit of the Enlightenment, Moses Mendelssohn was able to have a profound influence on the Jewish communities of Germany by introducing them to secular society. He brought the Jews into contact with stimulating currents of the European world both society and religiously. "European culture with which during the preceding two centuries Jews had failed to keep up owing to their forced migrations, increased persecutions, and social isolation."[98] The events of the Enlightenment enabled Jews to take advantage of the opportunities which were about to be offered to those willing to venture into Gentile society.

---

98 Joseph Jacobs, *Jewish Contributions to Civilization* (Philadelphia: Jewish Publication Society of America, 1919), 291.

CHAPTER TWO

MODERN BEGINNINGS OF THE ZIONIST MOVEMENT AND ITS CAUSES

Introduction

The foundations of the Jewish-Christian conflict are as old as the New Testament itself in creating an atmosphere of mistrust and competitive conflict, as was seen in the introduction. The Reformation alleviated little of the distrust between the Jews and the Church. A barrier still existed as the greater Jewish community elected to remain isolated within the context of both Eastern and Western Europe. "The ghetto also enabled the Jews psychologically to overcome medieval persecutions and Christian bigotry."[99] At this point of time (1600's), Restorationism (Zionism) would carry very little influence within western cultural changes as the Jews moved closer to assimilation. After the influx of a few Jews into the Ottoman lands, after the Spanish inquisitions, Palestine was still closed to the Jews into the twentieth century.

The Reformed Christian's relationship between the Jews made some definite progress in communication and acceptance within the Dutch communities of Holland through the fifteenth and sixteenth centuries. However, the influences of the Enlightenment took its toll on Orthodox Judaism as well as any interest in restoration. Jews found a home in Holland and Amsterdam.

"The integration into secular society impacted the religiosity of Dutch Jewry. Orthodoxy lost its influence to Liberalism, and the Jewish population gradually declined, due to conversions, intermarriage and a low birthrate. As a result, the Jewish nationalist movement never got a foothold in the region and Zionism never achieved the popularity that

---

99   Avineri, *The Making of Modern Zionism*, 104.

it did elsewhere in Europe."[100] Emancipation came to the Netherlands nearly two centuries before France and the rest of Europe.

The successful integration of the Jews into the Netherlands opened doors for Jews into other regions of Europe: "In 1622 Christian IV of Denmark invited a number of Jewish families to settle in his own cities, promising them every privilege."[101] The Jewish success in the Netherlands prompted England to allow the Jews to move to their country, thus creating at least the beginnings of communication between Christians and Jews in England. "Cromwell received the petition (from Manasseh Ben Israel for Jews to return to England) with genuine friendship like Charles before him; he required no persuasion to convince him of the commercial usefulness of the Jews."[102] The economic success of the East and West India companies convinced Cromwell of the economic benefits. In the midst of this political move, the Christian community was still reluctant to open its doors to the Jews. "The merchants of London and the clergy vigorously objected to a new Jewish immigration."[103] Though not initially well received, the English were much more civil in their treatment of the Jews than Central Europe. It would be through England in the coming centuries that the Zionist idea would be realized.

The 1700's was a time of transition and revolution throughout Western culture for Jews and Christians alike. Along with the American and French Revolutions, we witnessed the Enlightenment, which was a revelation and paradigm shift from a predominantly Christian worldview and Church-state relationship to a secular one. What was for the Church a time of reexamination and questions, the Jews found as a time of enlightenment and acceptance.

100　Shyovitz, David. "Virtual Jewish History Tour Netherlands: Emancipation Debate." *Encyclopedia Judaica.* (copyright 2013). www.jewishvirtuallibrary.org/jsource/vjw/netherlands.html. (accessed Sept. 24,2013).
101　Sachar, *A History of the Jews*, 230.
102　Sachar, *A History of the Jews*, 231.
103　Sachar, *A History of the Jews*, 231.

The Orthodox Jewish community lost some of its influence as result of several factors. First, was the failure of messianic mysticism of the sixteen hundreds pushing many Jews away from Judaism; as a result, many Jews moved toward a secular Renaissance. Next, was the French Revolution, followed closely by the Jewish Emancipation. As a result of these events, many Jews abandoned their Jewish religious roots in favor of entering the affairs of Western Europe without the hammer of the medieval church on one end and the extremes of Orthodox Judaism on the other. The political and secular recognition within Western society marked the beginning of Jewish assimilation into society from economic, political, and scholastic perspectives. "The emancipation of the Jews brought them political citizenship; enlarged economic opportunities, and new cultural influences."[104] The Jews would be accepted on equal bases, opening the doors to economic benefits while still maintaining their Jewish distinctiveness.

French Revolution

Unrest concerning old political systems gave rise to the French Revolution: " . . . the French revelations against monarchial, centuries-old forms of government. The promises of liberty fairly crackled in the air. The old order was uprooted."[105] The French Revolution had an impact on a much larger scale as the political impact spread Jewish emancipation across Western Europe; it " . . . let down political barriers and granted the Jews, at least temporarily, the opportunity to achieve the economic independence which is the prerequisite of a state cultural development."[106] Though the French Revolution had a negative impact on the influence of the Catholic Church, it opened many doors to European culture for many Jews. The French Revolution symbolized more than any other event equality of the Jews in France, just as for many Christians, the American Revolution represented a stand for religious freedoms and a break from the traditional state-church mentality of Europe.

---

104 Gordis, Robert. "The Rabbi," *National Jewish Monthly*, (July-August, 1957).
105 Epstein, *Zion's Call*, 15.
106 Sachar, *A History of the Jews*, 328.

The French Revolution marks the beginning of Jewish Modernism and emancipation (political and legal equality). "The Revolution and its political aftermath for the Jews—emancipation—are the starting points for modern Jewish history."[107] It marks the official point where the secular political establishment accepted the Jews within the national entities. It trails the acceptance of the Jews in Holland by about two hundred years, but through the wedge of the Enlightenment and the diminished influence of the Catholic Church, Jews found some relief from the prejudices and mistrust of both the Church and the secular political establishment.

The French Revolution accomplished the acceptance of the Jews by official proclamation by the French authorities. "In the French National Assembly of 1789 Clermont Tonnerre demanded that the Jews as individuals should be denied no rights."[108] Two years later the Jews were granted political emancipation and citizenship. "On September 28, 1791, the Jews of France found themselves full-fledged citizens, with rights and obligations equal to all other French men. It meant that Jews could continue as Jews in their religion and philosophy of life."[109] Some questions of loyalty still remained to be settled along with full economic freedoms; like the blacks in America, full emancipation sometimes requires time. What the law gives through proper political course is not always granted immediately within the hearts and minds of men.

Napoleon was perhaps the most influential person of the French Revolution in its aftermath. By the end of the eighteenth century when emancipation was being realized in Western Europe, Napoleon Bonaparte entered into the Restorationist mix. Epstein raises an interesting question concerning Napoleon's approach to the Jews. "Napoleon's plans rested on Restorationist thinking that had immediately preceded his emergence as emperor."[110] At first, it would be easy to question why Epstein would use Restorationist terminology with emancipation considering their

---

107 Sachar, *A History of the Jews*, 328.
108 Laqueur, *A History of Zionism, From the French Revolution to the Establishment of the State of Israel*, 3.
109 Menuhin, *The Decadence of Judaism in Our Time*, 295.
110 Epstein, *Zion's Call*, 17.

Modern Beginnings of the Zionist Movement and its Causes

contrast; restoration to the land of Israel would fly in the face of French nationalism. Yet Napoleon had ambitions far beyond Europe as he sought control of the Holy Land: " . . . after capturing Gaza and Jaffa, in 1799, he appealed to the Jews of Asia and Africa to rally to the French standard, promising them a homeland in Palestine when he had completely conquered it."[111] Conquering and holding the Holy Land proved to be too much for Napoleon. The Jews themselves gave little support to this early Restorationist movement as it flew in the face of emancipation. "The Jews were not dazzled, however. They continued to support their sovereign with loyalty, and those who lived in Jerusalem worked feverishly to throw up earthworks to repel Napoleon's invasion." [112] The Jews were quite satisfied with acceptance as citizens of France; Restorationism was not to play any role among the Jews for nearly a century.

Napoleon must still have had reservations concerning the Jews which may have become more acute after his failure to win Palestine. " . . . could Napoleon trust the Jews who were so prejudiced until now, as full-fledged citizens?"[113]

Napoleon was not looking for a restoration of the Jews but rather their full allegiance to France. On July 26, 1806, by permission of Napoleon Bonaparte, " . . . more than one hundred outstanding Jews from France, Germany and Italy gathered in Paris to take counsel and answer some of the questions Napoleon posed to them: "

1. Did the French Jews regard France as their country and Frenchmen as their brothers?

2. The problem of intermarriage presented a delicate situation: Judaism allowed such marriages. The rabbis, however, were opposed. Just as the Catholic priests were opposed to intermarriage . . . . [114]

---

111 Sachar, *A History of the Jews*, 281-282.
112 Sachar, *A History of the Jews*, 282.
113 Menuhin, *Decadence of Judaism in Our Time*, 296.
114 Menuhin, *Decadence of Judaism in Our Time*, 297-298. Some questions remain as to the exact date some sources give the date as July 29, 1806.

The questions raised verify the willingness of the Jews to assimilate into French culture and to identify as Frenchmen. The question of marriage was a sticky issue with Jews. Sachar raises the logical question that the Jews resistance to intermarriage is no different than the Catholic priests and created no major obstacles in that many Jews married outside their Jewish community. The final meetings of the Jewish Sanhedrin were completed. On February 9, 1807, at the Hotel de Ville in Paris, 71 men, a modern version of the Jewish Sanhedrin, offered all Jews citizenship. ". . . ghettoized autonomy of the Jews. . . . unlocked mobility of Jewish wealth and enterprise."[115] This gathering of Jews was instrumental in removing the obstacles that prevented acceptance, at least from a political perspective. Jews and Christians were to move closer together within the social climate of Western Europe.

Napoleon was responsible, through the cooperation of the Jews who by that time had abandoned some of their ideological exclusiveness and were accepting the national commitment to France, for baiting the Jews into adopting emancipation within the secular culture. Napoleon desired closer ties with Jews in bringing them into French society. The Jewish leadership declared themselves French, "In an enthusiastic affirmation the assembly said that Jews considered France their country and Frenchmen their brothers."[116] Napoleon's conditions had been met and Napoleon extended his support to the Jews. "France alone had claim on their political allegiance: French Jews . . . no longer formed a nation. . . . they had renounced forever their dream of collective exodus to the ancestral Land of Israel."[117] The French revolution had a profound effect on the Jews in that they were willing to submit to French rule.

Equality within secular society was too much for many Jews to deny and the secularization of the Jewish community was accelerated: along with it emancipation and assimilation. "We have at last obtained the benefits of which we have been deprived for eighteen centuries . . . .

115 Howard M. Sachar, *A History of Israel from the Rise of Zionism to Our Time* (New York: Alfred A. Knopf Inc Pub. Distributed: Random House, 1979), 3.
116 Menuhin, *The Decadence of Judaism in Our Time*, 297.
117 Sachar, *A History of Israel from the Rise of Zionism to Our Time*, 4.

This nation asks no thanks, except that we show ourselves worthy citizens . . . ."[118] The downside of such a statement points to a willingness on the part of the Jews to renounce any other allegiance to a greater Jewish nation (Zionism).

The French Revolution had an impact on a much larger scale as the political impact spread Jewish emancipation across Western Europe. "Napoleon's attitude toward Jews was copied, more or less, in other countries of Western Europe, and with the dissolution of the Holy Roman Empire, . . . to treat citizens all alike, irrespective of their faith, became universal in the West."[119] The walls of the ghetto continued to come down as the effects of the Enlightenment and the French Revolution converted the Jews from their exclusive devotion to Judaism to a broader nationalism of the countries where they were born and raised. It "let down political barriers and granted the Jews, at least temporarily, the opportunity to achieve economic independence."[120] Jews gained an open door to business and education that did not exist before under the confines of Judaism and the ghetto. Separation was no longer beneficial or desired by the majority within the Jewish community. The Jews were now free to act and participate in the greater secular culture and they succeeded.

Assimilation of Jews into Christian Europe

The French Revolution started in earnest the process of Jewish assimilation of a large portion of the Jewish population of Europe. The French Revolution symbolized a triumph and a new order for Western man. For most Jews, "it represented a new freedom as the ideas of the enlightenment percolated into the Jewish communities of Germany and France." [121] Though assimilation was taking place in Germany many years prior to the French Revolution, true equality in Germany took a

118 Menuhin, *Decadence of Judaism in Our Time*, 296. Quote from: Elmer Berger, *The Jewish Dilemma*, 198-99.
119 Sachar, *A History of the Jews*, 297-298.
120 Sachar, *A History of the Jews*, 328.
121 Menuhin, *Decadence of Judaism in Our Time*, 291.

bit more time. " . . . a Jew could not retain his Jewish identity and it (German political and sociological pressures) demanded that he convert and assimilate."[122] Equal citizenship for Jews in Germany did not come until 1869 with many strings attached.

Church-State influences still commanded a strong hold on the countries of Central and Eastern Europe, and the idea of full Jewish emancipation was not yet acceptable. Jewish emancipation brought a reaction under the Holy Alliance (Russia, Austria, and Prussia, in Paris, on September 26, 1815) who sought to revive the Church-State as a predominant force.

"Jews everywhere in Western Europe joined the liberal forces from whose triumph alone they could hope for a dispersal of the clouds which once more obscured the sun of liberty in which they had bask for a few short years. Jews soon ranked among the intellectual leaders of continental liberalism, and from 1815 to1848 exercised an appreciable influence on the course of public opinion."[123]

Jews became leaders within secular liberal society and in many cases opposed to Christian values which in reality were Jewish values. The abandonment of Orthodox Judaism played itself backwards and out of influence to the majority of Jews as they fled the influences of traditional Judaism in favor of a free secular life. "Thousands of young men threw over every restraint and became utter pagans.[124] Sachar continues to illustrate the dramatic changes that took place within the Jewish community as a result of emancipation. "Others, enamored by the apparent superiority of Christian beliefs, accepted baptism."[125] Some of the fears addressed by conservative Jews proved warranted.

Rabbis and teachers of Judaism saw the value of education and the benefits of the secular world for progress and opportunities. Isaac Bäer Levinsohn, rabbinical scholar and student of the classics, philosophy and Oriental languages, " . . . published Learning in Israel dedicated

122 Rausch, *Legacy of Hatred*, 36.
123 Jacobs, *Jewish Contributions to Civilization*, 298-299.
124 Sachar, *A History of the Jews*. 271.
125 Sachar, *A History of the Jews*. 271.

to Science, a vigorous appeal to link up Talmudic studies with the best in secular learning. He pointed out that the great Jewish teachers, authorities in their own fields, needed supplementing."[126] Levinsohn stressed that Art and Science are steadily progressing and Jewish education needed to catch up. "To perfect ourselves in them we must resort to non-Jewish sources . . . but the orthodox looked on sullenly. Only those who wished to be convinced were convinced." [127] Levinsohn now sought to explain the richness of traditional Judaism to the Christian world, " . . . to expose to Christian eyes the world of Jewish spiritual life, founded on the principles of the highest morality, a world then unknown to Russian Christians."[128] Levinsohn's work, *The House of Judah,* 1838 had more effect on Jews than Christians, but the opportunities to exit the Jewish ghetto into the secular world were increasing rapidly for the Jews."[129]

The ghetto was no longer enough for the Jews as they assimilated into greater European society. "The emancipation of the Jews brought them political citizenship, enlarged economic opportunities, and new cultural influences. At the same time it effectively destroyed the hegemony and cohesiveness of the organized Jewish community." [130] Moshe exaggerates the extent of Jewish transition into the greater European culture. The Jews have never completely lost their identity even to this day. However, the opportunities of a broader life within European culture stimulated many Jews toward the secular, minimizing the influence of Orthodox Judaism. What was changed, and continues into the twenty-first century is the determination by many Jews to receive the benefits of secular society while maintaining their distinctiveness and identity in the Jewish community in the midst of assimilation.

From the standpoint of the liberated Jew, Zionism was yet to play any role as the Western political community had given sanction to Jews equal rights under the law. Zionism and assimilation were at opposite

---

126 Sachar, *A History of the Jews,* 334.
127 Sachar, *A History of the Jews,* 334.
128 Sachar, *A History of the Jews,* 334.
129 Sachar, *A History of the Jews,* 334.
130 Rausch, *Legacy of Hatred,* 36.

ends of the sociological spectrum. Zionism symbolizes the traditional Jewish hope for self-preservation and nationalism in Palestine, though the results proved the opposite. "Nationalism actually initially had an unusual effect on the Restorationist movement: it increased Christian support and decreased Jewish support [for Zionism]."[131] While assimilation symbolizes the willingness or desire of Jews to merge into the Gentile culture; this does not sanction openness to the church even though larger numbers of Jews converted to Christianity at least out of convenience. Among the majority of Jews, the church was not to be trusted and was still a place to be avoided. Though Judaism was not easily accepted in Germany as in France many Jews elected to forsake the faith. "... to remain a complete Jew and a complete German is impossible."[132] For many Jews during the late seventeenth and eighteenth centuries, conversion and entering into secular society was not a problem. Though many conversions were done so out of convenience, the distinctiveness of being Jewish had lost some of its hold.

Just as the Protestant and Catholic reformers of the fourteenth and fifteenth centuries tried to put the Bible into the hands of the common people in their own language, the Jews accomplished this through Moses Mendelssohn in German and now in French. "In France, as in Germany, the Bible was translated into the national language. Jews began to discard their Yiddish and their segregation. Emancipation and integration began to flame in Jewish life all over France."[133] This included how the Jews lived from day to day as well as how they worshiped. They began to realize that the old patterns of Jewish worship would no longer meet the needs of the people within assimilated European culture.

Literacy was always a strong part of Judaism as the Jews wanted their children to succeed in life. The Torah offered a firm foundation concerning purpose and the necessity of learning to become useful in the Jewish community. With emancipation, the Jews were no longer bound to the Bible and Torah as their sole means of training. As the Christian community was undergoing the transition from a biblically

---

131 Epstein, *Zion's Call*, 15.
132 Rausch, *Legacy of hatred*, 36.
133 Menuhin, *Decadence of the Jews in Our Time*, 296.

centered education, the Jews also were seeking the benefits of a secular education. "The Jews threw off with avidity most of the shackles which prevented their joining in general European culture, and Jewish parents of means immediately began giving their sons, and what's more, their daughters, the secular education which would adapt them to the careers which now seemed to be open to them as publicists, lawyers, and civil servants."[134] Education became the ticket for many to leave the Jewish ghetto and enter into a more affluent lifestyle within European culture. Many Jews were very successful, such as Louis Brandeis, the first Jew appointed to the US Supreme Court and the genius inventor scientist, Albert Einstein being two examples. Jewish successes confirmed the role that education played for developing and prospering in Western culture. Educational success bred a larger Jewish response into the secular areas of education, business, industry, and politics.

Assimilation and the Development of Reformed Judaism

Following the French revolution and experiencing the grand cultural shift brought by the enlightenment, Jews were challenged in their faith and questioned the purpose of the synagogue and church in relation to culture and life. Moving into the nineteenth century Jews began to question the order and structure of Jewish worship. "The first few decades of the nineteenth century brought important changes in the structure and content of Judaism."[135] Through Reformed Judaism, they began to examine the purpose and function of their Jewish rituals to determine what place they had, if any, in the progressive secular society in which they were becoming a part. "Jewish leaders . . . helped their people to break up the old anachronistic hedges and safeguards, thus opening the way, by example and dedication, to preserving only the positive essential spiritual values by discarding the dross and the impedimenta of ghetto life with its redundancies of vestigial and effete rites, rituals, and precepts."[136] What was kept and what was discarded

---

134   Jacobs, *Jewish Contributions to Civilization,* 298-99.
135   Sachar, *A History of the Jews,* 291.
136   Menuhin, *The Decadences of Judaism in Our Time,* 291.

had profound effects upon Jewish life right up to the twenty-first century. The synagogue was no longer a place to escape secular society but rather a place to prepare and become equipped for the challenges of secular culture.

Religious assimilation of Jews to Christianity continued into the nineteenth century. Hebrew Christian Louis Meyer sought to reach out to the Jews. "The Father of Modern Jewish Missions established the London Society for Promoting Christianity among the Jews in 1809."[137] Meyer had moderate success as most Jews adapted their worship to modern culture. Others were challenged by the changes in the Reformed Synagogue and adaptations resembling traditional Christian worship were implemented; some of those changes reflected upon biblical interpretation. "Christians and Jews were bound by ancient prejudices and theological preconceptions."[138] Critical interpretations challenged the belief that the Bible was inspired of God and sought natural explanations within biblical texts. To counter this problem in 1819, "a number of earnest young men organized a society for the scientific study of Judaism."[139] Lead by Leopold Zunz, philosophical and doctrinal changes were made to reflect those interpretations based upon rationalist thought rather than inspiration. Sachar identifies Zunz as "the outstanding figure in the history of modern Jewish thought...."[140] Throughout the nineteenth century, Reformed Jews were embracing the naturalistic paradigms including Darwinism while seeking to maintain the treasure of biblical richness in the form of Jewish accomplishments, not as an inspired document. The Jewish Reformed movement paralleled much of the liberal Christian slide from orthodoxy through the nineteenth century.

For Jews in Medieval culture, separation from Gentiles was a way for life inside and outside the synagogue. Assimilation demanded a change in social interaction among Gentiles. "Many of the Jews who entered the European world wished to reshape Jewish practices to fit

---

137   Rausch, Legacy of Hatred, 30.
138   Sachar, A History of the Jews, 328.
139   Sachar, *A History of the Jews*, 330.
140   Sachar, *A History of the Jews*, 326.

Modern Beginnings of the Zionist Movement and its Causes

easily into European life. Too many of the traditional customs and ceremonies were obsolete; too many prevented intimate intercourse with the cultured men of other faiths. There was urgent need, therefore, to cut away those elements in the old faith which were no longer essential."[141] Since much of Jewish culture was designed to keep Jews separate from Gentiles, it became prudent to adapt, opening doors to interaction. This course required the Jews to open up to the world, to interact with Christians at work, in business and in education; much in the same way Christians are called to be in the world but not of it.[142]

The pressures of modern culture stressed the need for objective and rationalistic thought. "It came from groups of vigorous thinkers, deeply influenced by contemporary scientific developments, who sought to re-examine the very foundations of their religious faith. . . . This completely reconstructed Judaism until it seemed to be almost a new religion."[143] Through the influences of Zunz and later Darwin, secular science was in the process of naturalizing all explanations for creation and life. Leopold Zunz, lead the fight for the development of scientific Judaism. Zunz became "the outstanding figure in the history of modern Jewish thought."[144] Many Jews were in the process of changing their past for a new future, "the Jews had lost all knowledge of their past."[145] There was no longer room for a creation "Myth", within secular culture, and Jews within the Reformed traditions had little difficulty giving up on the six-day creation motif. Success in the sciences demanded a naturalistic approach to life and Jews perhaps more so than Christians were able to make that adjustment.

A positive aspect to Reformed Judaism that served as a benefit to the Jewish and Christian communities, was it opened up to dialogue with other faiths. "Many of the Jews who entered the European world wished to reshape Jewish practices to fit easily into European life. Too

---

141   Sachar, *A History of the Jews*, 329.
142   (John 17-21) deals with the responsibility of the church to interact with the world much as the Jews were seeking.
143   Sachar, *A History of the Jews*, 329.
144   Sachar, *A History of the Jews*, 326.
145   Sachar, *A History of the Jews*, 326.

many of the traditional customs and ceremonies were obsolete; too may prevented intimate interaction with the cultured men of other faiths. There was urgent need, therefore, to cut away those elements in the old faith which were no longer essential."[146] This is currently one of the social benefits of modern Reformed Judaism, in that the Gentile and Christian worlds were no longer closed doors. Rabbi Rick Jacobs, president of Union for Reformed Judaism, ". . . today has actively worked among the downcast in Haiti knowing full well there were no Jews among the suffering."[147] It was necessary for cooperation to take place, which Jews learned quickly through life among the Gentiles and the Christian community.

Another positive development from the Reformed position was the abandonment of Yiddish; Eliezer Ben-Yehuda was the one man most responsible for that transition. In a letter to Smolenskin, Ben-Yehuda writes: "But, sir, we cannot revive 'Hebrew' with translations; we must make it the tongue of our children, on the soil on which it once blossomed and bore ripe fruit!"[148] Ben-Yehuda promoted European languages along with Hebrew as a language among the Jews. The Haskalah (Enlightenment) cultural renaissance in Eastern Europe in the nineteenth century, though lagging behind Western Europe, was trying to catch up at least within the academic communities. In Judaism, Hebrew learning was encouraged. "It passed into a broad humanism which aimed to break through Jewish exclusiveness by bringing the cultural richness of the European world into Jewish life."[149] The Jews of Eastern Europe were also being influenced by the events in the West, though much slower as Jewish culture was being challenged across Europe.

---

146 Sachar, *A History of the Jews*, 329.
147 Jacobs, Rabbi Rick. "Shelach Lecha: A Glimpse of the Future." *Union for Reform Judaism*. (June 9, 2012). http://urj.org/about/union/leadership/rabbijacobs/?syspage=article&item_id=90580. (accessed Sept. 24, 2013).
148 Hertzberg, Arthur ed., *The Zionist Idea, A Historical Analysis and Reader* (New York: Doubleday & Co. Inc. Herzl Press, 1959), 164. Quote from a letter to the Editor of *Hashahar*, 4.
149 Sachar, A *History of the Jews*. 332.

Modern Beginnings of the Zionist Movement and its Causes

When we examine Zionism from the Reformed Jewish position, we must reflect upon the changes within Reformed Judaism and how those changes impacted the Zionist dream of the restoration of Israel. Shlomo Sand promotes the total dependence of Zionism on the Biblical mandate to return. "Zionist colonization could certainly not have been undertaken without an ideological preparation that gave rise to the blossoming and crystallization of myths."[150] Sand is clear from his interpretation that the Bible and Torah are myth and not relevant on their own; this reference to the Bible as myth is prevalent in revisionist history and literature. Without the promise and prediction of Jews returning to Palestine as the restoration of Israel, there would most likely not be any motive or challenge to go to Palestine. This historic hope provided a foundation for Zionism when circumstances prevailed. "It is also necessary to emphasize that the historical construction that has fuelled our national myths is not the specialty of the Zionist enterprise, but forms an intrinsic part of the formation of collective consciousness throughout the modern world."[151] Sand is correct; without the biblical mandate that he identifies as myth that the return of Israel as a nation in Palestine would most likely not have happened. The Jews would not have had this ethnic promise as leverage or motivation to claim the land. This explains in part why Jews in the reformed synagogue were not actively involved in the Zionist movements to come. It also gives some basis for why Reformed Judaism plays such a small part in the religious life of Jews in Israel today.

The Reformed Judaism movement moved to the United States early in the nineteenth century as immigration and opportunities for a new life challenged Jews and Gentiles alike. "As early as 1824 a group of Jews in Charlestown revised the service and the ritual, and in 1841 the first Reform temple was dedicated."[152] Most Jewish immigrants were connected to Rabbinic or Orthodox Judaism, but the same pressures pushing for conformity of Jews to modern culture came into play in the

---

150 Shlomo Sand, *The Invention of the Jewish People*, (New York: Verso Books 2009) Translated; by Yael Lotan, 314.
151 Sand, *The Invention of the Jewish People*, 325.
152 Sand, *The Invention of the Jewish People*, 314.

states as well. "Most of the immigrants were brought up in the tradition of Rabbinic Judaism, but the new conditions in America often made changes necessary."[153] Jews began to immigrate to the United States from Europe as a result of continued anti-Semitism; the reformed movement was carried along with it. " . . . the father of American Reform Judaism was Isaac Mayer Wise, who came to the United States from Bohemia in 1846."[154] Wise, "served as rabbi of Bene Yeshurun congregation for forty-five years. This was a ministry which profoundly influenced the development of religious life in America. Wise was a firm believer in adaptation, and despite the opposition of conservative elements (Orthodox Judaism), he introduced a great number of reforms in ritual and service."[155] Revolutions and persecution were to play a major part in Jewish immigration and the development of Reformed Judaism through the nineteen century. "The movement for reform gained headway after 1848, the impetus coming from the German liberals, who poured into the country when their revolution was crushed."[156] Today, Reformed Judaism constitutes about 42% of the Jewish population in the United States.[157]

What makes Reformed Judaism unique is its ability to maintain the form of Judaism, keeping the Jewish identity intact while leaving the residue of laws, rites, and rituals in the junk heap of history. "There was urgent need, therefore, to cut away those elements in the old faith which were no longer essential."[158] It helped the Jews maintain their distinctiveness and provided a stimulus to pursue secular activities within the greater Gentile culture: business, academics, and research without hindrances. These came at the expense of their traditional faith. "Too often, unfortunately, Reform Jews were little concerned with the

---

153 Sachar, *A History of the Jews*, 308.
154 Sachar, *A History of the Jews*, 308.
155 Sachar, *A History of the Jews*, 308.
156 Sand, *The Invention of the Jewish People*, 307-308.
157 "Reform Judaism: What is Reform Judaism?" *About the Union of Reform Judaism urj.org/about/* (May 21,1999). http://www.religion *facts.com/judaism/denominations/reform*
158 Sachar, *A History of the Jews*, 329.

true significance of their faith. They flocked to Reform because it made life more comfortable or because it enabled them to climb higher upon the social ladder."[159] Judaism found a home within secular culture, but without a foundational historical past or Zionist dream for the future.

Restorationists Try Again

The Christian Zionist movement of the mid-nineteenth century was determined to find a place for the Jews back in Palestine. Specific events in the Middle East triggered this movement to return Jews back to their ancestral homeland. "The political event that triggered off a re-evaluation of the Restorationists' hold on the real world, hitherto held to be tenuous, was the revolt of Mohammed Ali, an Egyptian leader, against Turkish rules in the Holy land."[160] For Great Britain, the issue was political control and security. "Turkey was viewed with suspicion because of its chaotic finances, infidel beliefs and Oriental customs."[161] Motives rode a purely political wave that carried very little in concern for the Jews outside the interests of Britain. Though this event had political implications, it was the Restorationists that provided the rationale. "Suddenly the Restorationists made a great deal of sense; the Jews should control the Holy land. The British viewed the Jews as having an inherent sense of sound economics, false but redeemable beliefs, and correctable social customs, in short, the Jews would be far more trustworthy than the Turks in control of Palestine."[162]

The political circumstances would seem to fit what had developed in the Middle East. One English Jew with means took interest in the possibility; a Jewish leader named Sir Moses Montefiore came up with a plan for Jewish control. After meeting with the British Counsel in Syria, Montefiore came up with strategy for returning Jews to Palestine. ". . . the Fund for cultivation of the Land in Palestine by the Jews . . . . I shall

---

159   Sachar, *A History of the Jews*, 332.
160   Epstein, *Zion's Call*, 29.
161   Epstein, *Zion's Call*, 30.
162   Epstein, *Zion's Call*, 29.

apply to Mohammed Ali for a grant of land for fifty years; some 100 or 200 villages; giving him an increased rent of from 10 to 20 per cent, and paying the whole in money annually in Alexandria, but the land and villages to be free, during the whole term, from every tax or rate either of Pasha or Governor of the several districts."[163] Ali initially agreed to the plan, but the deal never went through, as circumstances beyond their control closed the door to this opportunity. Though Montefiore went on to purchase land for development, the opportunity for a major immigration of Jews was closed.

Then there came the Damascus Blood Libel, an event from February 7, 1840. "A Capuchin friar, father Thomas (Padre Tomaso de Camangiano) disappeared from a street. One eyewitness had placed him near a Jewish-owned barber shop. The barber was arrested and tortured. The charge was that the Jews had ritually killed Father Thomas, drained his blood, and used the blood to celebrate Passover. The barber, of course, was forced by the horrors of his treatment to name other plotters."[164] Though rumors suggest a Turk killed Father Thomas for blasphemy against the prophet Muhammad, "Tomaso's fellow monks deliberately ignored this rumor, and preferred to spread the story that their Superior had been murdered by the Jews for ritual purposes."[165] It is unlikely this event had any merit or connection with the Jews and unfortunate that Jews suffered. Many Jews, ". . . were also arrested and tortured. Riots followed these arrests, an appeal was offered to Mohammed Ali who still controlled that area."[166] All hope for a movement of Jews to Palestine came to a quick end.

Full emancipation in Europe was short-lived, as the events of the Damascus Blood Libel showed. The door to Palestine for the Jews was closed once again as circumstances dictated. The events of the Blood

163   Epstein, *Zion's Call*, 30.
164   Epstein, *Zion's Call*, 31.
165   Fine, Arnold. "The Infamous Damascus Blood Libel: A Monk Disappears in Damascus." *Our Jerusalem Jewish Press* (January 18, 2002). http://www.ourjerusalem.com/history/story/history20020124.html. (accessed Sept. 24, 2013).
166   Epstein, *Zion's Call*, 31.

Libel prevented the possibility that could have allowed many thousands of Jews into Palestine with minimal conflict. However, the events that followed over the course of the next century demonstrated the precarious position which the Jews found themselves. ". . . the Russian pogroms of 1881, the Dreyfus Affair, and the Holocaust—provided, in the midst of horror, proof that the Jews needed to protect themselves."[167]

The Blood Libel demonstrated several points: Restorationists needed the help of a national entity with political connections. "Churchill made clear the implication of the Restorationist charge from purely a religious movement to one that was also political if the Restoration was not to be by the Anglican Church effecting a converted Israel. But a political effort, then the Jews themselves would have to enter the political struggle."[168] Though Montefiore provided the economic stimulus through purchasing land and establishing agricultural settlements, Jews needed to take charge of their own destiny with Christian and political support. "The Jews must take up the struggle . . . . The Jews themselves will take up the matter, universally and unanimously. . . . that the European powers will aid them in their views."[169] This statement proved to be somewhat prophetic as Herzl's work was not for another 50 years.

Few Jews picked up the Zionist mantle at this point of history; there may have been a great Aliyah (immigration) during the mid-nineteenth century. The fact remained; few Jews had any interest in a return to the Holy Land during the major part of the nineteenth century. Reformed Judaism and Orthodox Judaism had one thing in common: they both resisted Restorationism (Zionism). "For all the deep differences between East European Orthodoxy and the more liberal Reform movement in the West, both shared a fundamental opposition to Zionism, albeit for different reasons."[170] Reformed Judaism preferred assimilation, while Orthodox Judaism tended to be passive, holding solely to a Messianic hope of redemption and leaving Zionism as a future hope that would be

167 Epstein, *Zion's Call*, 31.
168 Epstein, *Zion's Call*, 35.
169 Epstein, *Zion's Call*, 36.
170 Avineri, *The Making of Modern Zionism*, 187. Quote by Rabbi Kook, *The Dialectics of Redemption*.

realized only through the coming of the Messiah. The Jews made little or no effort to return to Palestine except for a small effort in the fourth century with Restorationism playing a very small role. That condition was about to change as some Jews began to recognize the necessity of Jewish restoration.

Years of Favor for Zionist Activities: The First Aliyah

Throughout the early 1800's many Jews found some solitude within the enlightened Western culture; many Jews were against the Reformed movement and were still concerned about entanglements with Christians in general and Gentiles as a whole. Christianity was still viewed with suspicion and a deviation from true faith, which was Judaism, at least within the Orthodox Jewish community. They maintained a strong belief in an eschatological redemption. Some prominent Jews conjectured that the Messiah could not and would not come until Israel again possessed that land of Promise, Palestine. "It is important to realize that the most conservative Jews were anti-Zionists, believing that Palestine was not to become a Jewish land until made so by the coming of the Messiah."[171] Some Jews took issue to doing nothing and prompted the necessity of a Jewish return to Palestine.

These Jews were rethinking the necessity of a new Jewish exodus to the Holy Land. "The earliest forerunners of Zionism, pious rabbis like Alkali and Kalischer, who consisted on standing with the tradition, and to prove before the bar of the classical religious heritage that self-help was a necessary preamble to the miraculous day of the Messiah rather than a rebellion against heaven." [172] They actively promoted the need for Jews to take up the Zionist cause in the mid eighteen hundreds.

---

171 Jordan, James B. "Christian Zionism and Messianic Judaism." *Have Faith Productions Design.* (2007). http://endtimesmadness.com/CZandMJ.html. This viewpoint was dramatized in the recent and rewarding film, "The Chosen." (accessed Sept. 24, 2013).
172 Hertzberg, *Zionist Idea*, 16.

During the 1830's Rabbi Judah Alkalai, a Cabalist, challenged Jews to return to Israel before the 1840's. In his book <u>Darchei Noam</u> (Pleasant Paths), Alkalai emphasized, " . . . the need for establishing Jewish colonies in the Holy Land as a necessary prelude to the Redemption."[173] Conservative Judaism through history resisted any Zionistic goals. Alkalai along with another pious rabbi, Kalischer, challenged the Jews to take initiative. " . . . to prove before the bar of the classical religious heritage that self-help was a necessary preamble to the miraculous day of the Messiah . . . ."[174] This was to declare a favorable year for the Messiah and the belief was that Israel needed to be in the land for the coming of the Messiah (a flashback to the old Cabalist Judaism). This eschatological event prompted some Jews to pick up and move to Israel and Jerusalem.

Rabbi Zvi Hirsch Kalischer, like Rabbi Alkali, saw the need for Jewish involvement in the Zionist movement. "Kalischer apparently first expressed his Zionist ideas in a letter he wrote in 1836 to the head of the Berlin branch of the Rothschild family. He explained that the beginning of messianic redemption would be brought about by human effort and by the will of the governments to gather the scattered of Israel into the Holy Land."[175] Both Rabbi's saw the "emancipation of the Jews in France, Germany and Austria by Napoleon . . . as short-lived."[176] Both saw the necessity of developing Jewish communities in Palestine with emphasis on agriculture and defense. Kalischer proposed in 1870, "that the settlers organize guard units whose members would

---

173 Sachar, *A History of Israel*, 6.
174 Hertzberg, *Zionist Idea*, 15.
175 Isseroff, Ami. "Biography of Rabbi Zvi (Tsvi) Hirsch Kalischer." *MidEastWeb for Coexistence, RA* (2005) http://www.zionism-israel.com/bio/kalischer_biography.html. (accessed Sept. 24, 2013).
176 Isseroff, Ami. "Biography of Rabbi Zvi (Tsvi) Hirsch Kalischer." *MidEastWeb for Coexistence, RA* (2005) http://www.zionism-israel.com/bio/kalischer_biography.html. (accessed Sept. 24, 2013).

combine farm work with defense against attack."[177] These two Rabbis were instrumental in changing the attitude of passivity that existed among some Jews concerning the land of Palestine, the traditional view being to wait on a supernatural intervention.

The work of Rabbis Alkali and Kalischer contrasted with the Reformed Jews who rejected the historical foundations of traditional Judaism in regards to the Zionist movement and the Orthodox Jewish rabbis who saw the need for patience and passivity. Alkali and Kalischer recognized the need to maintain a clear perspective on Jewish history and the promises of a Jewish return as a people to the land of promise with an eschatological Messianic hope. At the same time they recognized the need to be active with God's help and the help of governments to secure that dream. Hertzberg clarifies the issue in contrast with Sand: " . . . the mainstream of Zionism sought a 'usable past' to act as a guideline for the great days to come . . . of an end days the Jewish perspective Messianism, of an ultimate release from the exile and a coming to rest in the land of Jewry's heroic age."[178] Even though Alkali came into the work through Cabalist Judaism, he still presented a more moderate Orthodox Judaism.

These Jews sought to establish a society under the harshest of conditions; however, the year of favor did not reveal the coming of the Messiah. The dates were revised and a six-year range was given as to the return of the Messiah, but again as history attests, the Messiah never came. These Jews remained, however, amidst difficulty and strife. This Jewish movement occurred about the same time as the Restorationists were seeking a return of the Jews to Palestine. The political circumstances would seem to fit what had developed in the Middle East "A Jewish leader named Sir Moses Montefiore came up with a plan for Jewish

---

177 Isseroff, Ami. "Biography of Rabbi Zvi (Tsvi) Hirsch Kalischer." *MidEastWeb for Coexistence, RA* (2005) http://www.zionism-israel.com/bio/kalischer_biography.html. (accessed Sept. 24, 2013).

178 Hertzberg, *Zionist Idea*, 16.

control. "the Fund for cultivation of the Land in Palestine by the Jews."[179] It was through this plan that some Jews were able to return to Palestine.

With the help and encouragement of these two rabbis and some financial assistance from Sir Montefiore and later Rothschild, progress was made raising interest, purchasing and establishing some settlements, and moving some Jews to Israel. It was not until after the Pogroms of Easter Europe and the rise of Jewish nationalism in conflict with European nationalism that the majority of Jews looked seriously at the prospect of a Jewish homeland.

Social and Nationalistic Zionism

By the mid nineteenth-century, assimilation had a profound impact upon many Jews and proved to be another turning point in Jewish-Christian relationships. Through the course of 200 years the Jews moved from committed Orthodox believers living in the ghetto, having a belief in the full inspiration of the Torah and biblical promises concerning the Jews, to a diverse mixture of Orthodox to Reformed Judaism, including a growing agnosticism and atheism. "Thus both liberalism and nationalism created for these Jews the beginning of a new self-awareness, no longer determined by any religious terms, but coequal to the emergence of modern, secular nationalism in Europe."[180] The creation of secular Jews resulted in a growing sense of nationalism, a byproduct of an increased disenchantment with the failure of emancipation through Central and Eastern Europe.

Events following the Damascus Blood Libel reenergized some Jews to pick up the Zionist dream. A second event that impacted many Jews concerning the fragile condition of emancipation was the German revolution of 1848 in central Europe. The purpose of this revolution was the unification of the 39 German provinces into one. For the Jews, that revolution never completely materialized, even after the influence of Moses Mendelssohn. As a result of the German revolution, some

---
179 Epstein, *Zion's Call*, 30.
180 Avineri, *The Making of Modern Zionism*, 123.

Jews took up the mantle in the form of social and nationalistic Zionism, in order to give the Jews a homeland and a return to Jewish pride and identity; another more practical reason was to protect the Jewish people from annihilation. In this development, Moses Hess became a champion for Social Zionism, seeking to develop a socialistic nationalist Zionism that would someday result in a Jewish state, independent and sovereign.

Many Jews participated in the German revolution for emancipation, dying side by side with Christians. " . . . Jews were killed fighting side by side with Christians attempting to bring about a new order, and the Jewish dead were buried in a common grave with the other martyrs."[181] The results were less than beneficial for the Jewish people. " . . . the 1848 uprisings ushered in a new more intense anti-Jewish hostility as many Christians feared that emancipation would be tantamount to Jewish domination."[182] Glenn Sharfman places much of conflict from the German revolution directly upon the fears within the Christian community. "Conservatives like Prussian Minister of the Interior von Thile argued against Jewish Emancipation by stating that granting Jews any rights in government was irreconcilable with Christendom because they would be expected to take part with the Christian spirit."[183] What was a political struggle seemed to have a great deal of Christian influence, resulting in a less-than-hoped-for outcome for most Jews. The failure of the secular and liberal forces pulled the revolution back within the Christian camp, putting most Jews back where they began.

The results of 1848 were ambiguous at best. The "Basic Rights of the German People" were abolished in 1851, and Jews were once again subject to discrimination. The idea of a "Christian state" reechoed in Prussia and many other states. Prussian law included a paragraph stating that: "The Christian religion shall be the basis in all government

---

181 Avineri, *The Making of Modern Zionism*, 123.
182 Sharfman, Glenn. "*Jewish Emancipation.*" *Encyclopedia of 1848 Revolutions*. (October 20, 2004). http://www.ohio.edu/chastain/ip/jewemanc.html. (accessed Sept. 24, 2013).
183 Sharfman, Glenn. "*Jewish Emancipation.*" *Encyclopedia of 1848 Revolutions*. (October 20, 2004). http://www.ohio.edu/chastain/ip/jewemanc.html. (accessed Sept. 24, 2013).

institutions that are associated with religion."[184] Jews would have to wait another twenty years for legal emancipation to take hold. "Yet in the decades following 1848, many Jews realized that the social and economic emancipation depended less on legalization and more on the willingness of the population at large to accept Jews as fellow citizens."[185] A strong barrier of mistrust still remained between the majority of Christians and Jews.

The German revolution did not bring emancipation for the Jews this time. Jewish leadership was hunted down, imprisoned, others were executed, or fled the country. "Many revolutionaries were arrested . . . sentenced to death . . . many other Jewish and non-Jewish revolutionaries, managed to escape to the United States." [186] "While most Jews were not political radicals, some prominent people of Jewish origin emerged as leaders of the nascent socialist movement."[187] To a large extent the socialist ideal was an offshoot of anti-Semitic injustice in Germany and Greater Europe.

Hess played an active role in the German revolution for emancipation; its failure impacted Hess negatively in regards to the future of the Jewish people. "Hess, the German Jew, after losing one battle, quickly arrived at the conclusion that he had lost the war."[188] Like many of his countrymen Hess fled the country, moving to France and becoming one of the idealistic socialist revolutionaries of the

184 Sharfman, Glenn. *"Jewish Emancipation." Encyclopedia of 1848 Revolutions.* (October 20, 2004). http://www.ohio.edu/chastain/ip/jewemanc.html. (accessed Sept. 24, 2013).

185 Sharfman, Glenn. "Jewish Emancipation." Encyclopedia of 1848 Revolutions. (October 20, 2004). http://www.ohio.edu/chastain/ip/jewemanc.html. (accessed Sept. 24, 2013).

186 Sharfman, Glenn. "Jewish Emancipation." Encyclopedia of 1848 Revolutions. (October 20, 2004). http://www.ohio.edu/chastain/ip/jewemanc.html. (accessed Sept. 24, 2013).

187 Sharfman, Glenn. "Jewish Emancipation." Encyclopedia of 1848 Revolutions. (October 20, 2004). http://www.ohio.edu/chastain/ip/jewemanc.html. (accessed Sept. 24, 2013).

188 Menuhin, *Decadence of Judaism in Our Time*, 37.

late nineteenth century along with Karl Marx and Friedrich Engels. According to Menuhin, Hess " . . . could never forget the sudden anti-Semitism, with its manifestations of discrimination and prejudice in all walks of life, that he discovered in his native Germany."[189] In part, as a result of the events in Germany, Hess became involved in the Zionist movement; more than any other individual, Hess became responsible for the rise of Zionism prior to Theodor Herzl. As a result, "Moses Hess is considered the father of socialist Zionism, since he was a pioneer in the socialist movement and a colleague of Karl Marx and Friedrich Engels."[190]

Hess' disillusionment with German emancipation turned the atheist scholar into a social Zionist. Hess determined to strategize the necessity of a Jewish state for the oppressed Jews of Europe. He saw the Jewish people having potential for great good and as lights to the world, the source of a future in the Middle-East. Moses Hess said, "Jewry alone was destined to play in fashioning the world of tomorrow. . . . and the new Jewish nation to act as the guardian of the crossroads of three continents and to be the teacher of the somnolent peoples of the East."[191] This high expectation prompted Hess to write *From Rome to Jerusalem,* where he lays out a strategy for the development of a Jewish national state in Palestine.

Nationalistic Zionism was not confined to Germany, but grew under the oppressive rule of the Czars in Russia. "Pinsker and Herzl, who appeared several decades later to preach the total evacuation of the land of the Gentiles, could make their case only by interpreting the whole of postexilic history as less of a problem to the extremist version of Zionism which crystallized in the early years of the twentieth century."[192] Pinsker promoted a purely secular nationalistic Zionism that left little room for religious Judaism. "Their program, total revolution, of a complete break with the entire earlier career of the Jew in favor of purely secular national life ('let us be like all the gentiles') required

---

189 Menuhin, *Decadence of Judaism in Our Time,* 26-27.
190 Menuhin, *Decadence of Judaism in Our Time,* 26.
191 Hertzberg, *Zionist Idea,* 19.
192 Hertzberg, *Zionist Idea,* 16.

the assumption that the eighteen centuries of life in exile had been a barren waste."[193] This form of Zionism completely removes any historic foundation based upon Torah; but leaves the Jewish identity intact. The Jews are like any other nationalistic country having their own identity.

Odessa in the Ukraine became the center for social Zionism in Russia. "Odessa Committee—as the Choivevei Zion organization was known henceforth in the Zionist world—opened a bureau in Jaffa . . . ."[194] Odessa became the academic epicenter of Jewish learning in Russia prior to the twentieth century. Jews in the Pale (Russian ghetto), the Orthodox, and conservative Jews remained passive toward any Scientific or Zionist goals. One rabbinical scholar, Isaac Baer Levinsohn "pointed out that the great Jewish teachers, authorities in their own fields, needed supplementing" [195] with art and science. Orthodox Jews were not convinced, "but the orthodox looked on sullenly. Only those who wished to be convinced were convinced."[196] Prominent Russians who trace their training through Odessa include Asher Ginzberg, (Ahad Ha-Am), father of spiritual Zionism; Peter Smolenskin, who wrote on Jewish nationalism *The Dawn*; and Lev Pinkster. Odessa became the center of socialism in the mid-to-late nineteenth century. Pinsker a Hebrew scholar and Medical Doctor, served with the Russian army in the Crimean War[197] and was decorated by the czar. Despite his record of service to Russia, Pinsker along with other Jews was driven from Odessa in 1871 as a result of earlier Pogroms to the southern regions of Russia. "Through the idea of Autoemancipation, or self-determination, Pinsker tries to reintegrate the Jews into the historical process, to make them one again an active factor in history, conscious of themselves and their historical activity."[198] Pinsker picks up on the writings of

---

193 Hertzberg, *Zionist Idea*, 16.
194 Sachar, *A History of Israel*, 32.
195 Sachar, *A History of the Jews*, 334.
196 Sachar, *A History of the Jews*, 334.
197 Crimean War //Sultan and Tsars: The battles raged between the Ottoman and churches of Greece, Armenian's, Latin's and Orthodox.
198 Avineri, *The Making of Modern Zionism*, 74.

Alkali and Kalischer in realizing the need for Jewish commitment to Zionism; in this case the circumstance contributes to the movement of the Jews a bit closer to a Zionist reality. "If I am not for myself, who will be for me? And the pamphlet's closing sentence, Pinsker echoes the sentiments of Alkali and Kalischer, "Help yourselves, and God will help you!"[199] The solution in Avineri's view of Pinsker, requires a nationalist mentality to rise among the Jews. "The solution to the Jewish problem should be found in a national manner, Pinsker argues, and education and philanthropy cannot solve it."[200] A wholesale change of attitude among the Jews was required; the Pogroms of the late 1800's served in part to create that attitude of urgency among some Jews that was previously missing.

For Reformed Jews, nationalism in the form of Zionism was not an issue; they were citizens of the countries in which they lived. The idea of a nationalist secular Jew did not fit into any currently active Jewish tradition, Cabalist Judaism included. Secular and Zion hardly fit into the same sentence without appearing contradictory. Another Jewish scholar, "Pines recognized the depth of this challenge of secular Zionism to the religious tradition by creating a new and modern focus for Jewish identity. They tried to prove that Jewish nationalism itself had religious connotations and cannot be based on a secular conception of nationalism."[201] This shows the difficulty of arriving at any consensus in regards to a Zionist policy and direction. The Jews still needed a central reason and focus to bring a majority of Jews together regarding the possibility of a Zionist Idea. Both of these reasons were about to come true by the end of the century.

The failure of German emancipation and the resistance to giving Jewish civil rights may be attributed to several factors. David Rausch presents the expectation under German leadership that the Jews assimilate. "A Jew could not retain his Jewish identity and it demanded

---

199   Leo Pinsker, Auto-Emancipation, (New York: Maccabaean Pub. Co. 1906), 4, 32.
200   Avineri, *The Making of Modern Zionism*, 82.
201   Avineri, *The Making of Modern Zionism*, 82.

that he convert and assimilate."[202] The failure to arrive at a strictly secular political structure can be attributed in part to a populist desire to remain close to the church. This does not suggest that secular and liberal forces were completely stymied; the Jews did gain equal rights and emancipation in the late 1860's and early 1870's in Germany. "Jews (were) granted equal citizenship in Germany in 1869 under Chancellor Otto Von Bismark."[203] From the Jewish perspective, the Church and the Christian influence still dominated.

The desire for Jewish emancipation came in a large part through the desire of the Jews to be accepted in the greater secular culture while remaining Jewish in practice and belief. It is not surprising that the sociologists of the nineteenth century reflected this socialistic desire to change the status quo of culture not only among the Jews but also among the Gentiles as well. Thus sociologists such as Pinkster, Hess, and Marx made a profound impact upon twentieth-century culture both East and West as socialism and the whole concept of fairness and equality present in today's culture were manifest. These same desires were also much of the impetus behind the rise of political and humanitarian Zionism.

Eastern Europe and the Pogroms

Following the events of the Enlightenment through the 1700's and 1800's, it appeared at least in many places that the Jews had found some relief. In Western Europe, with the development of industrialization and the influx of people to the cities, the Jews were able to adapt to the culture of the West and found success while maintaining their faith and customs.

Even in Russia the influence of Haskalah (Enlightenment) was evident and became more influential: Jews found some relief as educational opportunities opened up for the first time. "The most important impetus to the Haskalah was given by the early liberalism of Alexander II. Taking fullest advantage of his reform edicts, thousands

---

202   Rausch, *Legacy of Hatred*, 36.
203   Rausch. *Legacy of Hatred*, 291.

of young Jews flocked to the schools and universities and eagerly sharpened their intelligence on the whetstones of European culture."[204] Other motives were present for this openness toward the Jews concerning education. "The attempt during the regime of Nicholas I to wean Jews from the Talmud and to promote secular education seemed to give an impetus to the Haskalah."[205] The attempt was to assimilate Jews into the culture as Russians rather than Jews.

What this avenue to education did accomplish for the Jews was a new awareness of who they were as a people, or Jewish nationalism. It also provided the educational foundation and training necessary for Jewish immigration to other countries, including Palestine that needed the skills and the will to participate in the building of a new society. "It was natural that the Haskalah should arouse an intense nationalism among the Jews, just as it was aroused by the cultural revival among contemporary peoples . . . . Those who found the doors of Russian life closed upon them fed hungrily upon the new nationalistic literature, which gave the disillusioned a hope and the discontented a program. The Haskalah, in this sense, was a forerunner of Zionism."[206] As a result of this policy, the Russian government inadvertently equipped and trained many Jews for immigration and skilled labor for the building up of the Zionist movement.

Educational opportunities for Russian Jews did not remain open for long as over the course of the next three decades Jewish Pogroms would drive millions of Jews out of Russia, Romania, and Eastern Europe. Life in Russia became very difficult as the majority of Jews in Central and Eastern Europe were pushed to the edge of endurance, resulting eventually in a mass exodus to the West and to Palestine. "Russia . . . compelled thousands of young Jews to emigrate to better their economic condition."[207] The Pogroms of 1881 affected enlightened Odessa, Russia, influencing Pinkster and others toward Jewish nationalism and socialism. "Educated Odessa did not behave basically very differently

---

204 Sachar, *A History of the Jews*, 334.
205 Sachar, *A History of the Jews*, 334.
206 Sachar, *A History of the Jews*, 335.
207 Sachar, *A History of the Jews*, 306.

from the most backward village in the Pale of Settlement."[208] The Pogroms of 1881 were significantly more intensive, as they affected millions of Jews across Russia and Romania.

The failure or rather the refusal to assimilate the Jewish populace, created a sense of distrust which resulted in pressure to leave. The problem for many Jews on this exodus was the unwillingness of Western Europe to accept these wandering Jews. "The ablest of the eighteenth-century political philosophers, Montesquieu, also denounced the hypocrisy of a Europe which prided itself on its Christianity."[209] The Ottomans were unwilling to open up more land including Palestine for resentment or jealousy of Jewish commerce, "Ottoman authorities were systematically restricting immigration now and forbidding land sales to European Jews."[210] This resulted in a uniform rejection of the Jewish community, leaving them nowhere to go but west. Of these vast migrations at this time, few resulted in a settlement in Palestine; those doors were still closed, the vast majority ended up in the United States. The Jewish population in the United States by the end of the nineteenth century was well over a million Jews.

Throughout the history of the Jewish Diaspora, when Jews found acceptance within a particular culture, events changed and persecution came. The events of the mid-to-late 1800's were no different; the hope for people who were pulled into secular culture through assimilation began to unravel such that the Jews were no longer safe. The Pogroms of the mid-and-late century Europe forced many people from their homes into a situation that separated them from their culture. Germany demanded a patriotic devotion and a near renunciation of their Jewish faith. Russia demanded much the same, but still carried a strong religious bias that was used as a wedge against the Jews. For these Jews in Central and Eastern Europe, full assimilation into the culture or complete separation was the only option.

---

208   Avineri, *The Making of Modern Zionism*, 66.
209   Avineri, *The Making of Modern Zionism*, 275.
210   Sachar, *A History of Israel*, 29.

In Romania and Russia, the Pogroms resulted in millions of displaced people, many of whom crossed over the ocean to the Americas for a new life with the hopes of finding acceptance. "Early in the eighties the May laws and the violent pogrom epidemic in Russia set tens of thousands of Jews flying towards the United States. Whole communities migrated en masse, and more than twenty thousand Jews entered the United States annually."[211] Other displaced Jews found their way to Palestine under Ottoman rule. It was not necessarily the desire of the Jews to find a land of their own, for many were happy where they were; most of the immigrants left because of the hardships. "The great majority . . . of those who had come . . . left the country within a few months, returning to Russia or going on to America."[212] Those who remained in Palestine became the future leaders with a strong will and a determination to build a country of their own. These Jews would be considered the second Aliyah. "But those who remained eventually became the nucleus of Labor Zionism . . . they were to provide in later years the leadership of the Socialist parties, the Zionist movement, and the State of Israel."[213] It was the circumstances that forced the people to find a new home. The Zionist movement was not a calculated project by a few resourceful Jews. It became a source of survival for a race, a resourceful people whose situation cried out for relief that only a land or place of their own could resolve. It is in this circumstance that the Zionist movement took shape and the preservation of a race became such a priority.

Throughout Poland, Romania, and Russia, Jews were put into a position of inferiority. They were too successful for the common Gentile; therefore they were herded into "Pales."[214]

---

211   Sachar, *A History of the Jews*, 307.
212   Laqueur, *A History of Zionism, From the French Revolution to the Establishment of the State of Israel*, 282.
213   Laqueur, *A History of Zionism, From the French Revolution to the Establishment of the State of Israel*, 282.
214   Pales: Russian Reservations for Jews, similar to Indian Reservations in the United States.

"The masses of the people lived in poverty, hemmed into a narrow district, learning to subsist under an ever-increasing load of repression. . . . limited in business opportunities."[215]

". . . forbidding Jews to join merchant and artisan guilds in certain provinces practically confined them to a limited district."[216] Such unfair business restriction and outright discrimination was given no opportunity for appeal. Jews were no longer permitted to practice law or go to law school. No avenues remained but for them to pick up and leave resulting in mass movements of people during the harshest times.

Russia during the nineteenth century was the worst-case scenario for the Jewish people. Little room was provided for millions of people to live and prosper. The Jewish community came under harsher conditions than any groups in those countries. There was little thought given to how much the Jews contributed to Russian society. Why this discrimination became so fervent one can only guess. "The benighted policy of Russia was partly due to the colossal ignorance of the masses, to bigotry of the Church, and to the stupid incompetence of the rulers."[217] On top of this Sachar adds the resistance of any Orthodox and conservative Jews to assimilate into Russian culture. "It was assuredly complicated by the fact that the five million Jews of the empire refused to fall in line with the Russification policy of the panslavist. They (Jews) demanded the right to live their own lives in their own way."[218] The age-old excuse that the Jews would not assimilate and that they were responsible for the death of Jesus pans thin and leaves little rationale as to the ultimate objective.

These attacks were not limited to the Tsar or government officials; even the literary community felt compelled to offer hostility. "Russian novelists and poets of the period, the pride and glory of the country, joined in the crusade of Nicholas against the hated Jews."[219] It seems

---

215 Sachar, *A History of the Jews*, 313.
216 Sachar, *A History of the Jews*, 311.
217 Sachar, *A History of the Jews*, 309.
218 Sachar, *A History of the Jews*, 309.
219 Sachar, *A History of the Jews*, 315.

odd that a specific group of people would be singled out, but the fact remains that discrimination reached the highest levels of government and the Jewish people were singled out not for anything wrong, but for what they did right; they were perhaps too successful.

The Pogroms of 1881 and following were most influential in driving millions of Jews out of Eastern Europe to western countries and Palestine. As a result of restrictions placed upon Jews, the Jewish community as a whole was ordered to get out. "For nearly a century and a half the Jews of Russia had lived in darkness under the most brutal despotism in modern history."[220] Those forces pushed more Jews West and eventually to the United States rather than the more direct and shorter journey to the land of Israel. Zionism in this respect took a detour through the United States where by the century's end, many Jews found a new home.

The influx of Jews from Eastern Europe remained high throughout the late 1800's, moving Jews in mass. As the Jews, so hated by the Russians, were persecuted and forced from their homes, Russia, seeking to reinvent itself into its traditional culture, resisted westernization, leaving it behind the times. It was evident that the failure of Jews to assimilate into the culture created a sense of disharmony as had occurred many times before in history through many cultures. This disconnect has always left the Jewish people outside the cultural context among the people groups where they lived, eventually becoming subjected to restrictions and harassment usually reserved for criminals and rebels. The Jews were generally productive and beneficial to society. The problem in this case at least for the Russian Jews was that they were often too successful. Bitterness and jealously often resulted, leaving a backlash of retribution in the form of "Ukase,"[221] laws preventing commerce or at least restricting to such a degree as to remove any advantage, subjecting the Jews to poverty and disenchantment; this often resulted in the very thing Russian leadership was hoping would occur, the total evacuation of the Jewish population. "The Russian leaders looked forward to a

---

220   Sachar, *A History of the Jews*, 322.
221   Ukase laws – Government decrees.

Modern Beginnings of the Zionist Movement and its Causes

time when at least the larger cities would be as stated by Thomas Tully, (cleansed of Jews)."[222]

The movement of Jews across Eastern Europe brought some Jews to Palestine, but due to the restriction of the Ottoman Empire, "The Ottoman Turks allowed the settlement of no more than 200 to 250 families at a time in any one place . . . they could not establish themselves in Palestine. Furthermore, foreign nationality would have to be relinquished, Ottoman nationality adopted, and the immigrant would have to undertake to seek no special rights or privileges."[223] Most Jews still maintained their distinctive culture and were unwilling to make that sacrifice.

". . . to this offer, however, there was naturally no response. Jewish emigrants from Russia, Poland and Romania, who were set upon escape from present miseries and were concerned with their own private pain and individual salvation, left their homes. The great majority looked not east or south, in any case, but west. The minority, the men of Hibbat Zion, and the Zionists proper, with larger purposes in mind, had their eyes set exclusively on Ezra-Israel."[224] Those Jews who did find their way to Palestine in spite of the barriers began the hard task of building a country that was not yet theirs.

Christian Zionism Before Herzl

Zionism has been a part of many Evangelical Christian communities since the Puritans. Just as Sand emphasizes earlier in the chapter, "Zionist colonization could certainly not have been undertaken without an ideological preparation that gave rise to the blossoming and crystallization of myths."[225] The acceptance of a true biblical history of the Jews and the predictive power of scripture demands a Jewish return

---

222   Sachar, *A History of the Jews*, 319.
223   Richard Cohen, *Vision and Conflict in the Holy Land* (Jerusalem: Yac Ben-Zvi and St. Martin's Press, 1985), 52.
224   Cohen, *Vision and Conflict in the Holy Land*, 52.
225   Sand, *The Invention of the Jewish People*, 314.

to the Holy Land. Without a biblical historical perspective, Zionism would most likely never have developed either Orthodox or Cabalist Judaism. Epstein makes the same claim concerning Christian Zionism. " . . . without such a Puritan and Evangelical based religious temperament, Restorationism might have disappeared."[226] It was in part the influence of powerful Christian leaders that promoted the ideals of Zionism from both a practical and spiritual perspective. The belief that the biblical history was relevant was still vibrant in England and the United Sates; even as higher criticism was having its toll on the churches of Europe, Evangelical Christians along with Orthodox Judaism held to a biblical foundation.

Restorationism had some strong Christian support both in England and the United States. In England, Anthony Ashley Cooper, Seventh Earl of Shaftesbury, " . . . one of the most influential men of the Victorian Age in Britain,"[227] was a philanthropist, politician, and social activist who saw a need in helping the Jews. " . . . born wealthy and possessing family connections thought the British political hierarchy, Shaftesbury used his religious fervor as the basis of this entire life."[228] Shaftesbury worked all his life for the poor, oppressed, and downtrodden; " . . . he was the person primarily responsible for the Ten Hours bill limiting child labor."[229] Shaftesbury was a British Restorationist who acted when a need arose; they "never waited for Divine intervention nor had they relied on the Jews to restore themselves."[230] Christians at this point were not passive participants but realized the necessity for action. "Shaftesbury began the political steps necessary to realize his vision by visiting Lord Palmerston, the Secretary of State . . . ."[231] Lord Palmerston wrote to Ponsonby, the British Ambassador to Turkey. "There exists at the present time among the Jews dispersed over Europe, a strong notion that the time is approaching when their nation is to return

---

226 Epstein, *Zion's Call*, 29.
227 Epstein, *Zion's Call*, 36.
228 Epstein, *Zion's Call*, 36.
229 Epstein, *Zion's Call*, 32.
230 Epstein, *Zion's Call*, 33.
231 Epstein, *Zion's Call*, 33.

to Palestine.... It would be of manifest importance to Sultan to encourage the Jews to return and to settle in Palestine because the wealth which they would gain with them would increase the resources of the Sultan's dominions."[232] British wheels were turning, but without Jewish support, gained limited success within the Jewish community.

Those with influence also beseeched the Church to assist in helping the Jews. "Palmerston was beseeched by many others besides Shaftesbury. In 1841 ... the Church of Scotland requested that the Jews be allowed to return. Three hundred twenty citizens of Carlow, Ireland sent similar memorandum to Palmerston."[233] Some clergy tried to help, such as Clergyman Thomas Tully, a Restorationist, who established a *"British and Foreign Society of Promoting the Restoration."* Protestants recognized the need for Jews to return to accomplish the restoration to Palestine. He suggested a Biblical interpretation of the Promise of return, and suggested "the Jews need Protestant's help in order to effect that return." [234]

Christians in the United States also were open to help Jews return to Palestine. John Nelson Darby and the Plymouth Brethren, "had a profound effect on growth of American Christian Zionism."[235] "The latter Restorationist movement had a profound effect on growth of American Christian Zionism. The Jews, Darby argued, would be God's instrument through whom all Biblical prophecies could be fulfilled. Darby was hearkening back to Puritan admiration for the Jews and Jewish religious autonomy. Darby suggested boldly that the Jewish covenant with God had never been broken; nor had it been superseded by any Christian covenant. "[236] The New Testament gives biblical support to the claims made by Jesus that the first covenant was still active.[237] From this position there was a biblical mandate and spiritual necessity for a

232 Epstein, *Zion's Call*, 34.
233 Epstein, *Zion's Call*, 35.
234 Epstein, *Zion's Call*, 35.
235 Epstein, *Zion's Call,* 39.
236 Epstein, *Zion's Call*,39.
237 New Testament resources supporting the Old Covenant was still active: Matthew 5:17-18.

Jewish return to Palestine. The influence of many prominent Christians pushed the circumstances closer to reality. It was now time for the Jews to pick up responsibility as suggested by Alkali and Kalischer decades earlier and through the writings of Moses Hess to articulate the necessity for a national Jewish state. These events still took years and many circumstance to see their reality, but the ball was in full motion and the political, spiritual support of the Christians and Jews alike set up for the Jewish Zionist movement through the influence and work of Theodor Herzl.

Another instrumental Christian active in relieving Jewish suffering and a strong Restorationist was William Blackstone, a business man and student of D. L. Moody. After returning from a trip to the Holy Land, Blackstone organized a meeting of brother Christians and Jews. The First Methodist Church of Chicago was the scene. "Rabbi Emil Hirsch, a nationally prominent leader of Reform Jews in America, denounced Jewish nationalism, disclaimed any Jewish wish for restoration, and rejected Blackstone's efforts. Blackstone, for his part, pleaded for the right and necessity of such a return to ease Jewish suffering."[238]

Blackstone presented his petition to Harrison and Secretary of State James G. Blaine. "What shall be done for the Russian Jews? . . . but where shall 2,000,000 of such poor people go? It was at this point that Blackstone asked the question really on his mind: 'why not give Palestine back to them again?' "[239] "According to God's distribution of nations it is their home—an inalienable possession from which they were expelled by force."[240] After discussing Jewish farming success and the foreign politics of the day, Blackstone stated: "We believe this is an appropriate time for all nations, and especially the Christian nations of Europe, to show kindness to Israel."[241] "Blackstone petitioned Harrison and Blaine . . . to use their good offices and influence with a variety of world leaders, including Czar Alexander III of Russia, Queen Victoria, William II of Germany, and others, 'to secure the holding...of an

238   Epstein, *Zion's Call*, 110.
239   Epstein, *Zion's Call*, 110.
240   Epstein, *Zion's Call*, 110.
241   Epstein, *Zion's Call*, 111.

international conference to consider the conditions of the Israelites and their claims to Palestine as their ancient home, and to promote, in all other just and proper ways, the alleviation of their suffering condition.'"[242] In March 5, 1891, Blackstone ". . . gained 413 signatures for the Memorial. Czar Reed, speaker of the House of Representatives, J. Pierpont Morgan, John D. Rockefeller, Cyrus McCormick, Melville W. Fuller, then Chief Justice of the Supreme Court, Cyrus Field, William E. Dodge, Russell Sage, Charles Scribner, Philip Armour, Scores of ministers, Catholic leaders, and newspaper editors, but only 15 Jewish leaders."[243] President Harrison, "it turned out, was very sympathetic, though for political and economic reasons—he didn't relish the thought of welcoming several million penniless Jewish immigrants. In fact, Harrison had already begun to deal with the Russian government."[244] This document, it seems, should have carried an enormous amount of weight but with little Jewish support, Harrison had little motive to move forward.

The problem of Jewish participation or rather lack of it again derailed any attempt to push the Restorationist goal forward.

> "The real opposition to Blackstone's public plan, endorsed by so many, came from the Jews, both Reform and Orthodox. Rabbi Hirsch spoke for a group of Reform Rabbis in reiterating Reform ideology of the time; there was a divine purpose, or mission, in God's scattering of the Jews, so the Jews, therefore wanted to remain in the countries where they now lived as loyal citizens. Orthodox leaders, believing . . . Blackstone's scheme to be ultimately a conversionary one, and being very hostile to, or, in some cases, ignorant of, the fledgling nationalist movement among Jews, also expressed their displeasure. The strong Jewish rejection was among the

---

242 Epstein, *Zion's Call*, 111.
243 Epstein, *Zion's Call*, 111.
244 Epstein, *Zion's Call*, 111.

political reasons for Harrison's not following through on the plan."[245]

Blackstone's contribution, through profound, went no further. Blackstone shifted his work to serve in the United States Christian commission; William Blackstone made little headway into Jewish society. For his efforts, he was regarded by some as the "Father of American Christian Zionism."[246] Though Blackstone's efforts were notable, they barely merit mention by most historians concerning the historical events leading up to the Zionist movement due to lack of Jewish involvement.

Through the course of the 1800's, the Jews rode a roller coaster of political and social ideology through a maze of conflicts and contradictions. Emancipation was to be short-lived even within the confines of France, the Jew's most trusted ally. Ethnic nationalism was to play a much greater hand than many realized, and the ability to assimilate had its limits. Nationalism took on some rather interesting characteristics toward the end of the nineteenth century. "Nationalism actually initially had an unusual effect on the Restorationist Movement: it increased Christian support and decreased Jewish support. Some of the European Christians who were nationalists and anti-Semites saw in the Restorationist Movement an incredibly neat solution to the problem of having too many 'foreign'[247] Jews in their country disguised as a benevolent solution to the problem of Jewish exile. If Jews were removed, such a removal would obviate the need to grant Jews equality."[248] Epstein points out one of the major problems with Christian Zionism; from the Jewish perspective, the Christian's only true motive was to get rid of the Jews. It was viewed as self-serving and as less than favorable for the Jew. Assimilation was the only path to security. That assimilation was in the form of economic and political security that would enable the Jews to succeed within the national culture and in competition with Gentiles and Christians.

---

245   Epstein, *Zion's Call*, 112.
246   Epstein, *Zion's Call*, 112.
247   Epstein, *Zion's Call*, 15-16.
248   Epstein, *Zion's Call*, 15.

Modern Beginnings of the Zionist Movement and its Causes

In spite of the early Pogroms, most Jews saw little value in the restoration of Palestine. Except for a few exceptions among Cabalist Jews and academic socialists, most Jews, whether Orthodox, Reformed, or strictly secular, had little need or interest in Restorationism. "Despite the efforts of British Christian Restorationists, their major audiences didn't respond. World Jewry remained inert, unwilling to challenge the tacit agreement they had reached with European societies, exemplified by their relationship to Napoleon. Jews were unwilling to assert a specifically Jewish nationalism because it challenged both their purely religious as well as post-enlightenment identities."[249] In spite of their efforts, Christian Restorationists made little headway toward realizing any solid gains toward Jewish restoration. Even within Britain, anti-Semitism resisted efforts to help and facilitate Jews coming from Eastern Europe. " . . . The Christian Restorationist especially had to battle the deep-seated anti-Jewish prejudice throughout British society, a prejudice reflected in the literature, daily activities, and even the law."[250]

Condition of Jewish-Christian Relationships at the End of the Nineteenth Century

The Christian Church was not the official force behind the Pogroms and restrictions placed upon the Jews during the last half of the nineteenth century. However the Church, regardless of its form, had major influence upon the decisions that led to the politics involved. Pogroms as defined by the Jewish Virtual Library were, "attacks carried out by the Christian population against the Jews between 1881 and 1921 while the civil and military authorities remained neutral and occasionally provided their secret or open support."[251] This would seem to be the view held by many Jews today.

---

249   Epstein, *Zion's Call*, 46-47.
250   Epstein, *Zion's Call*, 47.
251   Slutsky, Yehuda. "Pogroms." *Encyclopaedia Judaica Jewish Virtual Library*, (2008) http://www.jewishvirtuallibrary.org/jsource/judaica/ejud_0002_0016_0_15895.html. (accessed Sept. 24, 2013)

For the Russians who were pressed under the heavy hand of the Tsars, traditional Orthodox Christian stereotypes were employed, keeping the Jews under the thumb of Christian fears. "To the tsarist government, no less than to the backward, largely illiterate native peasantry, the Jews were regarded in terms of their medieval stereotype: as Christ killers."[252] The Church as an institution fared little better than the Medieval Catholic Church in the eyes of many Jews, and trust in Christian institutions was still very low.

Throughout the Dark Ages, Poland was a place of refuge for Jews fleeing persecution and Inquisitions of Western Europe. "In the middle of the eighteenth century the Jewish population in eastern Europe totaled more than a million and a half, of whom the greatest numbers were concentrated in Poland. They were primarily the descendants of the refugees who had fled from the malevolence of Christian Europe during the Dark Ages."[253] For centuries they thrived under hospitable rules, and Poland remained the Promised Land. "Towards the middle of the seventeenth century, foreign merchants and grasping nobles combined with ubiquitous Jesuits to harass the Jewish population. Year by year as the Polish state degenerated into administrative anarchy, the burdens of Jewish life became heavier." [254] The presence of the Jesuits in addition to political and economic forces were in competition with the Jews.

In most of Europe it did not seem to matter what Church denomination was dominant. At least from the Jewish perspective, the Church was far from an example. Montesquieu makes a blanket statement concerning European Christians, that they were "guilty of practices towards Jews, harsher and infinitely more cruel."[255] The Catholic Church in Poland was not like the Catholic Church in France that was minimized within the backdrop of French secular society even though maintaining a church-state relationship into the twentieth century. Poland remained a prominent Catholic influence. Germans, mostly Lutheran, were very reluctant to grant Jews full emancipation without

---

252   Sachar, *A History of Israel from the Rise of Zionism to Our Time*, 4.
253   Sachar, *A History of the Jews*, 311.
254   Sachar, *A History of the Jews*, 309.
255   Sachar, *A History of the Jews*, 274.

some conditions. Jews were expected to become Christians. "... a Jew could not retain his Jewish identity and it demanded that he convert and assimilate."[256] Friedrich Paulsen, prominent Liberal humanist, in his *System of Ethics* stated, "To remain a complete Jew and a complete German is impossible."[257] Political and Religious ties were weakening many of the freedoms won by the Jews through emancipation.

The Jewish people made a choice on the whole to become part of Western culture in spite of their religious differences. Even though those differences are not as great as portrayed, they adjusted their religious practices to conform more to Western worship (Reformed Judaism) while assimilating into culture, education, and business. The Jews have effectively become part of Western culture, they are no longer isolationists, and they have contributed greatly to the advances of science and knowledge that have benefited all mankind. It stands to reason the Jews of the mid-and-later nineteenth century were reluctant to grasp at a hope (Zionism) they thought was out of reach or unwanted. Most Jews took hold of the promise or hope of emancipation and assimilation and saw going to Palestine as an unrealistic dream; though the realities were tantalizing, those doors closed quickly. In spite of the conflicts, Epstein presents a picture of Christians striving for a Zionist hope in the midst of Jewish passivity.

---

256 Rausch, *Legacy of Hatred*, 36.
257 Rausch, *Legacy of Hatred*, 36.

CHAPTER THREE

FROM HERZL TO INDEPENDENCE: THE GROWTH OF THE ZIONIST MOVEMENT

Early Roots of Modern Zionism

Zionism in the late 1800's grew out of desperation caused by internal political conflict among Eastern and Central European nations. "In such a Europe the Jews were unable to find peace. Everywhere they were looked upon as an alien group, a particularly stubborn, inassimilable group."[258] This failure to assimilate created a barrier between Jews and the leadership of these European countries, resulting in the Pogroms. On the political level, the emancipation of the Jews failed to give the Jews the acceptance they were seeking within secular culture.

The conflict between liberal Jews and the church continued within political and social institutions as well. Jewish liberals most often associated themselves with the anti-clerical causes with the church and Judaism; these causes were "Nurtured in the noble traditions of the rationalist philosophers . . . ." " . . . attacked denominational education and the ideal of a state officially dominated by sector creed."[259] Sachar states concerning Church groups, "They pilloried anti-clerical liberalism as a Jewish conspiracy and added their thunder to the denunciation of Jews and Judaism."[260] In fairness to those Jews who championed liberal freedoms in conflict with religious institutionalism, that resistance included both the church and the synagogue. Sect or creed was not restricted to Christian institutions. These battles affected more than religious institutions and also how public education was conducted.

---
258 Sachar, *A History of the Jews*, 338.
259 Sachar, *A History of the Jews*, 339.
260 Sachar, *A History of the Jews*, 338.

"Liberals in every land strove to emancipate education from Church control, to end the partnership of state and Church, to secularize the State."[261] These same battles continue into the 21st century. Jews and Gentiles both within Western and Eastern societies were questioning the foundations of biblical truth, the Old and New Testament, as well as the authority of the Church, and questioned as to whether they were able to meet the needs of a changing society.

With the influx of Jewish refugees into Western Europe and the United States, the rise of European nationalism had a profound effect on the Jews living in Western Europe. "Western European Jews insisted that Jewish nationalism was a delusion and a myth, that it could only endanger whatever position the Jews in Europe had already painfully won."[262] Those Jews who found their home in Western Europe and the United States wanted to protect their status as national citizens in the countries in which they lived."[263] Other Jews were simply seeking survival, " . . . those Jews who were seeking just survival and economic security immigrated to America in the wake of pogroms, and pauperization."[264] Jews who immigrated to Palestine were seeking self-determination and freedom. "Ottoman Palestine was hardly an economic paradise."[265] Many of these Jews were seeking self-determination, identity, and liberation within Eastern and Western European culture; this contrast in economic culture put some division between the Zionist Jews and Diaspora Jews committed to the countries where they found their success.

The events of the late nineteenth century created a post-emancipation Europe which in turn opened the doors to Zionism. "Zionism then is a post-emancipation phenomenon."[266] Avineri contends that this new emphasis on Zionism was the result of " . . . the challenges of liberalism and nationalism much more than a response merely to anti-

261 Sachar, *A History of the Jews,* 339.
262 Sachar, *A History of the Jews,* 254.
263 Sachar, *A History of the Jews,* 254.
264 Avineri, *The Making of Modern Zionism,* 13.
265 Avineri, *The Making of Modern Zionism,* 13.
266 Avineri, *The Making of Modern Zionism,* 13.

Semitism."[267] Increasing nationalism taking place during this period would add credibility to this statement; however, the events of Eastern European Pogroms compounded those nationalistic tendencies and drove the Jews to extreme solutions, one being Zionism. Many Diaspora Jews had found their security within Western society; however, events would occur that began to change that perspective. One man (Herzl) would prove the difference in changing the direction of a people and begin the process of creating a nation.

Theodor Herzl

The Pogroms of Eastern Europe along with the rise of anti-Semitism caused an awakening among the Jews that ignited the spark of Zionism that lay dormant through most of Jewish-Church history. Prior to 1895, the Zionist movement was spearheaded by the Christian community with little Jewish involvement. One of the most prominent individual of the late nineteenth and early twentieth century regarding Zionism was Theodor Herzl. A secular Jew from Bulgaria, Herzl raised the staff of hope for a Jewish nation and highlighted the necessity of establishing a Jewish homeland before the leaders of the world who were still reluctant to consider such a reality.

The Pogroms of Eastern Europe created extreme duress for millions of Jews; however, it was another event in France that got the attention of Theodor Herzl. The Dreyfus Affair turned Herzl from a secular assimilated Jew into a more passionate religious Jew. "For the first time in his adult life he began attending Jewish religious services."[268] "He was in Paris during the furious anti-Semitic campaign which was a concomitant of the Dreyfus case, and the affair may have touched a sensitive chord in him and accomplished his conversion. At any rate he began to analyze the Jewish question and as was usual with him, the whole problem was envisaged in a flash and a plan for its solution became

---

267   Avineri, *The Making of Modern Zionism*, 13.
268   Sachar, *A History of Israel, From the Rise of Zionism to Our Time*, 38.

clear."[269] The events of the Dreyfus Affair drove home a harsh reality that Jews were still not accepted, even in civilized Western Europe. "Nothing could have been a graver blow to the promise of emancipation and assimilation than this gut reaction: . . .true Frenchmen, true descendants of the ancient Gaul's, you are just Judas."[270] The unfortunate reality of this statement reflected a deep distrust for the Jews among the French, the birthplace of Jewish emancipation.

The impact upon Herzl produced a profound awakening as he began the process for finding a safe haven for all Jews; this event rang the alarm that social equality was only a piece of paper; many within the liberal secular leadership held stringently to an anti-Semitic bias. "Their equality before the law, granted by statute, has become practically a dead letter."[271] Herzl's faith in the secular state was shattered. " . . . the nations in whose midst Jews live are all, either covertly or openly, Anti-Semitic."[272] For many secular Jews like Herzl, the separation of church ideology from the secular political arena was not sufficient; there was still little security for the Jewish people in all of Europe. These events stirred the rise of modern Zionism within the Jewish community. To this point, the primary efforts promoting the return of Jews to the land of Palestine were a Christian venture alone with few exceptions.

Herzl fit the description of a completely secular Jew; if not for his heritage, he could have fit into the Gentile community without question. "He was thoroughly German, with scarcely a Jewish note to make him conscious of any other heritage. . . . If he ever thought of Jews, it was as of another people."[273] Herzl being a secular Jew carried no messianic trimmings to the Zionist table as he confronted the problems of Jewish banishment from a strictly practical Zionist position. Herzl took the Dreyfus Affair personally and reacted in defense of the Jewish people, restoring the schism he created in his drive for personal accomplishment.

269 Sachar, *A History of the Jews*, 353.
270 Avineri, *The Making of Modern Zionism*, 11.
271 Theodor Herzl, *The Jewish State* (New York: Scopus Publishing, 1941), 22.
272 Herzl, *The Jewish State,* 23.
273 Sachar, *A History of the Jews*, 353.

He was again a Jew with a renewed passion for protecting his people from the very culture his training had prepared him to embrace. He could no longer live as an emancipated Jew with little regard for the needs of the Jewish people.

Though Dreyfus was eventually exonerated when all the facts of the case became known, the fears of more reprisals against Jews in Western Europe were elevated. With Herzl at the head, many within Jewish society rang the alarm that an alternate evacuation plan was necessary to protect the Jews. The Jewish Zionist movement was in the process of being born with the primary objective to secure a home land, preferably in Palestine. "The object of Zionism is to establish for the Jewish people a publicly and legally assured home in Palestine."[274] The obstacles however would prove to be varied and formidable even within the Jewish community.

Herzl confronted the Jewish community on several levels. Orthodox Judaism on the most part still refused to act, depending upon the hope of a Messianic redemption. "Orthodox Jews still rested on the traditional Messianic ideas and refused to force the hand of Providence."[275] For many Jews, Herzl represented Jewish secularism, one who rejected Judaism. "Herzl and the leaders of Zionism were advocating a purely secular state in Palestine; they were themselves not observant religious Jews; in their hands Judaism could not be safe."[276] Winning over the many factions of the Jewish community proved to be a daunting challenge.

For Zionism to succeed, Herzl needed to gain financial backing. Money would be necessary for purchasing land, building enterprises and moving large numbers of Jewish immigrants who as a result of the Pogroms had little monetary means. Diaspora Jews saw little benefit to their security with any news of a Jewish state in the Middle East. "The great Jewish financiers fled at his approach as from a plague."[277]

---

274   Sachar, *A History of the Jews*, 354.
275   Sachar, *A History of the Jews*, 355.
276   Sachar, *A History of the Jews*, 355.
277   Sachar, *A History of the Jews*, 356.

The future outlook for any long term Palestinian venture looked extremely doubtful. "He had nothing to offer in return for the grant of an autonomous Jewish life in Palestine."[278] For Diaspora Jews, there was little interest in a Jewish homeland; they were not personally affected by Eastern European Pogroms.

William Henry Hechler

It was apparent more would be required of Christian Zionists for any foothold to take place in the public arena and among skeptical Jews. Epstein writes, one Christian rose to the task, coming to the aid of Herzl. William Hechler was a missionary from India having almost nothing in common with Theodor Herzl as far as occupation, faith, or background. William Henry Hechler (1845-1931) was born in Benares, India, of a missionary family connected to the Evangelical Church. His father being German and his mother British gave Hechler a bi-lingual upbringing. Hechler served as a missionary in India from 1871 to 1874 but had differing interests from his missionary family. Hechler was influenced by Evangelical Christianity, becoming a Christian Zionist seeking to solve the Jewish problem with an eschatological focus on the future.

Hechler's interests lay elsewhere as he left missionary work to follow his passion for helping the Jews. "After the Russian Pogroms of the 1880's, Hechler went to Odessa and met with Leo Pinsker."[279] Though little is made of this meeting, Hechler was well aware of the problems facing the Jews in the late 1800's. Herzl himself, however, had little knowledge of earlier Jewish scholars concerning the Zionist movement within Eastern Europe. According to Sachar, "Herzl was completely unaware of the work of Hess, Pinsker, and other nationalist leaders."[280] A Jew with the stature of Herzl knowing little of the Zionist movement within Judaism shows the extent of Herzl's assimilation into secular life. Through his writing: *The Jewish State*, Herzl articulated

278   Sachar, *A History of the Jews*, 356.
279   Epstein, *Zion's Call*, 77.
280   Sachar, *A History of the Jews*, 353.

many of the same issues from the earlier Zionist writers. "When Herzl read Hess for the first time, soon after completing his *Judenstaat*, he noted ...'Everything we tried is already there in his book.'."[281] Hechler's previous visit with Pinsker informed Herzl regarding the problems faced by Jews in Eastern Europe. Epstein relates Hechler's response as a most likely encouragement. "We have prepared the ground for you!"[282] Hechler was more aware of previous work helping Herzl lay some of the groundwork for the Zionist cause.

Herzl and Hechler proved to be a microcosm of the Jewish-Christian paradox in relationships; a secular liberal Jew and a conservative evangelical Christian working together for a common cause. Theodor Herzl became acquainted with William Hechler through their common connection to Zionism, each possessing a portion of the solution to a problem neither could resolve individually. Hechler was operating on a future eschatological framework that saw the outcome from a Christian perspective. Herzl's remark reflects concern, "I take him for a naïve visionary . . . ."[283] Herzl, a secularist, was operating completely within practical and political Zionism. Herzl was the pragmatist who saw the problem and derived a solution based upon facts and function. The two men though opposites still came to a unified purpose, to open the road to Palestine just a bit wider for the Jews; a unity of opposites demonstrating that a common objective can accomplish much. In this case, it accelerated the rise of Zionism within the minds of many Jews and awakened the need for a Jewish homeland among the leaders of Europe, issues that would later take root and produce results.

Through Hechler's contacts, doors opened slowly through Europe, Germany and Britain being the most open. The only door, however, that mattered for Herzl was Great Britain; it was through the British that the Zionist movement came to life (The Balfour Declaration). Still, gaining financial support was a barrier; even those with whom Herzl made a positive impact were reluctant to help. Chancellor Bülow

---

281 Laqueur, *History of Zionism, From the French Revolution to the Establishment of the State of Israel*, 53.

282 Epstein, *Zion's Call*, 79.

283 Epstein, *Zion's Call*, 78. Quote taken from Herzl's Diaries.

said, "Dr. Herzl made an excellent impression upon me, but I did not believe in his cause. His people have no money. The rich Jews would not aid, and nothing can be done with the lousy Polish Jews."[284] The failure of the wealthy Jewish community had few exceptions, one being Baron Walter Rothschild, who helped the struggling Zionist cause by purchasing land in Palestine. "Only the venality of the Ottoman officials made settlements possible-and a grant of money from Baron Edmond de Rothschild."[285] Besides the help of Rothschild, land purchases were limited.

With the exception of Epstein, few Jewish writers make reference to Hechler's support of Herzl. In their histories of Zionism and Israel, Walter Laqueur and Howard Sachar make very brief references to Hechler. Hechler had a much greater impact on early political Zionism than is credited by many within the Jewish community. Jewish literature on Zionism makes very little reference to the Christian, or church support. "Zionism and the Jewish people forgot the great debt owed to Rev. William Henry Hechler, the man Herzl termed the first Christian Zionist."[286] Herzl's perspective on Hechler demonstrates a reluctance to accept help from a religious simpleton. "I take him for a naïve visionary with a collector's quirks. However there is something charming about his naïve enthusiasm."[287] Hechler seemed undeterred as he was diligent in his task of opening doors. Herzl accepted Hechler's services in spite of their differences.

Herzl left no stone unturned in his quests to find a solution to the Jewish problem of mass expulsions and homelessness. A home land was

284 Sachar, *A History Jews*, 357.Taken from De Haas: *Theodor Herzl I*, 271.
285 Geoffrey Lewis, *Balfour and Weizmann: The Zionist, the Zealot and the Emergence of Israel* (London: Continuum Books, 2009), 11.
286 Klinger, Jerry. "A Zionist debt fulfilled," http://www.ourjerusalem.com/history/story/rev-william-hechler-theodor-herzl.html. Klinger, a Viennese Jewish journalist was responsible for placing a marker stone on Hechler's unmarked grave site in London, (February, 2011).(accessed May 2013).
287 Epstein, *Zion's Call*, 78.

the logical solution, with the possible extinction of his renewed family (the Jews). Sachar even mentions the possibility of Herzl challenging the Jews to accept Christianity as a possible solution for their continued rejection. "Once he even thought that a mass conversion to Christianity might solve the problem."[288] This is a profound step to even consider coming from a completely secular Jew. This view, however, shows a somewhat limited perspective on the Christian faith, as if it is no more relevant than one's signature. Within the context given by Epstein, Hechler is a sort of John the Baptist who is opening the doors to Herzl and giving him access while getting little or no credit himself.

While Herzl and Hechler were working diligently for the Zionist cause, the institutional church did little to instill confidence that organized Christianity would be a significant partner in any respect. For example: "The Pope sternly refused to lend any sanction to Herzl's program. The Jews denied the divinity of Christ. The Church could not declare itself for them without stultifying its principles. He would do nothing in opposition, however, and if the Jews did come to Palestine, 'we will have priests and churches ready to baptize all of you.' "[289] This statement does not suggest any openness in dialogue or cooperation. The Pope in this case closed the doors to any open receptiveness among Jews.

Uganda Plan

British colonial secretary Joseph Chamberlain came up with another plan to help displaced Jews exiting from Eastern Europe. England's colonial connections in Eastern Africa provided other options to Herzl rather than Palestine. " . . . the idea that the attractive lands in Uganda, in British East Africa, could serve as a Jewish homeland."[290] Herzl however died before the decision was made to reject the Uganda plan in the Zionist congress of 1905. "The opposition led by the Russian delegates themselves, representing the millions whom it was intended

---

288 Sachar, *A History of the Jews*, 353.
289 Sachar, *A History of the Jews*, 358.
290 Sachar, *A History of the Jews*, 358.

to relieve."[291] The idea of creating a land for the Jews anyplace other than Palestine was too much for many Eastern European Jews, the same ones who were suffering under the pogroms. One major road block to the Uganda plan that may have turn many Zionists away. " . . . as to the management of religious and purely domestic matters, such local autonomy being conditional upon the right of His Majesty's Governments to exercise general control."[292] This condition was hardly palatable to many Jews but the greater concern was no land could substitute for Palestine, the traditional biblical home of the Jews. The Jews were locked into a Palestinian solution; Zionism was fiercely connected to the tract of land in Jerusalem from which the name Zionism comes.

Herzl became known universally as the Father of Modern Zionism by opening awareness of the need to help Jewish refugees. He was the one individual most responsible for the establishment of the Zionist congresses that began in 1897. "Herzl convened a small committee in Vienna which decided to call a Zionist congress in Basle."[293] The Zionist Congress continued until the establishment of the Jewish state in Israel in 1948. With the help of Hechler, one of the few Zionist Christians who attended the first Jewish congress, the Jews became involved in the Zionist movement in a more active way than any time in previous history. Previous to Herzl, Christians spearheaded the Restorationist (Zionist) movement with little help or interest from the Jews; Herzl changed that.

World War I

The years following the death of Herzl were difficult for the fledgling Zionist movement as little land was purchased and few Jews were willing or able to move to Palestine prior to the War. As the Zionist movement grew during this period, the ideals of practical Zionism became tangled up in the affairs of reality; the land of Palestine was

291   Sachar, *A History of the Jews*, 359.
292   Sachar, *A History of the Jews*, 359.
293   Laqueur, *A History of Zionism, From the French Revolution to the Establishment of the State of Israel*, 103.

occupied. Herzl fails to reflect in his *Jewish State* the stark reality that Palestine was occupied. No reference is made concerning the Arabs already living in Palestine. "Herzl largely ignored the presence of Arabs or other minorities in the prospective Jewish State." [294] The Jews had their hearts set on a land that belonged to the Arabs. For Zionist Jews, the realization that political Zionism would be necessary for any chance of prying an indigenous population (Arabs) from their land; political Zionism would require the assistance of a major power, ready to assist the Jews in that transition from a wondering people into a nation state.

Alan Hart brings up one area of contention with the Jews handling of the issue of a Jewish state among secular nations in which Zionist leaders were seeking support; the word 'state' was seldom mentioned in the early days of the movement. "Herzl was among the first to appreciate the need for dropping the word state from all public policy statements and in effect, telling a tactical lie about the real intentions."[295] Hart's reference to Herzl's removal of "state" as a lie contributes to the problem of distrust at least with many within mainstream journalism today. For Zionists, the dialogue served to reduce the threat in as much as the Balfour agreement used the words "national home" as being less threatening.

In spite of the Arab presence, the Jewish population of Palestine grew steadily up to the beginning of WWI in spite of the restrictions put on Jewish immigration.[296] There were a number of struggling new colonies before the Great War. Life in Palestine was very hard and survival required extreme endurance. Most Jews moved to the cities with little room and resources to work with. Those who moved to the country did soon find rocky or sandy farm land. "The land that was purchased

[294] Herzl, *The Jewish State*, 1896. Translated from German by Sylvie D'Avigdor, American Zionists Emergency Council, 1946. PDF e-book, MidEastWeb, www.MidEastweb.org, preface by Ami Isseroff, 3.(accessed Sept. 24, 2013).

[295] Alan Hart, Zionism, The Real enemy of the Jews, Vol.1, The False Messiah (Atlanta, GA: Clarity Press, 2009), 65.

[296] Cohen, *Vision and Conflict in the Holy Land* (Jerusalem: Yac Ben-Zvi and St. Martin's Press, 1985), 52.

was not good ground. Most of the land was owned by Arab landowners and worked by the indigenous Arab workers."[297] All the good aridable land belonged to the Arab community who on the most part, refused to sell such land or were restricted by the Ottomans and latter British White Papers. The Ottoman Empire prior to WWI restricted immigration and land sales to the Jews. For anyone wanting to enter the Ottoman Empire, they must be willing to serve the Empire; a condition most Jews would reject. The Ottoman Turks allowed few Jewish settlements. "They would be settled only in groups of 200 or 250 families and on largely unoccupied lands in Mesopotamia," "They could not establish themselves in Palestine."[298] Still the Jewish population continued to grow slowly in Palestine in spite of the restrictions, difficulties and lack of industry. The determination and spirit of those Jews who managed to enter Palestine during this period gave testimony to the growing influence of the Zionist movement.

The biggest obstacle facing Zionist Jews was the population difference between Arabs Palestinians already living in Palestine. "Before the war the Jewish population had risen to nearly a hundred thousand."[299] This was far from the size of the indigenous Arab community of nearly one million during WWI. "When the War burst upon the world, it seemed a certainty that the frail little structure of Zionism would be shattered and cast to the winds."[300] Life for Jews during World War I was clouded with uncertainty as Jews were being thrust out of Western Europe, having no place to go. Most Jews ventured west, to the United States and Canada. "Those Jewish emigrants from Russia, Poland, and Romania who were set upon escape from present miseries and were concerned with their own private pain and individual salvation, the great majority looked not east or south, in any case, but west."[301] Most Jews elected to go west, to the United States where there

---

297   Menuhin, *The Decadence of Judaism in Our Time*, 56-57.
298   Cohen, *Vision and Conflict in the Holy Land*, 52.
299   Sachar, *A History of the Jews*, 361.
300   Sachar, *A History of the Jews*, 361.
301   Cohen, *Vision and Conflict in the Holy Land*, 52.

was room and opportunity for success; there was little room for Jews in Palestine.

Wiseman and Balfour

The new leader of the Zionist movement after the war became Chaim Weizmann, a Russian Jew, from the province of Belarus, who later became a British citizen and contributed in part to the war effort. Weizmann moved to "London to work for the Ministry of Munitions."[302] His development of acetone aided in the production of bombs for the war. Weizmann lost his own son during the war and laid stake to his British loyalty. Like Herzl, much debate surrounds the extent of Weizmann's contribution to the war effort and the legitimacy of Jewish rights and claims to Palestine. Weizmann like Herzl recognized the necessity of political Zionism for the success of any Jewish state in Palestine. "Modern or political Zionism began in 1897 when Theodor Herzl convened the First Zionist Congress and reached its culmination in 1948 when the State of Israel was born."[303] Britain became the door through which the Zionist dream would be achieved.

Arthur Balfour served previously as Prime minister of Britain, who came from a Scottish Christian background. According to Balfour's niece Blanche Dugdale, Balfour was a Christian having a keen interest in Jewish affairs. The British Christian influence remained a fairly steadfast ally through the nineteenth century in spite of the roller coaster politics of most European nations. Balfour was a product of that Christian influence, contributing to the cause of Jewish Zionism.[304] "As he grew up, his intellectual admiration and sympathy for certain aspects of Jewish philosophy and culture grew also, and the problem of the Jews

---

302   Laqueur, *History of Zionism, From the French Revolution to the Establishment of the State of Israel*, 187.
303   Learsi, *Fulfillment, The Epic Story of Zionist*, Foreword, vii.
304   Klinger, Jerry. "Beyond Balfour," *Jerusalem Post* (August 21, 2010)9+-*/, http://www.jpost.com/ChristianInIsrael/Features/Article.aspx?id=185477 (accessed Sept. 26, 2013).

in the modern world seemed to him of immense importance."[305] "He always talked eagerly on this, and I remember in childhood imbibing from him the idea that Christian religion and civilization owe to Judaism an immeasurable debt, shamefully ill repaid."[306] Balfour's Christian background contributed to the political assistance given the Jews and had a major impact upon the continued rise of Zionism and the eventual completion of the Balfour Declaration.

Christian involvement in the Zionist movement became less active during the early years of the twentieth century while Jewish participation accelerated. Arthur Balfour was a key factor influencing British interests in his support for the Jewish people in gaining a secure homeland; though these interests were much more complex, they will be addressed later. In much the same way as Herschel assisted Herzl in the rise of the Zionist movement among the Jews, so Balfour came to the assistance of Chaim Weizmann providing a political footing to raise the cause of Zionism as a necessity for the Jewish people. Herzl's work was coming closer to being realized through the assistance of the Christian political community.

Weizmann's contacts with the British enabled him to bridge the gap of influence others, including Herzl were unable to secure. "The chief architect of the alliance between the Zionist movement and Great Britain was Chaim Weizmann (1874-1952)."[307] The alliance with Britain proved invaluable to the eventual success of Zionism and the goal of Jewish independence. As a result of this commitment to the British, Weizmann is credited with securing the Balfour Declaration and opening the doors to Palestine for the Jews. With the conquest of Palestine by the British, the way was cleared at least in perception for

305 Klinger, Jerry. "Beyond Balfour," *Jerusalem Post* (August 21, 2010), http://www.jpost.com/ChristianInIsrael/Features/Article.aspx?id=185477 (accessed Sept. 26, 2013).

306 Klinger, Jerry. "Beyond Balfour," *Jerusalem Post* (August 21, 2010), http://www.jpost.com/ChristianInIsrael/Features/Article.aspx?id=185477 (accessed Sept. 26, 2013).

307 Avi Shlaim, *The Iron Wall Israel and the Arab World* (New York: W.W. Norton & Company, 2001), 5.

a larger Jewish immigration into Palestine. Balfour Declaration: "His Majesty's Government view with favor the establishment in Palestine of a national home for the Jewish people, and will use their best endeavors to facilitate the achievement of this object, it being clearly understood that nothing shall be done which may prejudice the civil and religious rights of existing non-Jewish communities in Palestine, or the rights and political status enjoyed by the Jews in any other country."[308]

The agreement between Zionists and the British government was not a clear victory as is often portrayed by history in that many hooks were attached to the document with conditions riding on other factors. Expectations were elevated for many Zionists. It would seem that Balfour understood the problem of Arab participation and the need for some type of cooperation to make possible a movement of Jews into Palestine. The population difference of nearly 9:1 would require a massive displacement of the Arab population for any substantial immigration to take place. "Considering that the Arabs constituted over 90 percent of the population, the promise "not to prejudice their civil and religious rights. . . ."[309] " . . . had a distinctly hollow ring about it, since it totally ignored their political rights."[310] Shlaim's hindsight does not take away from the early recognition that the Palestinian Arabs had rights and these problems needed to be addressed. The Arab community had already allied with Britain during World War I and was also bound by agreements to establish an Arab state. British diplomacy created a diplomatic nightmare that was to be tested in the decades to follow.

---

[308] Balfour, Arthur J. "Balfour Declaration," *American - Israeli Cooperative Enterprise*, (2013). Foreign Secretary Arthur J. Balfour wrote to Lord Rothschild, 2 Nov. 1917. http://www.jewishvirtuallibrary.org/jsource/History/balfour.html. (accessed Sept. 18, 2013)

[309] Balfour, Arthur J. "Balfour Declaration," *American - Israeli Cooperative Enterprise*, (2013). Foreign Secretary Arthur J. Balfour wrote to Lord Rothschild, 2 Nov. 1917. http://www.jewishvirtuallibrary.org/jsource/History/balfour.html. (accessed Sept. 18, 2013)

[310] Shlaim, *The Iron Wall Israel and the Arab World*, 7.

British Commitments

Christian influence was not the only factor affecting Britain's foreign policies. Previous agreements made by Britain put obligations on the Empire that carried both political and military significance. These policies would have ramifications not only to the Jews but also to the Arabs and the western alliances as well. Jewish support was necessary in the eyes of British military strategists; the Balfour Declaration was a necessary strategic alliance. Weizmann took every advantage of those pressures to open those doors. "To a very great extent Weizmann's attitude toward the Palestine Arabs was shaped by his broader strategy of gaining British support for Zionism."[311] Though Christian influence may have played a factor, it was political military necessity that carried the weight. The British became the legal administrative authority of Palestine between World Wars I and II. It was their responsibility to maintain peace and to keep the agreements they made with both the Arab peoples of Palestine and the Jewish community at large within the Palestine geography and domain.

The Allies concerns about the War placed pressure on the British to work with the Arab peoples in resistance to the Ottoman Turks who had sided with Germany. ". . . the war went steadily against the Allies and it became necessary to redistribute the spoils in the East to bring in Arab support . . . . a new treaty was now worked out which won the Arabs to the Allied side."[312] The result of these agreements made the Balfour Agreement an impossible contradiction; these agreements gave little room for a Jewish home land let alone an open door to Palestine sought by many Jews fleeing from the East who had settled in Western Europe. "During the Pogrom years thousands of Jews had migrated and had settled in the western countries and in Palestine without becoming naturalized. When the war came they were expelled as enemy aliens, or deported as war slackers."[313] England signed itself into a corner that they would not escape from for another 30 years.

---

311   Shlaim, *The Iron Wall Israel and the Arab World*, 7.
312   Shlaim, *The Iron Wall Israel and the Arab World*, 7.
313   Shlaim, *The Iron Wall Israel and the Arab World*, 364.

Besides the Balfour Declaration, other agreements made by Britain during World War I came into play making peace with the Arab countries strategically important. The British promised Hussein bin Ali, Sharif of Mecca control over the majority of lands in the Middle East though Palestine was not mentioned specifically. "The Hussein-McMahon correspondence made in 1915, prior to the Balfour Declaration also promised the Arabs rights in the Middle East. The new British government following World War I saw little benefit in supporting the Jews."[314] Giving Hussein control over Arab lands required compromise which resulted in a more restrained attitude toward Palestinian Arabs than what the Jews had hoped concerning Palestine. The stage was set for the coming conflicts between Arabs and Jews orchestrated by British over-commitment. The stage was now set for conflict that would continue to infect Palestine well into the 21st century.

Arab Jewish Conflict

Zionists following WWI and the Balfour Declaration had the ambitious plan of establishing a Jewish state regardless of the circumstances surrounding the Arab population. "The Jews' best hope, Feinberg and Aaronsohn were convinced, was simply to wrest Palestine away for themselves."[315] The only official ruling body of Palestine was the British, who had promised to them a homeland in Palestine. For most Zionists, the conditions regarding the Arabs were of little concern. The only issue was to bring as many Jews into Palestine as possible. The difficult task was complicated in the fact that the Jews owned only about 10% of the land in 1920; the country in all practical purposes was still Arab.

It took a few years before the Arab population realized the danger surrounding the Zionist movement and the desire of Jews to immigrate in mass numbers. Where would these people go, the conflicts between

---

314   Shlaim, *The Iron Wall Israel and the Arab World,* 9.
315   Sachar, *A History of Israel, From the rise of Zionism to Our Time,* 103.

Arabs and Jews were already becoming intense and the immigration issue was heating the pot to the boiling point. Conflict was inevitable, "... the restlessness of the Arab population in Palestine itself which had erupted in violent riots in April 1920."[316] The first Arab riots took place only 3 years after Balfour and pushed the British into a compromise with the Arab population.

Churchill White Papers

The 1922 Churchill White Papers drafted by Winston Churchill was a clarification of the Balfour Declaration; it recognized the desire of the Jews for a national home only and not a national Jewish state. "The White papers recognized the progress that the Zionist community was making but made it clear that they do not support a Jewish national home and would like to see it as only a community within Palestine."[317] This was an apparent step back from the original agreement made to satisfy the growing Arab unrest in the region. This agreement limited the extent of the Palestinian geography to West of the Jordan leaving the East solely to the Hussein leadership and what is Jordan today. This is one of the promises made to the Arabs that was kept. These White Papers limited the immigration to the economic conditions of the state. "... the maximum limit of immigration is not to exceed the absorptive capacity of economic state of the country."[318] The bottom line in this document emphasized a reduction in Jewish immigration to maintain peace among Arabs in the region; this did not help the Jewish problem of Western Europe and served only to placate the Arabs unrest.

British sought a political and rationale solution to the problems rising in the Middle East, since they were given the Mandate by the

316 Cohen, *Vision and Conflict in the Holy Land,* 193.
317 "White Paper of 1922: What was the White Paper of 1922?" (2013) *Palestine Facts.* www.palestinefacts.org/of-mandate-whitepaper-1922.php.(accessed Sept. 27, 2013).
318 "White Paper of 1922: What was the White Paper of 1922?" (2013) *Palestine Facts.* www.palestinefacts.org/of-mandate-whitepaper-1922.php.(accessed Sept. 27, 2013).

League of Nations, having gained physical control over the land by conquest of the Ottoman Empire at the conclusion of World War I. British Leadership had in the years that followed changed hands. "All the persons who had issued the declaration in 1917 weren't in power."[319] Those within British government even tried to repeal the statements of support in the Balfour Declaration with the hopes of stalemating the continuing conflicts. Political considerations were to gain the upper hand as the new government sought to regulate and abolish the Balfour Declaration. "House of Lords and House of Commons raised motions to cancel the Balfour Declaration and although they were rejected, British realized that they would have to reach a compromise sooner or later."[320] The British were no longer whole heartedly behind the Balfour Declaration leaving many Jews with no course but conflict.

The White Papers became a clear retreat from the Balfour Declaration and indicated to the Jews that the British were no longer supportive of the Zionist program except on a very small and limited basis. The Christian perspective as indicated by Colonel Wedgwood[321] was no longer the predominant view, as the British elected pragmatic and rationale views over a biblical view. The Jews were in a sense on their own leaving the military option the only door for any hope of gaining control of Palestine.

Revisionist Zionism and Haganah (Jewish Military)

Two competing ideologies surfaced following the signing of the Balfour Declaration and the end of World War I. Revisionist Zionism sought to protect Jewish interests through Militia and arms. "The Zionist movement was driven to develop its own military power through the

---

319 www.palestinefacts.org/of-mandate-whitepaper-1922.php.
320 www.palestinefacts.org/of-mandate-whitepaper-1922.php
321 The New York Times February 4,1918. Colonel Josiah Wedgwood M.P. and avid Christian Zionist campaigned vigorously for the Zionist cause and a homeland for the Jews in Palestine.

paramilitary organization called the Haganah (defense)."[322] The Arabs influenced the British by way of riots and threats; these did not point to a smooth transition of any sort into Palestine. In addition to the Arabs, the British in a sense became the enemy as well.

The Jewish response to Arab riots and increased hostilities provoked Vladimir Jabotinsky, a Russian Jew, to develop a military underground resistance which insisted on continued immigration. "When his own disciples set out to achieve the independence of Israel, they did it through a rebellion against British rule, not through cooperation with it."[323] He lead the fight for building a strong Jewish militia to defend against the Arabs attacks that grew over the course of post and pre war Palestine between the Arab populations that were becoming increasingly restless. This form of Zionism was to encourage the Jews to fight back leading to development of several underground military organizations.

Jabotinsky argued, " . . . that the Jews should be prepared to defend themselves; defying the Mandate administration's ban on arms, he'd embarked on training a Jewish militia."[324] Jabotinsky's work with the Jewish militia enabled the Jews to maintain some control of their land but also created a condition of concern among Arabs. Jabotinsky was responsible in part for setting the course for future Zionism that would place a greater emphasis on military action rather than political dependency. Irgun became the military arm of the Revisionist movement. "Irgun, originally little more than a branch of revisionism, became increasingly independent in its actions and policy."[325] As will be discussed later, Irgun "became a factor of some significance in the Palestinian Jewish community."[326] The Revisionist Zionism movement

---

322 Shlaim, *The Iron Wall, Israel and the Arab World*, 22.
323 Avineri, *The Making of Modern Zionism*, 186.
324 Victoria Clark, *Allies for Armageddon: The Rise Of Christian Zionism* (New Haven, CN: Yale University Press, 2007), 130.
325 Laqueur, *A History of Zionism, From the French Revolution to the Establishment of the State of Israel*, 373.
326 Laqueur, *A History of Zionism, From the French Revolution to the Establishment of the State of Israel*, 374.

was launched, leading eventually to the successful control of Palestine without the West bank and without Arab cooperation.

The primary issue between the Jews and Arabs in this case was control of the land. The vast majority of the land was owned by Arab absentee landlords, known as the 'Effendi'.[327] "The Arabs . . . gradually were being driven off the soil by Jewish land purchases and by the JNF policy of not reselling to Arabs or allowing them employment on Jewish tracts."[328] However, the White Papers (from 1922, 1929, 1937) restricted Jewish land purchase and Jewish immigration to Palestine. It became apparent quickly that Israel was not going to be granted an open door. The restriction on land sales would indicate that the free market was being closed; gaining control of the land by purchase was not possible at this point under the British. Arabs were willing to sell the land for the right price but British restriction squeezed the market. " . . . it was from the effendis that the JNF purchased their tracts—at exorbitant prices."[329] Alan Hart raises a question regarding legal rights to the land of Palestine based on historical tradition. In modern society, rights to possession does not justify any Jewish claims concerning ancient history, only signifies that two people groups desired to live on the land. "In the Western world the Arab-Israeli conflict is perceived as a struggle between two peoples with an equal claim to the same land. As we shall now see, the notion of there being two equal claims to the same land does not bear serious examination."[330] Hart missed the point, the issue that two claims are made for the land by Palestinian Arabs and Zionist Jews suggests that the Jews following World War I were seeking

---

327 Effendi is a Turkish term referring to an educated man or man of standing, in this case, Arab landowners.
328 Sachar, *A History of Israel, From the Rise of Zionist to Our Time*, 176. A reference to Hope Simpson's conclusion that Palestinian land was becoming less available to the Arabs. JNF - Jewish National Fund.
329 Sachar, *A History of Israel, From the Rise of Zionist to Our Time*, 172.
330 Hart, *Zionism, The Real enemy of the Jews, Vol.1, The False Messiah*, 65.

the land without compensation. Jews were actively purchasing land until land purchases were restricted. With the mounting Arab unrest, survival became the focus for Jews over the course of the next three decades while control of Palestine was the Arabs concern.

Spiritual Zionism 1930

Rabbi Judah Magnes (former president of Hebrew University) warned that by establishing a political dominion in Palestine against the wishes and without the consent of the Arabs, " . . . we shall be sewing the seed of an eternal hatred of such dimensions that Jews will not be able to live in this part of the world for centuries to come."[331] Another voice seeking a positive relationship with the Arab community was Ahad Ha-am (Arthur Ginsberg); he wrote with more urgency. "They treat the Arabs with hostility and cruelty, deprive them of their rights, offend them without cause and even boast of these deeds; and nobody among us opposes this despicable and dangerous inclination."[332] Ha'am appealed to the Jews to take time in developing a positive relationship with their Arab neighbors. "But the time has come for the Jews to take into account the Arab factor as the most important facing us."[333] Most of Ha'am's words fell on deaf ears as conflict became the predominant course of action.

Passfield White Papers

The White Papers of 1930 were a result of attacks on Jewish worshipers at the Western Wall in Jerusalem in 1929 and were again the more instrumental in restricting both immigration and land purchases. "Arab riots, August 1929 raised ill feeling against the Mandate

---

331 Hart, *Zionism, The Real enemy of the Jews, Vol.1, The False Messiah*, 107.

332 Hart, *Zionism, The Real enemy of the Jews, Vol.1, The False Messiah*, 65.

333 Hart, *Zionism, The Real enemy of the Jews, Vol.1, The False Messiah* , 108.

authorities...."[334] Britain was losing its grip on the Palestinian situation in Palestine. "The Shaw Commission of Inquiry (Command 3530, 30 March 1930) found that Jewish immigration and land purchases were immediate causes of 'the Arab feeling of disappointment of their political and national aspirations and fear for their economic future.'"[335] The British intervened politically again to control the market regarding land purchases. While the intentions seem admirable as all politically motivated policies are, the result was further restricting Jewish participation in the market place and artificially limiting their ability to purchase land. If the Jews had not been restricted since the markets were there, much of Palestine could have been bought by the Jews prior to WWII and a safe haven for Jewish immigration may have made the events of the Holocaust and Jewish Independence less catastrophic. The report declared that the government must issue clear statements safeguarding Arab rights and regulating Jewish immigration and land purchases. These regulations served only to prolong the inevitable which was the displacement of the Arab community following the UN mandate of 1947.

Jewish Entrepreneurship

The development of Palestine was greatly accelerated by Jewish involvement as immigration was permitted. "By 1910 the settlers were owners of plantations employing mainly Arab workers."[336] This trend continued, for many Jewish settlers, general labor was a hard thing to find. Most Jewish entrepreneurs preferred, "the cheaper and more experienced Arab labor."[337] The result of these trends, "Arab immigrants,

---

334 Hart, *Zionism, The Real enemy of the Jews, Vol.1, The False Messiah*, 108.

335 "The White Papers on Palestine." http://www.answers.com/topic/white-papers-on-palestine. (accessed Sept. 27, 2013).

336 Laqueur, *A History of Zionism, From the French Revolution to the Establishment of the State of Israel*, 79.

337 Laqueur, *A History of Zionism, From the French Revolution to the Establishment of the State of Israel*, 79.

no less than Jews, were flooding into the country as a result of new economic opportunities provided by the Jewish National Home."[338] These conditions made possible meetings between Weizmann and the Prime Minister Malcolm MacDonald, some of the conditions restricting immigration were lifted while the 1930 White Papers remained in effect, though limited.

With the right mix of skill education and development, "There was endless hope for the future, if only Jewish scientific resourcefulness and energy were given full play." [339] Sachar discusses, that the Holy Land would be able " . . . to support a population of at least 5 million in the ensuing decades."[340] Such a condition would not have displaced the Arabs as the White Papers envisioned. Such a condition would have benefited Jews and Arabs alike. These conditions did not occur even though Arab and Jewish immigration continued through the thirties, the distrust in the greater Jewish presence resulted in more discontentment among many Palestinian Arabs.

The MacDonald White Papers of 1939

Arab Jewish conflicts continued up to WWII and Arab riots along British capitulation resulted in more White Papers restricting Jewish immigration back to lower levels. "The White Papers of 1939 kept legal immigration to Palestine at a farcically minimum level. This infamous document declared, at the very moment when millions of European Jews were facing merciless destruction that, " . . . within the next five years only 75,000 Jews would be allowed into Palestine and that hereafter none would be admitted without Arab consent."[341] At a time when the Jewish population in Germany was at the most risk, the restrictions on Jewish immigration to Palestine became more prohibitive.

---

338 Sachar, *A History of Israel from the Rise of Zionism to Our Time*, 176.
339 Sachar, *A History of the Jews*, 408.
340 Sachar, *A History of Israel from the Rise of Zionism to Our Time*, 519.
341 David Ben-Gurion, *Israel: Years of Challenge* 1st ed. (New York: Henry Holt & Company Inc. June 1963),15-16.

What proved to be disaster for Jews throughout Europe was also enforced in North America as it seemed no Western country was willing to accept any more Jews than necessary at the time of their greatest need. Hindsight provides no solace to Western Christians who must take part of the blame for events of which they had little awareness until after the War.

"The nations in whose midst Jews lives are all, either covertly or openly, Anti-Semitic."[342] Though these words come from Theodor Herzl who died several decades earlier, the meaning became more significant to those who suffered through the tragic events of World War II. What was most unfortunate for the Jews during the late 1930's, when the beginning of the Nazis reign of terror was just beginning, was that restrictions on immigration were strictly and forcefully maintained for the next 10 years. Millions of lives were lost as a result of these decisions.

Christian Zionists Influence and Jewish Military

During the early stages of World War II, British forces were instrumental in training Jewish servicemen to help with the war effort. The Jewish Defense Force, later to be known as the IDF was established and trained by experienced British military officers. Many of these men were Christians, who were given the charge of building up the Jewish military for the war with Germany. In addition to the training supplied to the Jews living in Israel, was the support given by those in the Zionist movement. Two individuals rise to the surface in the discussion of Christian influence on Jewish military preparedness. Colonel Josiah C. Wedgwood, MP (Member of Parliament), a British Christian Zionist gave expression to the necessity of military preparedness on the part of the Jews. Wedgwood was a prominent Member of Parliament who gave a voice to Zionism in the early twenties. The second was Orde Wingate from a Plymouth Brethren background with family connections to the mission field. Orde Wingate, a " . . . descendant of missionaries and soldiers, raised as a Nonconformist member of the Plymouth 'brethren,'"[343]

342 Herzl, *The Jewish State*, 23.
343 Joshua B. Stein, *Our Great Solicitor: Josiah C. Wedgwood and the Jews (Selinsgrove, PA.: Susquehanna University Press, 1991)*, 132.

Both men influenced the development of the Israeli Military along with its special forces.

Wedgwood was not in agreement with the limitations on Palestinian borders as documented in the White Papers. "The Jewish homeland should comprise territory on both sides of the Jordan River – both Israel and Jordan."[344] Wedgwood would have fit into the mode of an extreme Christian Zionist who saw no wrong with pushing the Arab population out of Palestine altogether much like Rabbi Benny Elon's suggestion today, "Christian Zionists today who back the radical right-winger Rabbi Benny Elon's plan for a mass 'transfer' of the Palestinians from the West Bank to neighboring Arab states are true heirs of Josiah Wedgwood."[345] Clark pictures Wedgwood, as a military man, who saw no problem using military force to gain an objective, conflict being crucial to gaining Palestine.

The second prominent British officer, Orde Wingate was converted to Zionism after his arrival in Palestine. According to Virginia Clark, Wingate came to Palestine without any Zionist convictions. "Wingate had arrived in Palestine in the middle of the Arab Revolt, fluent in Arabic and experienced in Arab affairs, but was almost instantaneously converted to Zionism."[346] As a military man, he was trained to win the battle and find the peace, in the case of Palestine, that peace was yet to be found as the conflicts continued.

Both British leaders were in agreement that the military was the only option for the Jews. ". . . [Wingate] was as adamant as Wedgwood that the Jews be armed." Clark clarifies this position. "Wingate devoted himself to training what would become the core of Israel's army today, the Haganah. Soon he was spying for the Zionists and leading 'Special Night Squads' in pre-emptive raids on Arab villages or on missions to

---

344 Clark, *Allies for Armageddon: The Rise Of Christian Zionism*, 131.
345 Clark, *Allies for Armageddon: The Rise Of Christian Zionism*, 130. Rabbi Benny Elon was a member of the Israeli Knesset, who supported continuation of Jewish settlements in the West Bank and Gaza, in addition to the transfer of Palestinians.
346 Clark, *Allies for Armageddon: The Rise Of Christian Zionism*, 132.

deliver scandalously brutal reprisal."[347] Regardless what one thinks of this military individual, Wingate set the stage for the development of the Irgun and later, the Stern group that became the terrorist arm of the IDF. This is not to suggest an official endorsement of terrorism from the Jews which placed them in a precarious position of extremist and outside any legal or political structure from which to make a case for any rights to Palestine.

Following the results of the Peel Commission, rulings were initiated in 1937 to determine how to resolve the continuing Arab Jewish conflicts that persisted since the end of the first war. These rulings being consistent with previous White Papers, " . . . urging an abridgment of future Jewish land purchases . . . . [and] curtailment of Jewish immigration to a limit of 12,000 annually for the next five years."[348] This ruling played significantly into the magnitude of the approaching Holocaust, leaving little place for Jews to go.

The Commission, " . . . acknowledged that Arabs and Jews could not share Palestine and recommended a speedy division of the country into two states."[349] It is appropriate at this point to consider Ahad Ha'am's solution of spiritual Zionism. Would it have been more effective to have let the Arabs remain, then to allow a slow gradual entry by Jews as conditions would allow? This would have allowed the Arabs to remain in control yet without any significant economic growth. Any influx of new Jews would be unlikely. Jerusalem would have been no more than a tourist spot much like for the Christian today. "While Weizmann, Jabotinsky and Ben-Gurion reluctantly accepted the scheme as a basis from which to negotiate at some future date, Wedgwood, like thousands of millenarian Christian Zionists, resolutely opposed it."[350] Wedgwood became a mentor to hard-line Zionists. "In May 1938, he received a letter from a group named the Association of Former Jewish Army Officers, begging for his advice and support for opposition to

347 Clark, *Allies for Armageddon: The Rise Of Christian Zionism*, 132.
348 Sachar, *A History of Israel, From the Rise of Zionism to Our Time*, 204.
349 Clark, *Allies for Armageddon: The Rise Of Christian Zionism*, 133.
350 Clark, *Allies for Armageddon: The Rise Of Christian Zionism*, 133.

partition."[351] Wingate was banging the same drum, preaching resistance to Britain and telling his elite squads, "There will be no Jewish state unless you fight for it, . . . it is the English you will have to fight."[352] England was no longer an ally to the Jews or any Jewish state in the Middle East. Any hopes for a Zionist state at the onset of World War II seemed bleak.

Wingate parted company with the mainline politicians of British government, for Britain was no longer interested in the Zionist cause. Wingate stated that "God's Englishmen' such as himself were hopelessly few and powerless now to assist them, that they would have to find another advocate: 'I have tried to save for my own countrymen the Glory of rebuilding Jerusalem, of doing justice, of creating freedom. It is no use, they won't do it. I can't help. You must run to America and take on the job yourselves. Ask no more from Britain . . . . "[353] Christian Zionists were the minority in Britain and their voices could not trump the political realities of Palestine at the time of greatest need for Jews in Europe. Like Wingate and Westcott, the Christian Zionists in Britain were silenced. The battle for the Jews however continued.

British military in the late 1930's and early 1940's spread across the Middle East including Jordan and Egypt. With the exception of Glubb Pasha in Jordan these men were committed to a Jewish state and were prepared to help the Jews accomplish it. For these reasons the British reassigned Colonel Wedgwood, so as to prevent further damage to the Mandate, "Wingate himself was considered expendable, his pro-Zionist views were becoming an embarrassment to the government."[354], while keeping close ties to the Arabs who in all practical purposes had

---

351   Clark, *Allies for Armageddon: The Rise Of Christian Zionism,* 133.

352   Clark, *Allies for Armageddon: The Rise Of Christian Zionism,* 39. Reference: Leonard Mosley, *Gideon goes to War: The Story of Wingate,* London, Hamish Hamilton, 1957 (1955), P. 58.

353   Clark, *Allies for Armageddon: The Rise Of Christian Zionism,* 134. Reference: Stein, p.40, 143.

354   Sachar, *A History of Israel from the Rise of Zionism to Our Time,* 216.

sided with the Nazis in WWII. "No courtship of the Axis was more avid, than the one carried out by the émigré Mufti of Jerusalem."[355] For the Arabs, the war sided with who would give the Palestinians the best change for independence. For the Jews, their livelihood still rested with the British, at least until the war effort was completed.

Arab Leadership Supports the Nazis

Arab leadership so hated the British that they would become accomplices with the Nazis' for the destruction of the Jews and in conflict with the British. "It committed the two Axis governments to recognize the sovereignty and independence of the Arab countries and promised Axis help in "the elimination of the Jewish National home in Palestine."[356] Arab leadership who allied with Britain in World War I chose to support the Nazis in World War II. "The Arab rulers sided with the Nazis, continually recognizing in Hitler the most blood thirsty and brutal enemy of the Jews in the pages of history."[357] Had Arab leadership remained loyal to the Allies during World War II, as they were in World War I, the outcome for Palestine might have been different.

As mentioned, the Arab leadership which included the Mufti of Jerusalem were Nazi collaborators. "The Fuhrer added, the Mufti would become the chief spokesman for the Arab world."[358] Arab leadership had failed the Palestinian Arabs. Had they remained in Palestine, it is quite possible they would have maintained control of Palestine or been given adequate compensation for their properties, now the issue was lost. The conflict that arose as a result of partition was not going to go away until the Jews were gone.

---

355   Sachar, *A History of Israel from the Rise of Zionism to Our Time*, 228.
356   Sachar, *A History of Israel from the Rise of Zionism to Our Time*, 229.
357   Ben-Gurion, *Israel Years of Challenge*, 16.
358   Sachar, *A History of Israel from the Rise of Zionism to Our Time*, 229.

Jewish Terrorism

The Jews fought on two fronts during World War II; "All through the war period the Jews of Palestine toiled loyally and fought gallantly under British direction, confident that victory would bring recompense through the abrogation of the White Papers and the other creatures of the appeasement era."[359] While the Yishuv supported Britain and the Allies, "Arabs had done virtually nothing for the war effort."[360] In spite of this, British support for a Jewish homeland however never fully materialized. Immigration barriers were enforced while Jews were being displaced and killed throughout Europe. The backlash of these events prompted the continued harassment by the Jewish underground. The Irgun, an offshoot off Jabotinsky's militia and the Stern group created by Abraham Stern in response to Arab riots of the late thirties turned their hostilities on the British, the backlash of persistent British crackdowns were responsible for numerous attacks on the British as well as the Arabs. During the war years, these groups worked actively to smuggle Jews into Palestine despite British navel blockades.

On the surface, the Jewish military sanctioned no terror. "Haganah sanctioned no terror . . . there were smaller dissident groups, Irgunists and Sternists, who became intractable and refused to accept any such discipline."[361] These forces however, contributed greatly to the eventual success of the Jews in pushing Britain out and in securing the UN Mandate for a Jewish state. The Stern group, also called Lehi, along with the Irgun were responsible for many terrorist attacks including the destruction of Deir Yassin west of Jerusalem. It is this attack more than any that elevated Arab fears to flee the country in the face of conflict. Deir Yassin became "the epicenter of the catastrophe – a warning to all Palestinians that a similar fate awaited them if they refused to abandon their homes and take flight."[362] Though condemned at the time, the

---

359 Sachar, *A History of the Jews*, 428.
360 Sachar, *A History of the Jews*, 246.
361 Sachar, *A History of the Jews*, 430.
362 Ian Pappé, *The Ethnic Cleansing of Palestine* (Oxford England: Oneworld Publications, 2006), 91. Quote taken from: Menachem Begin, *The Revolt*, 164.

Jewish leadership realized the benefits of that attack and seemed to make no real effort to stop the resistance from that wing of the military. Another major attack carried out by the Irgun was the bombing and destruction of the King David hotel where dozens of British were killed, resulting in the continued crack down on Jewish resistance.

Both underground organizations were led by future Prime Ministers; the Irgun by future Prime Minister Menachem Begin, while Lehi leadership included future Prime Minister Yitzhak Shamir. Shamir " . . . had led the rightist underground organization Lehi (the Stern group),[363] The most interesting thing about both groups, though condemned by the Jewish leadership, was that neither group was held accountable for their acts. Israel granted general amnesty to Irgun and Lehi members on the 14th of February, 1949. How could former terrorist leaders advance to Prime Minister status of the country unless they were committed members of the established leadership? These facts become difficult for many Arabs who do not trust the Jews, leaving a legacy of mistrust that goes well beyond Israeli Independence.

End of the British Mandate

The British, though experienced in foreign affairs having the British Empire as a badge of honor, were entering into a situation no power on earth was equipped to solve. The Arab-Jew issue was in fact a blood feud going back nearly 4,000 years. The Christian influence in the creation of the Balfour Declaration had little effect on the outcome of Mandate. The contradictory statements within the document concerning the Arabs could not be settled. ". . . it being clearly understood that nothing shall be done which may prejudice the civil and religious rights of existing non-Jewish communities in Palestine."[364] The British were

---

363 Yoram Hazony, *The Jewish State Struggle for Israel's Soul* (New York: Basic Books, 2000), preface xvi.
364 Klinger, Jerry. "Beyond Balfour," *Jerusalem Post* (August 21, 2010), http://www.jpost.com/ChristianInIsrael/Features/Article.aspx?id=185477 (accessed Sept. 26, 2013).

unable to accommodate both Arabs and Jews within that document as the conflict continued up to the end of the British Mandate.

The management of Palestine proved to be a nightmare of conflict for the British. "For thirty years, while Britain tried to govern Palestine under first a military authority and then a League of Nations mandate that endorsed the impossibly contradictory terms of the Balfour Declaration."[365] The British tried to appease both the Jews and the Arabs in their search for a solution. "While Zionist Jews struggled to establish their Jewish state, and Palestine's Arabs fought to retain their land, Britain began ruling the day Allenby had conquered the Holy Land for Christendom."[366] Was Allenby wrong in conquering Palestine? It would seem like a shallow argument by Clark to suggest the conquests of Palestine and the Turks was the wrong course after seeing the suffering placed upon the Albanian Christian community during World War I.

To criticize Allenby and Christendom is to avoid the greater problem; what to do with displaced Jews in Europe? Clark admits the Christian connection, to the Balfour agreement and the desire within the Jewish and Christian communities both, was to see a safe haven for the Jews. "Nonconformist Christianity played in the personal formation of the politicians whose combined efforts led to the Balfour Declaration of 1917."[367] These were noble goals that were being sought; the solution to the complex problem of the Middle East however carried no easy fixes. Christianity from this context appears to have two faces; one whose influence in the political process drove Jews out of Eastern Europe and the other seeking a solution.

In Britain, "The Labor Government decided that Palestine had become too great a liability, and announced that it planned to surrender the Mandate. In making the sensational statement, Britain threw the

---

365   Clark, *Allies for Armageddon: The Rise Of Christian Zionism*, 129.
366   Clark, *Allies for Armageddon: The Rise Of Christian Zionism*, 129.
367   Clark, *Allies for Armageddon: The Rise Of Christian Zionism*, 70. Quote from: Jill Hamilton, *God, Guns and Israel: Britain, the First world War and the Jews in the Holy Land,* Stroud, Sutton, 2004, x.

responsibility for failure on the other nations. According to British secretary Bevin, 'The real difficulty, he said, was that no country, including the United States, was willing to admit Jews.'"[368] Bevin's statement being true is somewhat hypocritical in light of Britain's naval blockade to keep Jews out of Palestine. "There has been a failure of international moral consciousness. Bevin felt that such shirking of moral responsibility makes it intolerably hard for Britain. The United Nations would now have to take over the problem and work towards a settlement of its own."[369] While the United States had little contact with the Zionist cause early in Israeli history, it became more prominent during the course of the following decades, up to the Six Day War.

The White Papers would turn the Jews away from Britain, even though they fought with the British, during WWII against the Germans. "for Ben Gurion the Peel partition plan marked the beginning of the end of the British mandate in Palestine and the birth of a Jewish state as a realistic political program."[370] In spite of Jewish support for the British during World War II, the British continued to enforce restrictions on Jewish immigration. "The rigor with which mandatory officials continued to enforce the White Paper, suggested that political considerations alone were now dictating British policy."[371] Both issues prevented the Jews from entering and gaining a strong foothold in Palestine during a time of great upheaval in Germany. The Labor Government flatly repudiated its own Committee and refused to yield any interim concessions. "This policy was applied just when the pressure from the camps had become overwhelming, when the years of suffering and hopelessness should have been an irresistible compulsion on the Christian conscience."[372] Most people did not know of the magnitude of this problem of European Jews until after the War. The British Mandate in a sense failed leaving the upcoming UN mandate the Arab-Jewish problem. The Arabs eventually

---

368 Clark, *Allies for Armageddon: The Rise Of Christian Zionism*, 129.
369 Sachar, *A History of the Jews*, 431.
370 Shlaim, *The Iron Wall, Israel and the Arab World*, 19.
371 Sachar, *A History of the Israel from the Rise of Zionism to Our Time*, 232.
372 Sachar, *A History of the Jews*, 428.

submitted to the Jews but only in the face of military force. Concerning the land of Palestine, the Holocaust would become a major factor in opening the doors to a Jewish homeland, something war and politics alone could not do.

The Palestinian Arabs along with the underground activity of the Jewish militia cells contributed to Britain's detachment from Palestine; their mixed loyalties would contribute to the ambivalence of the British toward both, Arabs and Jews prior to the UN. Mandate of 1947 and after. The Balfour Declaration had become a dead document as Britain had abandoned any hope of a solution to the conflicts in Palestine.

The Holocaust and the German Church

The events of the Holocaust go well beyond rationale; there is little explanation for what happened there. How this event affected Christian -Jewish relationships and the eventual return of the Jewish state in Palestine was profound. The Holocaust comes as a tragedy with a positive ending. Without the Holocaust, it is most likely the Jews would not have gained the foothold needed in Palestine at least for decades. "The tragedy of the European Jewry became a source of strength for Zionism. The moral case for the Jewish people in Palestine was widely accepted from the beginning; after the Holocaust it became unassailable."[373] The magnitude of devastation upon the Jews was beyond endurance, giving the fledgling Zionist movement all the ammunition it needed to gain access to Palestine.

The sobering reality of the brutality of man came front and center during the aftermath of World War II. Man's inhumanity to man took a stark turn downward as the realization that there are few limits on man's capacity for evil when the circumstances are right. The irony and absurdity of Hitler's SS squads and Gestapo, make one wonder, how educated men could perform such acts of horror, as many wore the symbol of the cross and gave lip service to God while treating others with contempt.

---

373 Shlaim, *The Iron Wall, Israel and the Arab World*, 24.

Another unfortunate consequence, of the Holocaust, was a monstrous fall of respect for the Christian community at least among the Jews. "The 'plausible' argument offered the heartbroken and depressed Jews of the West when they learned of the German crematoriums of the Jews in the decency, morality and sense of common humanity of the Christian world was misplaced."[374] Not that there existed a lot of trust between Christians and Jews at this time. Even though the Christian community was not directly responsible for the events of WWII and the Holocaust, it is obvious, that Christian Germany could have done much more to stymie Hitler and the Nazi run over a population that surrendered its influence without a fight.

The Liberal Church

The Holocaust represents to many a failure of the Church to stand behind the Jews against the Nazis. Quoting Eric Metaxas, the German Church stood, " . . . solidly behind Hitler's rise to power and blithely tossed two millennia of Christian orthodoxy overboard."[375] One reason for this slide from orthodoxy according to Metaxas was the slide from a universal church to a national church. "For many Germans, their national identity had become so melted together with whatever Lutheran Christian faith they had that it was impossible to see either clearly."[376] Since most Lutherans were of Aryan decent, many Germans had difficulty seeing beyond their racial condition to see the larger picture of the Jews in the historical context. "After four hundred years of taking for granted that all Germans were Lutheran Christians, no one really knew what Christianity was anymore."[377] Complacency and ignorance can creep into any faith system, and such seems to be the case for the German church during the Nazi rise to power.

---

374   Menuhin, *Decadence of Judaism in Our Time*, 329.
375   Eric Metaxas, *Bonhoeffer, Pastor, Martyr, Prophet, Spy* (Nashville, TN.: Thomas Nelson Publisher, 2010), 174.
376   Metaxas, *Bonhoeffer, Pastor, Martyr, Prophet, Spy*, 174.
377   Metaxas, *Bonhoeffer, Pastor, Martyr, Prophet, Spy*, 174.

The Enlightenment not only affected Judaism but the Christian Church as well. "There's little question that the liberal theological school of Schleiermacher and Harnack helped push things along in this direction (the questioning of the canonicity of the Old Testament)."[378] For many within the established church of Western Europe, they had abandoned much of the historical foundations of Christianity before WWII just as the Jews had given away much of their faith in the Old Testament (Tanakh) and moved away from their traditional historic faith.

The sad reality was the Church had failed to understand its strategic relationship to the Jews well before the Nazis came. "There were few denunciations of anti-Semitism in German pulpits in the 1920's or for that matter in most pulpits of the Christian world."[379] The German Church had lost its focus on its biblical mandate to go into the entire world, to show compassion, or to expect God's Kingdom. From this vantage, it is easier to see how the Nazis replaced God's Kingdom for another; it represented a movement away from a solid faith and commitment to historical Christianity.

In some respects, the Church was not the most respected institution in Germany during the early and mid nineteen hundreds. Many Germans had reservations about the church and the relevance to their lives. "As far as many of them were concerned, the church was a corrupt institution, and if their kids could ladle out a bit of grief to their soft, golden-haired cleric, perhaps he had it coming."[380] Metaxas indicated that many within German culture were simply using the church for convenience as many had little respect for it. This would explain in part why there was little interest in fighting injustices amidst social pressures. The church played a very minute role in the lives of most people, it was a cultural stigma. As a result, personal security and safety became the greater issue for many within the Church.

---

378 Metaxas, *Bonhoeffer, Pastor, Martyr, Prophet, Spy*, 174.
379 Rausch, *Legacy of Hatred*, 48.
380 Metaxas, *Bonheoffer Pastor, Martyr, Prophet, Spy*, 318.

The Church of Germany became split, as the Riche Church (German Lutheran Church) came under Nazi control, " . . . the plight of the German church under the Nazis shows us the immense hardships and difficult decisions Christian leaders have to make under impossible conditions. . . . decisions the American church may likely face someday."[381] Without a firm foundation or faith, the Church capitulated to Nazi rule. The Riche Church was sanctioned by the Nazis before the War and was the Church in name only.

Confessing Church

The events that took place during WWII were difficult not only for the Jews along with the horrors of the Holocaust; they were difficult for all countries involved. The events of WWII destroyed millions of lives. For the Jewish community, the events of the Holocaust became the source of increased mistrust for the Christian communities' failure to protect and defend. It is true that the larger Christian community failed to speak out against Nazi abuses that became more profound in the late 1930's and early 1940's.

The smaller confessing church split with the German church during the same period as abuses were beginning to be seen in the streets. Martin Niemoller, one of the leaders of the Confessing Church, was more forthright when he realized Hitler's intentions. "When Niemoller finally turned against Hitler, he did so without any fear, and the sermons he gave at this overfilled church in Dahlem, . . . were listened to with great interest not least by members of the Gestapo."[382] The Confessing Church in Germany did stand up for the Jews in opposition to Nazi tyranny.

The Confessing Church resisted Nazi control and as a result, was not recognized by the Nazis. The confessing Church endured persecution as it operated primarily underground; it still exercised biblical Christianity and became one of the few institutional supports

---

[381] Rausch, *Legacy of Hatred*, 3.
[382] Metaxas, *Bonhoeffer Martyr, Prophet, Pastor, Spy*, 177.

for the Jews of Germany before and during WWII. "There is no question that the confessing church had resisted the rise of Nazism and suffered for it. . . . One can ask if they could have done more short of being killed as many were including (*Dietrich*) Bonhoeffer."[383] Metaxas adds, "By war's end more than 80 of the 150 young men from Finkenwade and the collective pastorates had been killed."[384] These pastors, many of whom were students of Bonhoeffer, were part of the Confessing Church.

Christian Support During World War II

Even through Christians have been accused of passivity or indifference to the events of the Holocaust, many Christians rallied around to assist Jewish refugees, even though many governments did little to relieve the pain of Europe's insanity to the Jews. There were many who risked their lives for the Jews within and outside of Christianity while the larger institutional Church failed.

In addition to the confessing Church, the Dutch Reformed Church took a strong stand against the Nazi takeover of Holland. "The General Synod of the Dutch Reformed Church reaffirmed its solidarity with the Jews: According to God's providence, the Jews have lived among us for centuries and are bound up with us in a common history and a common responsibility."[385] The Reformed Church took a hard line against persecution of the Jews and made numerous strides to resist efforts to persecute Jews. "The Christians of the Dutch Church saved hundreds of their Jewish brothers from the Nazis."[386] Many Jewish lives were saved through the underground efforts of Christians and non-Christians alike in Holland as testified by Corrie ten Boom's book, *The Hiding Place*, as she recalls her life's story of saving Jews and then surviving a Nazi prison camp. Acts of defiance against German cruelty to Jews were seen across Western Europe during the War. "In France,

383 Metaxas, *Bonhoeffer Martyr, Prophet, Pastor, Spy*, 318.
384 Metaxas, *Bonhoeffer Martyr, Prophet, Pastor, Spy* 349.
385 Arthur Roy Echardt, *Christianity and the Children of ISRAEL* (Morning Heights, NY.: King's Crown Press, 1948), 99.
386 Echardt, *Christianity and the Children of ISRAEL*, 174.

Belgium, and Holland, declaration of solidarity, and help for the Jews were almost universally regarded as signs of patriotism."[387] Though the German Church became tangled in the web of Nazi propaganda, the greater Church still acted in defense of the Jews.

The Holocaust was one of the greatest tragedies of history for many peoples. After emancipation and assimilation within Germany and other western democracies, anti-Semitism still played a huge role in the systematic destruction of a people to satisfy unwarranted prejudices. However, the events of the Holocaust played a major role in making the dream of a Jewish state possible. "The tragedy of the European Jewry became a source of strength for Zionism."[388] Shlaim brings into focus the impact of the Holocaust on the eventual success of the Zionist movement. "Few people disputed the right of the Jews to a home after the trauma to which they had been subjected in Central Europe."[389] The Holocaust was instrumental in the establishment of the Jewish state and the realization of the Zionist dream.

Biltmore Conference

The Biltmore Conference brings into focus one Jewish perspective, on the oppression that was taking place in both Germany and the United States that prevented an increase in immigration. Menuhin presents Rabbi Abba Hillel Silver of Cleveland as being angry with the Christian community's failure to help the Jews demanding that the restrictive immigration policies be lifted. Rabbi Silver's statements were made at the Biltmore Hotel May 6 to May 11, 1942. "With a defiant, angry and determined approach, purporting to solve the Jewish problem of homelessness while the Christian world was beginning to suffer a collective guilt-penitence for its stained heritage of bestiality toward the Jewish people, there descended upon New York."[390] What Rabbi

387 Conway, *The Nazi Persecution of the Churches, 1933-45* (Vancouver BC: Regent College Publishing, 1997), 266.
388 Shlaim, *The Iron Wall, Israel and the Arab World*, 23.
389 Shlaim, *The Iron Wall, Israel and the Arab World*, 24.
390 Menuhin, *Decadence of Judaism in Our Time*, 330.

Silver represented was a condemnation of the entire Christian enterprise without any distinction. This would include the Confessing Church of Germany and the thousands who suffered or died for the Jews while maintaining their Christians witness. Stereo types to this extent do no justice to the individuals who suffered in the name of Christ for the Jews.

Menuhin made emphasis on the fact that little credit is given the hundreds who helped the Jews during the war. "Little was ever mentioned at the Eichmann trial in Jerusalem of the thousands of self-sacrificing Christians in Hitler's occupied Europe, who risked or lost their lives in the process of saving or hiding Jews. A spirit of anti-Christianity spreads out of Zion in our time, instead of 'Love they fellow man as thyself.'"[391] Even though the larger institutional Church failed to make a strong stand against injustices against the Jews, many Christians stood and sacrificed for the Jews out of a deep commitment to Christian values.

Immigration Policies of the West

In March 1933, the Jewish community in Palestine contacted the German government and offered a break in the boycott as far as Palestine was concerned provided it was combined with Jewish emigration from Germany. As a result, the "Haavara" or "Transfer" agreement was signed by the Germans and Jews in May 1933. "The Haavara transfer was a major factor in making possible the immigration of approximately 60,000 German Jews to Palestine in the years 1933–1939." The significance of this event opened the doors to Jewish emigration, only there was no place for displaced Jews to go. The West was limiting the number of emigrants and Palestine under the harsh restrictions of the White Papers limited entrance into Palestine. The reasons given for limiting immigration was many people were out of work in the United State creating large scale suffering during the depression. "The United States, wracked by the Depression, refused to allow in new immigrants

---

391   Menuhin, *Decadence of Judaism in Our Time*, 478.

while millions of its own citizens remained unemployed."[392] This conflict kept thousands of Jews out of the United States, a situation that could have limited the depth of the Holocaust.

After emancipation and assimilation within Germany and other western democracies, anti-Semitism still played a huge role in the systematic destruction of a people to satisfy unwarranted prejudices. However, the events of the Holocaust played a major role in making the dream of a Jewish state possible. " . . . the tragedy of the European Jewry became a source of strength for Zionism."[393] Shlaim brings into focus the impact of the Holocaust on the eventual success of the Zionist movement. "Few people disputed the right of the Jews to a home after the trauma to which they had been subjected in Central Europe."[394] There is little question that the Holocaust was instrumental in the realization of the Zionist dream.

Truman and the UN Mandate

Following World War II, victims of the Holocaust were still living in refugee camps; in much the same way displaced Jews from the Pogroms of Eastern Europe, which left thousands of Jews seeking refuge during and after WWI. The practical implications of the Zionist cause needed to be addressed. "Truman believed that Zionism required the support of every true Christian."[395] However, the decisions of President Truman, just like that of Balfour and his political reasons for the Balfour Declaration, weighed heavily on the political implications. Had Truman not been so quick to recognize Israel as a nation, he might have lost the elections to Dewey in 1948 because the Republicans were very critical of the Democratic handling of the Jews that contributed to the high numbers during the Holocaust. Very rarely are motives pure by

---

392   Melvin Urofsky, *We are One: American Jewry and Israel* (Norwell, MA: Anchor Press Inc., 1978), 4.
393   Shlaim, *The Iron Wall, Israel and the Arab World*, 23.
394   Shlaim, *The Iron Wall, Israel and the Arab World*, 24.
395   Menuhin, *Decadence of Judaism in Our Time*, 330.

any political entity: " . . . even a determination to secure the Jewish vote for his re-election in 1948, sullied Truman's Christian Zionism."[396]

Truman was, in the beginning, reluctant to do anything to promote or foster support for the mandate. Clark presents a rather harsh picture of Truman concerning his attitude toward the Jews. Truman said, " . . . concerning the Jews, 'Jesus Christ couldn't please them when he was here on earth so could anyone expect that I would have any luck?'"[397] Truman would have preferred not to deal with this directly but circumstance forced their way. It was through the efforts of Jewish allies and the charm of Chaim Weizmann that the President was turned and responded positively in support for the Zionist cause. "The persistence of a few of the extreme Zionist leaders-actuated by political motives and engaging in political threats-disturbed and annoyed me."[398] In the end, Truman came through for the Jewish Zionist cause.

The Holocaust continued to cast a long shadow upon the events of Palestine following World War II. "President Truman recognized the necessity of supporting a Jewish state in light of the events of the Holocaust. Truman at first resisted pressures by Jewish interests to promote the UN mandate but eventually bent. . . . the sense of a historic injustice crying out to be righted, the emotional conviction that the Jews must have their ancient homeland again, the awareness of the underdog and the belief that there was a rare opportunity to forsake the mundane murk of conventions politics . . . ."[399] In the end, Truman stood in support of the Zionist cause and the partition resolution. "President Truman took a firm stand for partition and worked zealously to line up the other

---

396 Clark, *Allies for Armageddon: The Rise Of Christian Zionism*, 140.

397 Clark, *Allies for Armageddon: The Rise Of Christian Zionism*, 151: McCullough, David, *Truman*, (New York: Simon & Schuster, 1992), 52.

398 Truman, Harry S. *Memoirs of Harry S. Truman Volume Two: Years of Trial and* Hope (New York: Smithmark Publishers Inc., 1996), 251.

399 Truman, Harry S. *Memoirs of Harry S. Truman Volume Two: Years of Trial and* Hope, 140.

delegations."[400] Through the influence he had with many UN nations, the mandate for partition won the day and the hope of Israel was finally to be realized again after nearly 2,000 years. "The Partition Resolution of November 29 was followed by a revolutionary change in the British strategy. Within a few weeks the Colonial Office declared that it was the intention of the government to relinquish the mandate over Palestine as of May 15, 1948. The Foreign Minister, his prestige at stake, doubtless hoped that the ensuing civil war between Jews and Arabs would end in the overwhelming defeat of the Jews."[401] This could be considered the end result of Britain's departure from the Zionist mandate. The Christian influence as predicted by Wedgewood came to its conclusion. The political realities of maintaining control of Palestine became too much of a liability and Britain abandoned its promise or pledge to help the Jews establish a homeland.

The most imposing problem before the Zionist goal now was the Arab peoples. It was the Arab people whose land would be sacrificed to settle the "moral conscience" of the Western democracies. "The Arabs had denounced the action that placed the discussion on the United Nations agenda; they had attempted to block the right of the Jews to be heard; they threatened to boycott the hearing of the commission."[402] The Jews were caught in the middle of an impossible situation. The remaining Jews of Europe had nowhere to go. Many Jews lost everything; it would be years before any restitution would be implemented to help settle the survivors. One could hardly blame the Arabs for wanting to protect their land, but the Arabs made several serious mistakes. Their leadership sided with the Nazis during World War II. That mistake contributed in part toward Jewish sympathies and inhibiting consideration to the Palestinian Arabs.

The Zionists presented a case for Jewish autonomy that included their historic rights to the land as well as a reminder to the UN committee of the generous land grants given the Arabs following WWI. "Nor could they by-pass the historic claims of the Jewish people, especially when

---

400   Sachar, *A History of the Jews*, 433.
401   Sachar, *A History of the Jews*, 434.
402   Sachar, *A History of the Jews*, 432.

they were placed against the overgenerous territorial grants that the Arabs had received after World War I."[403] What is forgotten by Sachar is the grants were given to land of which 90 percent were already owned by the Arabs.

For the Jews in Palestine who committed themselves to the Zionist dream of a Jewish state, the military was the only option left. Political Zionism had only opened the door. It would be their responsibility to go through it and in a biblical sense, possess the land. "Ben-Gurion's confidence that his military forces could beat the Arabs in war - at least to the extent of taking by force more Arab land than had been allotted to the Jewish state in the partition plan."[404] He was happy that " . . . the final struggle would be between the Jews and the Arabs, with military force determining their outcome."[405] "But the sympathy of the world for the stunned and heartsick Jewish people was at its zenith. Practically anything was to be had for the asking, and the leaders of "Jewish" nationalism did not miss their unique opportunity."[406] The Jews had the leverage to play the UN for their advantage in Palestine. With the British gone, and the world having witnessed the tragedy of the Holocaust, the possibility of obtaining at least a piece of Palestine was now possible for the first time in 2,000 years.

UN Mandate

In the case of the Jews and the establishment of a Jewish state, the circumstances of the Holocaust made possible the impossible. "Few people disputed the right of the Jews to a home after the trauma to which they had been subjected in Central Europe."[407] As indicated earlier by Hart and other scholars, the likelihood of the Jews being given control

403   Sachar, *A History of the Jews*, 432.
404   Menachem Begin, *The Revolt* (Plainview, New York: Publishing Corporation, 1978), 246.
405   Hart, *Zionism: The Real Enemy of the Jews, Vol.I, The False Messiah*, 42-43.
406   Menuhin, *Decadence of Judaism in Our Time*, 328.
407   Shlaim, *The Iron Wall Israel and the Arab world*, 24.

over an indigenous foreign population would have seemed like reckless diplomacy. The events of World War II gave precedence to the Jews and a Zionist dream that both Jews and Gentile alike could embrace, at least for the moment. "The moral case for the Jewish people in Palestine was widely accepted from the beginning; after the Holocaust it became unassailable".[408] Zionism for the time being had won the day; the celebration was to be short lived at least in the sense of a peaceful conclusion. In the case of the fledgling nation of Israel, the Jews would have to fight to maintain their right to remain; a fight that stills continues into the 21th century.

Battle for Independence

The Zionist (Jewish) battle for Independence began well before Independence was declared. About six months went by between November of 1947 with the United Nations Mandate to May of 1948 when Israeli Independence was announced. Most world leaders gave little chance for a Jewish victory due to the Arab attitudes toward the Jews taking over Palestine. "There were few responsible statesmen among the nations of the world who doubted that the Arab victory would be quick and decisive. For the odds seemed to be overwhelming."[409] Sachar's statement supports Ben-Gurion's statement of confidence. "Ben-Gurion's confidence that his military forces could beat the Arabs in war-at least to the extent of taking by force more Arab land than had been allotted to the Jewish state in the partition plan."[410] Jewish strategists proved successful in their assessments.

The Jews had been planning this time for decades. The ultimate desire of the Jews to return to the land goes back to the first and second centuries. The Arabs would not surrender their ground easily; Palestine would be won at the end of a sword. ". . . the final struggle would be between the Jews and the Arabs, with military force determining their

---

408 Shlaim, *The Iron Wall Israel and the Arab world*, 23.
409 Sachar, *A History of the Jews*, 444.
410 Ben-Gurion, *Israel: Years of Challenge*, 246.

From Herzl to Independence: The Growth of the Zioist Movement

outcome."[411] Jewish determination verses Arab numbers: "The Arabs drew from a population of about 30,000,000; the total Israeli population was approximately 650,000."[412] Jewish determination won the day as those serving with the Jewish military had no other option but to fight. "The period between the first Arab attacks and the final withdrawal of the British offered the largest challenge to Jewish fortitude and tenacity. The basic strategy was a delaying action, an action to hold the territory that had been assigned by partition, to protect the laboriously created Jewish settlements that were marooned in the proposed Arab Zones, and to keep open all lines of communication, especially the lines to Jerusalem."[413] It was this plan that led to the destruction Deir Yassin, located on high ground west or Jerusalem. It was the attack on this village that set the stage for the Arab evacuations and a new refugee problem for many Palestinian Arabs.[414]

Sachar documents the radical change in population resulting from the early stages of the war. "The most decisive change was in the status of the Arab population.... All but 60,000 had fled precipitously during the preliminary skirmishes and the month of all-out war. A Jewish state, with almost as many Arabs in it as Jews, had been part of every plan and had been resignedly accepted by the Israeli leaders. The battlefield was apparently resolving issues that all the delicately balanced diplomatic settlements had until now only complicated." [415] With the status of war, most people fled in fear. "Arab population in the Jewish areas had been virtually resolved by the action of the Arabs themselves, who had fled into the surrounding Arab lands."[416] The down side to these positive events was the displacement of 700,000 refugees who were not allowed to return to their homes and land. Jewish Zionist gained their victory, they had won a piece of Zion but not without cost; along with the

---

411 Hart, *Zionism: The Real Enemy of the Jews, Vol. I, The False Messiah*, 246.
412 Sachar, *A History of the Jews*, 444.
413 Sachar, *A History of the Jews*, 444.
414 Sachar, *A History of the Jews*, 120.
415 Sachar, *A History of the Jews*, 446.
416 Sachar, *A History of the Jews*, 449.

victory came the refugee problem and a deepening of resentment by Arab Neighbors who saw no justice in Jewish actions.

Independence

The Jews of Palestine declared their Independence on May 14th of 1948; the day after Britain ended it's nearly 30 years of control. For Britain, it was a relief to rid itself of a political liability that only served to remind the English of their failures. Churchill, however, was gracious in his response to Jewish Independence and the fulfillment of the Zionist dream showing the influence of Zionism in spite of British resistance in following through with the Balfour Declaration. "When the state of Israel was proclaimed in 1948, Winston Churchill cabled Chaim Weizmann, the states' venerable first president, declaring what a fine moment it was 'for an old Zionist like me!'"[417] This statement from Avishai concerning Churchill carries some irony, in face of the early White Papers submitted by Churchill restricting Jewish movement into Palestine, while limiting the purchase of land by the Jews. These restriction lead directly to the problems faced by the Jews and Arabs just prior to the UN Mandate. It also rides in stark contrast to Britain's restrictive policies over the Jews during the 30 years of the British mandate.[418]

However viewed, Churchill gave a diplomatic response to a very difficult 30 years that exasperated many British leaders including Churchill as the first White Papers suggest. In spite of these conflicts, the Jews of Israel eventually honored Churchill for his contributions to Zionism, with a statue in Israel for his part, despite the British lapses.

For Churchill and many world leaders, the idea of an independent Jewish state must have seemed surreal. "In Churchill's sense, certainly, Zionism had been a source of fascination and good will not only for Jews, but also for non-Jewish Western leaders and intellectuals since

---

[417] Bernard Avishai, *The Tragedy of Zionism How Its Revolutionary Past Haunts Israeli Democracy*, (New York: Helios Press, 2002), Prologue.

[418] Avishai, *The Tragedy of Zionism How Its Revolutionary Past Haunts Israeli Democracy*, Prologue.

England's Balfour Declaration of 1917 authorized a Jewish national home in Palestine."[419] The events leading up to Independence including the tragedy of the Holocaust made possible this event along with another tragedy, displacing a people (Palestinian Arabs). The Palestinian Arabs were the big losers in this event. Zionism became a cry for justice to the Arabs community; to this day we have experienced the affects of those events of 1948. Many of the troubles in the Middle East and terrorist activities have their roots in the successes of Zionism.

---

419   Avishai, *The Tragedy of Zionism How Its Revolutionary Past Haunts Israeli Democracy*, Prologue.

CHAPTER FOUR

JEWISH-CHRISTIAN RELATIONS TODAY

Reflection

Chapter Three brought into view the rise of Zionism following the terrible events of European Pogroms and the Holocaust. The hope that emancipation would allow full Jewish participation among Gentiles within secular Western and Eastern culture was stalled. The success of Zionism can be attributed to several factors: first, the Pogroms pressed the Jews into seeking a solution to the Jewish problem of security, and finding a safe haven. Through the work of Herzl, and the help of Hechler, the Zionist cause was brought before the nations as a tangible need to find a homeland for the Jews.

Second, the events of World War I brought the British to the forefront of the Jewish problem. With the British gaining control of Palestine after the fall of the Ottoman Empire, they moved to assist the Jews in acquiring their homeland. Britain at this time was still being influenced by its Christian heritage, and through the work and influence of Chaim Weismann, and Arthur Balfour, the Balfour Declaration was established to help open the door to Palestine for the Jews The British, however, failed to follow through on their commitment to the Jews; a series of White Papers aimed at restricting immigration, and land purchases, could have alleviated concerns about Arab ownership, as well as providing a place for displaced Jews.

Third, Nazi Germany implemented an extermination program for the Jews before and during World War II. The Holocaust was one of the greatest travesties committed to any people group in history; this occurred while the majority within the German church passively stepped aside.

The Christian community failed miserably within Germany, except for the Confessing Church, which stood by the Jews during this period. Many Christians and non-Christians risked their lives for the sake of the Jews during and before WWII; these people were still a minority, and failed to shine sufficient light on Christian charity. The few examples of Christian sacrifice, were but a remnant, and insignificant in the eyes of many Jews; the Christian community could have done much more.

Fourth, Christians in the United States, along with Britain, though supportive of the Zionist movement, failed to influence the leadership of their perspective governments, which restricted immigration at the very time the Jews needed a refuge. It is true that Jewish and Christian organizations in the West protested against Nazi tactics against the Jews, but little was accomplished on the bureaucratic level. In the United States, one effort included The Wagner Bill which would have admitted twenty thousand refugee children from Germany, but support failed to materialize. Friedman presents the bill as "a token of our sympathy," and also "as a symbol of our faith in the ideals of human brotherhood."[420] David Rausch conceded, "The widespread public outcry he envisioned never materialized."[421] The Western democracies, including the church, failed the Jewish people in their greatest time of need.

A Christian Defense

Christian Zionism supported Israel long before its Declaration of Independence in 1948. The argument that the Christian community could have done much more has merit, but the extent of influence that Christian communities of the Western nations had on the political establishment may be exaggerated. "American Christian committee for German Refugees ACCGR tried desperately to garner support to alleviate the plight of the refugee."[422] Unfortunately, little was accomplished. David

---

420 Saul S. Friedman, *No Haven for the Oppressed; United States Policy Toward Jewish Refugees, 1938-1945*. (Detroit, MI: Wayne State University Press, 1973), 103.
421 Rausch, *A Legacy of Hatred*, 90.
422 Rausch, *Legacy of Hatred*, 90. American Christian committee ACCGR

Rausch writes, "The deeply concerned actions of these few individuals and organizations were unable either to help their refugees or pressure the government."[423] The influence of those who did try was not enough to offset the policy makers.

A point often missed with regard to many Jews, not all Gentiles are Christians. "Jews tend to view most non-Jews as Christians."[424] In addition to the failure of Gentiles, and Christians, most Diaspora Jews prior to the rise of Nazism and World War II were not Zionists. Support for Zionism, and the demand to open the way to Palestine occurred in the late 1930's and 1940's. "Zionism, would not have secured enough Jewish support to succeed with its Palestine project but for the Nazi Holocaust."[425] Zionism had a tall hill to climb regardless from where one's perspective was drawn.

Gaining and Maintaining the Jewish State

This chapter will examine more closely the aftermath of the Holocaust, and the events following World War II. The eventual successes of Jewish Independence, created another set of problems that shaped and affected Jewish-Christian relationships today. The success of Zionism, in gaining part of Palestine, was not won without a price; it cost the loss of peace among their Arab neighbors, along with it a diminishing hope of having a positive relationship with the outside world. The UN mandate stipulated that the Jews treat the Arab people within the Jewish Partition with respect, and restraint giving any compensation

---

423 Rausch, *Legacy of Hatred*, 90.
424 Eckstein, Rabbi Yechiel. "Jew-Christian Relations: What is the Most Important Thing Christians Should Know About Jews and Jews About Christians? *International Fellowship of Christians and Jews.* (2013) American-Israeli Cooperative Enterprise. http://www.jewishvirtuallibrary.org/jsource/anti-semitism/christjew.html.(accessed Sept. 27,2013).
425 Hart, *Zionism, The Real enemy of the Jews, Vol.1, The False Messiah*, 64.

for lands gained. "No expropriation of land owned by an Arab in the Jewish State (by a Jew in the Arab State)(4) shall be allowed except for public purposes. In all cases of expropriation full compensation as fixed by the Supreme Court shall be said previous to dispossession."[426] This request was not possible in the aftermath of three decades of conflict. Following the events of the Holocaust, by the time the Jews won their Independence, there was little trust left for Gentile (Arab) or Christian cooperation.

Following Independence, there was no going back on the military option. War was the only course left for the Zionist community. One major question, occupying the minds of many Jews and Zionist Christians today, is how to maintain and, keep the Jewish state? With the rise of Arab-Jewish tensions, before and after the UN mandate for partition of Palestine, and Jewish Independence, the situation in the Middle East seems no closer to a solution today than it did in 1953. "There's an ongoing painful side of life here, the sense that we're embroiled in a conflict that has no resolution."[427] Gordis clarifies the tension that still exists among Jews and Arabs alike in Palestine.

The Zionist leadership of Palestine put little or no faith in the Gentile community after the tragic events of World War II. This included the Christian community who, in the sight of many Jews, were partly responsible for the Holocaust. Rabbi Abba Hillel Silver stated. "The Christian world was beginning to suffer a collective guilt-penitence for its stained heritage of bestiality toward the Jewish people, there descended upon New York."[428] Silver's comments present a sweeping condemnation of Christians even as the Holocaust was occurring.

---

426   United Nations Mandate 181. Chapter 2. *UN General* Assembly (Nov. 29, 1947). http://www.mideastweb.org/181.htm. (accessed Sept. 27, 2013).

427   Daniel Gordis, *Home to Stay: One American Family's Chronicle of Miracles and Struggles in Contemporary Israel*, (New York: Three Rivers Press, 2003),123.

428   Menuhin, *Decadence of Judaism in Our Time*, 330.

The Arab Refugee Problem and Zionism

One part of the Zionist agenda that has been mostly ignored by both Christians and Jews has been the refugee problem. On this issue, both agree, in respect to the biblical promise that the land of Palestine belongs to the Jews as an inheritance. " . . . for all the land which you see, I will give it to you and to your descendants forever."[429] The result of the UN mandate, in November of 1947, was the ensuing fight to define and secure the boarders of the UN partition. Since the Arabs failed to agree with the UN mandate, there was never any consensus on Jewish rights, or borders. These lines would be drawn by military action, and not diplomacy, as exhibited by Ben-Gurion's "cavalier attitude toward the independence, sovereignty, and territorial integrity of the neighboring Arab states."[430] According to Avi Shlaim, and Gurion the Jewish leadership placed high priority on maintaining Israeli security.

The Arab community resisted implementation, not only of the UN mandate, but any influx of Jewish immigration from the end of World War I onward, as noted in Chapter Three. Since the Arabs owned the majority of the land given the Jews by Partition, "only a small area of current Israel had been in Jewish hands in November 1947."[431] The Arab community became very united on the issue to resist Jewish implementation of a Jewish state, yet they did little to prepare themselves. "The Palestine Arabs, who unlike the Jews had done very little to prepare themselves for statehood, rejected the UN partition plan out of hand."[432] The Jews desire to declare independence alienated the Palestinian Arabs from the beginning.

During and after the battle for Independence, the question of what would happen to the Arabs living in the Jewish Partition of Palestine was an unanswered question. It was expected, that the Arabs living in all of Palestine, would continue to live there as the

---

429 (Genesis 13:15)
430 Shlaim, *The Iron Wall, Israel and the Arab World*, 178.
431 Sachar, *A History of Israel from the Rise of Zionism to Our Time*, 387.
432 Shlaim, *The Iron Wall, Israel and the Arab World*, 27.

UN mandate stipulated. "The moral case for the establishment of an independent Jewish state was strong, explicitly in the aftermath of the Holocaust. But, there is no denying that the establishment of the State of Israel involved a massive injustice to the Palestinians. Half a century later, Israel still had to arrive at the reckoning of its own sins against Palestine's recognition that it owed the Palestinians a debt that must at some point be repaid."[433] The problem for Jews of Israel was to deal with the moral injustice committed against the Arab community who suffered the loss of their land through war. The Zionist goal was won at the tip of the sword. The long-term danger of this scenario is the necessity of maintaining the Zionist dream, with the dependence upon the sword, a strong military, being central to maintaining a secure nation.

Was the Jewish portion of Palestine secured legally by the Jews? UN Resolution 181's validity hinged on acceptance by both parties of the General Assembly's recommendation.[434] The Arab delegates never ratified the resolution leaving the Partition agreement as a dead document. From the Arab's perspective, since the UN Partition agreement was not ratified by both parties, technically, it was not a legal agreement. The second point to ponder, is the purchase of the land. "The land which the Society of Jews will have secured by international law must, of course, be privately acquired."[435] This condition stated by Theodore Herzl was never realized in an official sense. The land acquired through war was never given restitution to the innocent among the refugees. The Arabs lost the assets through war, yet a majority of those suffering in the refugee camps were victims, and not necessarily the agitators. "I'd been taken around the refugee camps and was outraged by what I saw. I saw only human tragedy, not the politics that caused these wretched people to be used as a whipping

---

433 Shlaim, *The Iron Wall, Israel and the Arab World*, 598.

434 United Nations Mandate 181. Chapter 2. *UN General* Assembly (Nov. 29, 1947). http://www.mideastweb.org/181.htm. (accessed Sept. 27, 2013).

435 Herzl, *The Jewish State*, 34.

post against Israel."[436] Both Arab and Jewish leadership is to be blamed to a large extent for their mishandling of the Middle East problem. The question still remains, what about the refugees?

Within the United States, the Arab question was a part of the political platform in the 1948 elections. Because of Zionist influence, the Democratic platform advocated , " . . . the resettlement of Arab refugees in lands where there is room and opportunity to them."[437] The resettlement of the Arab population was never carried out, and the refugee problem among the countries in and around Israel still exists in a state of unrest that looks unlikely to go away anytime soon.

Much of the conflict we see in the Middle East today can be drawn directly to the perception of injustices against Arab Palestinians, creating the Refugee problem. It is unfortunate that the Arab community failed to take care of the refugees, leaving them in camps for decades. The constant reminder remains a critical barrier to Arab-Jewish relationships today. The failure of the Jewish community to recognize its obligations has caused a rift that has prevented any peaceful solution to the crises in the Middle East today. In a letter to the Jewish Distribution Judah Magnus communicates his concern through his resignation. "Here was an opportunity for the JDC (Joint Distribution Committee) which would have made it the most important factor in bringing peace to the distracted Holy Land. "[438] The 'Joint' has failed to avail itself of an opportunity to become a factor of the first magnitude in bringing peace to the war-torn

---

436 McWhirter, Joan. *Israel Scene*, August, 1981, p.22 ff. In reference to husband James concerning UNRWA (the United National Agency concerned with Refugees); www.unrwa.org. (accessed Oct.6, 2013).

437 Alan Hart, *Zionism: The Real Enemy of the Jews, David Become Goliath, Vol. II* (Atlanta GA: Clarity Press, 2009), 262. i.e. outside Israel-despite UN Resolution 194.1.

438 Magnus, Judah L."Letter of Resignation - To the Chairman and Members of the Board, The American Jewish Joint Distribution Committee, Inc." *JDC (Joint Distribution Committee) Archives,* (Oct. 8, 1948). www.search.archives.jdc.org/multimedia/documents/ny_ar_45-54.pdf. (accessed Oct. 4, 2013).

Holy Land. This could have been an opportunity to extend the helping hand of a Jewish brother to thousands in distress--in the very same way in which the 'Joint' used to enlist the aid of others in helping Jews in distress. In many ways this could have been the most glorious chapter in the glorious history of the 'Joint.' "[439] The reality was the unwillingness of the Jewish Joint Distribution Committee to even consider helping those (Arabs) who were driven from their homes for no fault of their own.

This problem ties to both the Jewish and Christian communities, who continue to support an exclusive Jewish connection to the land of Palestine, and serves as a barrier to resolving any conflicts in the Middle East. "Israel's moral obligations will only be met when the refugees receive adequate financial compensation for the losses they have suffered . . . ."[440] Menuhin recognizes the depth of the refugee problem in resolving, at least in part, some of the Middle East peace problems. "Receive adequate financial compensation for the losses . . . . and what about their homeland as well as their homes and their properties: What about their political rights as well as their economic and financial rights in their homeland? Jews and non-Jews must support such a fund, if and when it is established."[441] The solution to the refugee problem can be found in compensation for those refugees and their children.

Judah Magnes seems to be in agreement with Ahad Ha'am's assessment thirty years earlier; how the Zionist Jews treated the Arabs was critical to the future.[442] As it turns out, the Jewish-Christian conflict expanded into the Jewish-Arab conflict and continues to affect not only the Middle East but all of Western society. Many Jewish scholars, place the blame for the Palestinian evacuation on the Arab nations, who told

439   Magnus, Judah L."Letter of Resignation - To the Chairman and Members of the Board, The American Jewish Joint Distribution Committee, Inc." *JDC (Joint Distribution Committee) Archives*, (Oct. 8, 1948). www.search.archives.jdc.org/multimedia/documents/ny_ar_45-54.pdf. (accessed Oct. 4, 2013).
440   *New York Times*, Dec. 5, 1958.
441   Menuhin, *Decadence of Judaism in Our Time*, 321.
442   Menuhin, *Decadence of Judaism in Our Time*, 108.

the local Palestinians to leave the country, thus resulting in a vacuum for the immigrant Jews to fill. "Many Zionist historians claim that in the early months of the war the Arab leaders encouraged the Palestinians to leave their homes. Their only evidence, however, is a vaguely worded statement by the Arab League urging the member states to give shelter to 'women, the elderly and children." [443] Those who remained were then allowed to stay while those who left were not given permission to return.

From a Christian perspective, little thought is given to how the Arab displacement took place, the emphasis being placed on the implementation of the UN mandate, or resolution 181. For Christians, a biblical view is the lens used for discerning Israel's right to the land based upon biblical promises. What becomes the more interesting dilemma is what perspective is taken by Palestinian Christians, "Like it or not the fact is that there are two peoples living in the geographic territory of Palestine, and their fates can no longer be separated."[444] Palestinian Arabs continue to battle for their right to remain within Israel.

Following the War for Independence, the Arabs demanded compensation for land, and allowing refugees who wanted to return back to their homes. "The Arab league reveals that the official position was that the territory of the Jewish state should be as defined in the UN Partition Resolution, but with two provisos. First, some parts of the Jewish state should be served to make room for the refugees. Second, if Israel chose to keep some of the territories it captures in the war, it had to compensate the Arabs."[445] Within Israel, compensation is not seriously considered. When World War II was completed, the question of compensation for the Jews became an issue among world leaders. "Of more dubious value was the completion of negotiations with Western Germany for a grant to cover some of the costs of resettling the victims of the Nazi Holocaust. It was made clear, as far as the Jews were concerned, no monetary payment would wipe out the monstrous guilt of the Nazi regime. But

---

443   Michael Palumbo, "The Palestinian Catastrophe", *Al HaMishmar*, April 5, 1985: 42.
444   Mitri Rabeb, *I Am a Palestinian Christian*, Translated by Ruth C. Gritsch, (Minneapolis, MN: Fortress Press, 1995), 80.
445   Shlaim, *The Iron Wall Israel and the Arab World*, 58.

the material indemnity would at least make the task of rehabilitation a little easier. The claim was set at one and a half billion dollars."[446] Such compensation only gives some solace to the enormity of the crimes, but the action does bring some acknowledgement of guilt and can result in some satisfaction.

For the Jews, just as it was for the Germans, the idea of compensation was not a popular idea. Many Germans considered themselves victims of the same Nazi regime. The German government capitulated and agreed to compensate. "The Federal government is prepared, joining with representatives of Jewry and the State of Israel, which has admitted many homeless Jewish refugees, to bring about a solution of the material reparation problem in order to facilitate the way to a spiritual purging of unheard-of suffering. The Bonn parliament, by a standing vote, endorsed the offer."[447] Germany was restored in a sense as a member of the world community. Such an appeasement would remove some barriers to a possible peace settlement between the Jews and Arabs.

Jewish Immigration

For the many Jews living in Arab nations, Jewish Independence created new barriers between them and the Arab countries in which they resided for centuries. "Migrations from the Arab lands of the Near East, and North Africa were severely limited by hostile government restrictions. There was no love for the native Jews, and their departure was devoutly sought by the discredited Arab effendis."[448] What was ironic in this situation, was that these Jews had lived in relative peace with the Arab communities for a millennium. This forced migration to Israel, was not universally accepted among those living in Arab-controlled countries. Jewish leadership in Israel necessitated, they replace the displaced Arabs as quickly as possible. Having unoccupied Arab land populated with Jewish refugees would reduce pressures of allowing the return of Arab refugees.

446 Sachar, *A History of the Jews*, 458.
447 Sachar, *A History of the Jews*, 459.
448 Sachar, *A History of the Jews*, 455.

The immigration of Jews was carried out at great difficulty and expense for a country with so few resources. "Every migration plan, whether, managed individually or by accredited Jewish international agencies, became a nightmare combination of negotiation and blackmail . . . . Tens of thousands of Jews in the Arab lands managed to get out."[449] The removal of Jews from Yemen is an example of the difficulties faced by the young nation. "Here, nearly fifty thousand Jews lived, in incredible misery and degradation. Their roots in the land went back to Biblical days, . . . permission was obtained for them to leave for Israel if they forfeited their possessions and paid a silver tax of three dollars per person."[450] This operation, called Magic Carpet, required one hundred and fifty C-54 Sky Mater transports to go to Israel. Jews were yet unwilling to consider restitution for the Arabs when they went to such lengths to take care of Jews living in Arab's countries.

Early Jewish Leadership

Early Jewish leaders such as Ben-Gurion and Golda Meir were hawks in the military sense, seeing no option but to fight for the land. Gurion and Meir fit the mold for what constituted many Israeli leaders during the first few decades of the Israeli state. Sachar describes Meir, her "personality, being imperious, overbearing, and intolerant of opposition." " . . . she saw the world in black-and-white, without intermediate shades of gray. Her confidence that in any debate her party, her country, and she were in the right was without limits." ". . . it was always being in the right that made it so difficult to reason with her."[451] Her attitude toward the Arabs was based on emotion and intuition rather than on reason and reflection. "Golda was afraid of the Arabs. And these fears were connected with her memories of Pogroms and the Holocaust . . . she could not come to terms with the thought that maybe the Arabs

---

449   Sachar, *A History of the Jews*, 455.
450   Sachar, *A History of the Jews*, 455.
451   Shlaim, *Iron Wall Israel and the Arab World*, 284.

felt that an injustice had been committed against them."[452] It needed to be the Arabs, or the Jews, no middle ground existed.

The strong hawkish demeanor of early Jewish leadership was instrumental in keeping the Israeli military at the forefront of all Arab-Jewish relationships, without which, the Jews would not have survived in Palestine. The down side is the perpetual state of war that now exists between Israel and the Arab nations. Jewish leadership knew their limits: "For Golda the only realistic solution to the Palestinian problem, from the demographic and the geographic point of view was to place them under Jordan's jurisdiction."[453] It was through negotiations with King Hussein of Jordan that the Jordanian military kept its presence in the West bank that helped the Jews in the War for Independence. While Westcott and Wingate were instrumental in building up a strong disciplined military in Israel, Glubb Pasha was responsible for the military buildup in Jordan with British help. It was this potential conflict that prompted Meir to negotiate a truce with King Hussein prior to the War for Independence with the promise to leave the West bank for the Arabs.

Through the last half of the twentieth century, Jewish leaders were concerned about two primary issues: first, the security of Israel from what was considered the Arab threat. For Israeli leadership, extreme emphasis was placed on survival and minimizing risks to the well being of the fledgling state. The down side of demonizing the Arab community was that it alienated them from any possible hope for a positive future relationship. Such an approach left the Israeli leadership with little trust in anyone besides themselves. The second issue that was most elusive for Israel was their desire for peace; that became even more elusive as the century drew to a close leaving little room for error in regards to its neighbors.

---

452 Shlaim, *Iron Wall Israel and the Arab World*, 284.
453 Shlaim, *Iron Wall Israel and the Arab World*, 311.

Jewish Injustices

There is no doubt that many injustices were committed by the Jews against the Arab population during and after the War of Independence. Moshe Dayan, leader of the Jewish Military, was clearly not insensitive to Arab feelings. According to Shlaim, "He recognized the injustice that his country had inflicted on hundreds of thousands of Arabs."[454] But like Meir, he was pessimistic concerning the possibility of an accommodation with the Arabs. "Israel's survival was at stake and that led him to reject any magnanimity. Dayan's was the philosophy of a man who was born in war; who lived all his life in war, and for whom war had always been the focus of his thoughts."[455] Survival at all costs seemed the rule in that early leadership with the strong emphasis on maintaining control. Dayan displayed a very aggressive policy toward the Arabs, creating an even higher level of tension that continues to permeate the Middle East.

The creation of the Arab refugee problem and the failure or unwillingness of the Arab neighbors to receive those refugees has left the situation unresolved. The refugee problem opens another door to the Zionist condition and the current state of Israel. Gary Burge raises a spiritual problem concerning Jewish faithfulness and possessing the land. "If, however, possessing the land is tied to Israel's fidelity to the covenant, it is not surprising that when the prophets looked to the future, they predicted a new generation that would embrace the covenant with zeal and reclaim the land at the same time."[456] Burge suggests that the prophetic voice points to a dual reclamation of a spiritual inheritance, along with the land, as the Jews would enter into a new relationship with God. This, however, is not the case, as we see, 70% of the Jews living in Israel are secularists.

Jewish fears of Arab population growth have prompted Israeli leaders to keep Israeli Arabs out areas in Israel that are crucial to Israeli

---

454 Shlaim, *Iron Wall Israel and the Arab World,* 102.
455 Shlaim, *Iron Wall Israel and the Arab World,* 102.
456 Gary Burge, *Whose Land? Whose Promise? What Christians Are Not Being Told about Israel and the Palestinians* (Cleveland, OH: Pilgrims Press, 2004), *103.*

security. Amnesty International states concerning Israel. "Palestinian Bedouin who are citizens of Israel have suffered the repeated demolition of their homes as a consequence of discriminatory policies that do not recognize the legality of some 35 villages in the Negev/Naqab; region."[457] According to Amnesty International, today in East Jerusalem alone, nearly 5,000 homes within the Palestinian section of Jerusalem are threatened with demolition orders. "An estimated 4,800 demolition orders are thought to be pending."[458] More Palestinian refugees are being created today through various restoration projects in Israel.

Survival

The Arab nations at this point had little love for Israel and the bitterness Israel caused in relationship to the Palestinian problem. Zionism became a catch word for imperialism and colonialism amongst Palestinian refugees and the Arab community in general. "The Arab states surrounding Israel have been consistent in their resistance to Israel's statehood. They are sympathetic to the Palestinian loss of land and see Israel as one more extension of Western imperialism in the Middle East .... Israel is viewed as an offense to Arab sensibility and pride."[459] It is of no surprise that peace is so fragile and hard to find. The bitterness created by the wars of the last half of the century left little doubt that a peace settlement, if found at all, would only be on paper, but not in the hearts and minds of the Arab people. This is not surprising, however, in

---

457 Amnesty International, "Submission for the Universal Periodic Review of Israel", 17th session of the UPR Working group, (October-November 2013). www.amnesty.org/en'library/assest/MDE15/015/2013/en/c88f325d-74b-434e-9db0-44b544eb732b/mde150152013en.pdf. (accessed Oct.4, 2013).

458 Amnesty International Press release, June 16, 2010, http://www.amnestyusa.org/news/press-releases/israel-amnesty-international-urges-israeli-authorities-to-stop-demolitions-of-pales. (accessed Oct. 5, 2013).

459 Burge, *Whose Land? Whose Promise? What Christians Are Not Being Told about Israel and the Palestinians*, 31.

that the Israel of old was always surrounded by its enemies and relief was found only in the hands of God for deliverance.[460] A secular Israel however, does not seek refuge in God.

This brings the words of Theodore Herzl crashing down on the realities of current Zionist hopes: "But the Jews, once settled in their own State, would probably have no more enemies, and since prosperity enfeebles and causes them to diminish, they would soon disappear altogether. The Jews will always have sufficient enemies, much as every other nation has. But once fixed in their own land, it will no longer be possible for them to scatter all over the world."[461] Wishful thinking on Herzl's part, as the Zionist community ignored the Arabs' sense of nationality and pride. Enemies were to be a way of life in the new Israel, with little hope in the immediate future for any relief.

Jewish Renewal

One positive result coming from the Zionist movement and the return of the Jewish state is a sense of renewal and purpose among many Jews. "Even nonreligious Jews did not oppose the Orthodox drive. For one reason, it seemed peculiarly fitting that Israel, as Jewish state, should follow traditional practices."[462] The Jewish people in Israel have committed themselves to the establishment and maintenance of Israel as a nation. The return of the land brings a sense of closure to many Jews as a fulfillment in terms of purpose and direction. Many Jews who return to Israel either temporarily or permanently confess to a renewed enthusiasm for their Jewish heritage, including the necessity of learning Hebrew, their ancient language, and their faith, which consists of several special days of festivals in celebration of Judaism. The land of Israel has to some extent provided a spiritual renewal to many Jews. "It's about feeling that we belong here, fit in here better than we ever did

---

460 (Deuteronomy 1:1-25)
461 Herzl, *The Jewish State,* 76.
462 Urofsky, *We are One: American Jewry and Israel*, 250.

in the States."[463] Daniel Gordis reflects upon settling in Israel from the United States.

For many Jews, Zionism became a renewed sense of worth in their Jewish pride. "The Zionist movement has revived among Jews the sense of community."[464] Their Jewish heritage was renewed and awakened as a result of their possession of the land of Palestine and the renewal of their language. Each of these has brought many Jews closer to their faith and a desire for many a restored sense of their ethnicity. Jews coming from the Diaspora have developed a deeper sense of belonging in Israel, and the Jews carry a special longing for the land that spreads across many millennia.

Six-Day War and Yom Kippur

The early leadership of Israel was controlled predominantly by a hawkish relationship with the Arabs. Many of the conflicts which occurred were provoked. "I know how at least 80 percent of the clashes there started by agitating the Syrians."[465] "Dayan's 1976 comments on Israel's behavior were rather sweeping and simplistic. They may have been colored by his disgrace and resignation as defense minister following his failure to anticipate the Arab attack on October 1973. It appeared that Dayan and some of his fellow officers did not accept the armistice line with Syria as final. Hertzberg adds regarding Israeli leadership, they "hoped to change them [armistice line] by means that fell short of war, by 'snatching bits of territory and holding on to it until the enemy despairs and gives it to us.' This may have been naïve on their part, said Dayan, but at the atrium they did not have much experience in diplomacy among sovereign states."[466] From all appearances they

463 Gordis, *Home to Stay: One American Family's Chronicle of Miracles and Struggles in Contemporary Israel*, 85.
464 Albert Einstein, *Out of My Later Years* (New York: Edition by Open Road Integrated Media, 2011 : From the Estate of Albert Einstein, 195), 262.
465 Hertzberg, *Zionist Idea*, 235-236.
466 Hertzberg, *Zionist Idea*, 236.

really did not try. On top of this, the Arabs were as inexperienced as the Israelites at diplomacy. In fact, for the most part, they were less educated than most Israeli Jews. They should have considered their methods more carefully; as a result, they have deepened the resentment of the Arabs. Peace initiatives have become less likely as the conflicts continue between Jews and Arabs.

The Palestine Liberation Organization (PLO)

The PLO entered the scene in 1974, as the body representing all Palestinian interests, with one of its objectives being the return (liberation) of Palestine to Arab control, along with the refugees in surrounding camps. This organization has as its primary function the dismantling of Zionism, and the Zionist dream, meaning the departure of the Jews from Palestine. The primary goal implies, the Liberation of Palestine from Jewish control. ". . . the liberation of Palestine as the principal goal of this movement."[467] It was the wish of Jewish leadership that Jordan would take custody of the Palestinian Arab problem; this scenario never occurred. In October of 1974, the Arab League summit meeting was held in Rabat, the capitol of Morocco. King Hussein suffered a major defeat because the summit endorsed the claim of the PLO to be, "the sole legitimate representative of the Palestinian peoples."[468] The Arab League summit reaffirmed the right of the Palestinian people, to set up an independent nation authority, led by the PLO, on any part of Palestine that was liberated. "Some State Department officials were sympathetic to the view that the Palestinian issue was at the heart of the Middle Eastern problem and that the PLO position could evolve in a moderate direction."[469] The PLO with Yasser Arafat as its leader became the spokesman for Palestinian Arabs. As the name implies, the liberation of Palestine from Jewish control back into Arab hand is still the primary objective for the organization.

---

467 Shlaim, *The Iron Wall, Israel and the Arab World*, 187.
468 Hertzberg, *Zionist Idea*, 333.
469 Hertzberg, *Zionist Idea*, 341.

Failed Treaties - Camp David Accords

The success of Zionism, as desired by Christians and Jews seeks to have one objective, a stable and secure Palestine under Jewish control. Any treaty between Arabs and Jews would be a welcome event, if such a treaty would give security to the Jewish people. One agreement was significant only within the context of its claim for success and reflects on most Jewish-Arab peace talks. The Camp David "Accords", were facilitated by President Jimmy Carter, a Christian. He hosted both Menachem Begin, who was the prime minister of Israel, and a former terrorist leader of the Ingram, together with Anwar El Sadat, leader of Egypt and the one responsible for the Yom Kippur War against Israel. Without discussing any of the details, both parties shook hands, took pictures, and received Nobel Peace Prizes for coming together in an agreement. What makes this agreement so interesting is that the US promised billions of dollars to each party if they would agree. "While he was wary of "buying peace," Carter realized that he could use America's "vast economic and military resources [to] help to change the calculus of benefit and risk for the parties to the conflict by making bilateral commitments to them."[470] In a sense, the agreement is little more than a costly bribe by the United States, giving away billions of dollars every year to two leaders who were intimately involved in war.

While most agreements have some substance to their purpose and the handshake between Jewish and Palestinian leaders was monumental, the agreement made, served primarily as a cosmetic function. Israel deeply desires peace however they are at perpetual war with the Arab nations; there is little interest within the Arab community to make peace with Israel. Any agreement would bind the Arabs to recognize Israel and would put them in a difficult situation to restore Palestine to Arab control, which is the ultimate goal of the Arabs. Intifadas, which are

---

[470] William B. Quandt, "Camp David and Peacemaking in the Middle East, Political Science Quarterly, Vol. 101, No. 3 (1986), 359. Jonathan Oakman, The Camp David Accords, A Case Study on International Negotiation, 2002, 6. www.princeton.edu/research/cases/campdavid/pdf.

small-scale Arab uprisings, served as a half measure to keep pressure on the Jews within Israel and have served to breed a measure of despair.

The Oslo Accords

The Oslo Accords brought some hope for a peace settlement as Yitzhak Rabin and Yasser Arafat came to an agreement. "Every Israeli concession, however minor, was made only after exhausting negotiations, deliberate delays, and protracted crises. Every small step forward involved brinksmanship and increased the bitterness felt by both sides."[471] Israeli Jews and Palestinian Arabs live in close proximity as neighbors but having completely different objectives. For any possibility of peace, recognition of each other's rights was a critical step. "The Oslo Accords carried the kernel of an understanding that Israel would have no peace unless it recognized the Palestinian right to national self-determination."[472] "For all their shortcomings, these Accords contained the basis for a historic compromise between the two principal parties in the century–old struggle for Palestine."[473]

Peace talks brought more uncertainty; even as leaders agreed, tensions increased. Israel, which committed itself to Revisionist Zionism, requires a strong military to survive. The people within Israel today are tired of war and the hope of peace is becoming less visible under current conditions. Once Israel committed itself to the military option of taking and maintaining its hold on Palestine, the hope for peace was diminished. With Arab intifadas and the rise of Hamas inside the Gaza strip, the desire for any peace seems more distant. Both Arabs and Jews have committed themselves to tracts that will be nearly impossible to change without major restructuring.

Arab and Jewish leadership recognize the need to tread a fine line in seeking solutions to Jewish Arab relations. Yasser Arafat remembered to tread this fine line in avoiding any significant commitments and

---

471   Shlaim, *The Iron Wall Israel and the Arab World*, 602.
472   Shlaim, *The Iron Wall Israel and the Arab World*, 602.
473   Shlaim, *The Iron Wall Israel and the Arab World*, 603.

agreements with Israel, which may have saved his life, because Anwar Sadat and Yitzhak Rabin were both assassinated shortly following the treaties they signed bringing closer ties between Jews and Arabs. Factions exist within both Jewish and Arab communities that have no desire for improved relations and seek only the destruction of the other. Under such circumstances, any agreements would be most difficult to achieve.

Palestinian Christians

Arab's resistance to Zionism is not based upon religious ideology as can be seen, when we consider the camaraderie between Arab Christians and Muslims on this subject. Being Christian does not necessitate support for Zionism, as many Catholic and liberal Christians would testify. "Christian Arabs--and there are many hundreds of thousands of them in the Arab world--are in absolute agreement with all other Arabs in opposing the Zionist invasion of Palestine."[474] The loss of land and property goes a long way in bringing people with common needs together. Religious ideology in this case plays very little part when personal livelihood is at stake. A sense of justice can unite differing faiths.

Hart paints a rather bleak picture of Palestinian Christians and the Jews as he defines the existence of Israel. His description of the Christian community is accurate; Christian Palestinian Arabs are under the oppression of Israeli control to the same degree as Arab Muslims. From the Jewish perspective, there seems to be little difference. The native Palestinian Arabs, regardless of faith, are not trusted. One consensus rings true for both Arab Muslims, and Arab Christians, both oppose Zionism.

Though most of the land was granted by way of United Nations Partition, the Jews won possession of the land through war. Most of the land granted to the Jews was never purchased, a result of the British

---
474 Hart, *Zionism: The Real Enemy of the Jews, David Become Goliath, Vol. II* , 21.

White Papers. Legal land purchases would have diverted some tension between Arabs and Jews. Bitterness and anger rose among Palestinian Arabs for having lost their land while being driven out of their homes. For the Jews, the reality was survival, to Palestinian Arabs a tragedy. Palestinians lost their land and their future hope, Jews lost the peace.

Review of Spiritual, Political/Practical, and Revisionist Zionism

Zionist philosophies, before, and after World War II took on three basic forms, these included: Political Zionism, Spiritual Zionism, and Revisionist Zionism. Each carried a distinct characteristic regarding the ultimate goal of Zionism, which would be a safe haven for the Jews in Palestine as a Jewish state. This ultimate goal has yet to be achieved; even though the Jews possess the majority of Palestine, they have yet to gain the entire region. They still have a large minority of indigenous Arabs possessing a large portion of land and many more living as legal citizens within Israel itself. A peaceful settlement between the Arabs and Jews has yet to be resolved. The hope of a safe haven without the constant threat of war still remains to be seen.

A second direction is Spiritual Zionism which will be discussed in more detail later. This form of Zionism was promoted by Ahad Ha'am, a Jewish writer (Asher Ginsberg), who was heavily involved in the early development of Jewish Palestine. Concerning Ha'am, he warned "all the way from the very beginning of Jewish colonization in Palestine, about the relations of the Jews to the Arabs of Palestine." [475] Ha'am recognized early the urgency of working with the Arabs and building a relationship with them in order to build a slow and progressive foothold in the land without disrupting the entire culture and atmosphere of the Arab community. "He was the only one in the Zionist organization who dwelt on the 'Arab problem ' . . . from a moral and humane point of view as behooves a Jew."[476] According to Menuhin, Ahad reminded the Jews that the land was occupied and the Arabs would not give it up easily. This form of Zionism, called Spiritual Zionism, put the emphasis on a

475 Menuhin, *Decadence of Judaism in Our Time*, 63.
476 Menuhin, *Decadence of Judaism in Our Time*, 63.

slow adjustment into Palestine, and more cooperation with the Arabs. His emphasis was on gaining a spiritual renewal in the land without necessarily possessing the land. "We must not strive for our Holy Land, but to our own land."[477] The spiritual emphasis was to encourage a spiritual renewal of the Jews which had fallen heavily into secularism and away from the Jewish faith.

The third form of Zionism, called Revisionist Zionism was discussed in Chapter three, it demanded a strong military response to Arab attacks. The failure of the British to help with Jewish immigration into Palestine put heavy restrictions on the possession of weapons designed to keep the Jews and Arabs under control and to reduce conflicts. The opposite occurred, leaving the Jews in a very compromising position. This form of aggressive Zionism was promoted by Ze'ev Jabotinsky, who was later captured and imprisoned to prevent the Jews from gaining any military advantages. It is through Jabotinsky's influence and direction that Revisionist Zionism took up the battle for the land that ultimately resulted in the War for Independence.

Revisionist Zionism won the day for the Jews, who saw no other solution to gaining the land. The Jews fought Arab attacks, resisting the strict quotas maintained by the British throughout World War II and after. The ultimate result of this strategy succeeded in pushing the British out of Palestine and turning over of the Palestine Mandate to the United Nations.

Zionism Today

The Zionist movement has become somewhat split between the secular and spiritual within Israel today. The Israeli government and institutions are very secular, while the religious community has become

---

477 Menuhin, *Decadence of Judaism in Our Time*, 57. Menuhin from Pinskers' Auto-Emancipation, reflected, Ahad Ha'am Ahad (Jerusalem: Yavneh, 1925. VI.) 216-233.

predominantly Orthodox. This spectrum of religious indifference to religious fervor can only be explained by the intense nature of Jewish extremes that seem to reflect on its national life. "Even nonreligious Jews did not oppose the Orthodox drive. For one reason, it seemed peculiarly fitting that Israel, as a Jewish state, should follow traditional practices."[478] Even though secular Jews resisted traditional Orthodox Judaism, within the boundaries of the new Israel, it seemed fitting to incorporate Jewish religious tradition even among the secular Jewish community.

The whole objective of the Enlightenment was to separate these two factors and explains why Jews today are so liberal in views; they are only protecting their religious life from the scrutiny of pro-Christian governments. In essence, there is still little trust in the Christian community to do the right thing for the Jews. This distrust is built on 2,000 years of history, which the past century has had little impact in changing. Tolerance and openness, virtues in the West, are often negated by those who seek a stronger, more focused Judaism, with its emphasis on exclusivism. Israel exists today in the midst of this secular Orthodox conflict.

Secular Zionism

Secular Zionism is much the same as the practical Zionism of Theodor Herzl, except for the added emphasis on the military. It operates on the rational realities of life as they are seen from the world of men. They seek to maintain a strong military (Revisionist Zionism), knowing that without it Israel would fall quickly.[479] The Secularists place a high value on tolerance and pluralism, the two being in some form of conflict with Orthodox Judaism, the standard faith of Israel. The conflict places some barriers between the Secularists within the leadership of Israel and the religious Orthodox Jews.

---

478 Urofsky, *We are One: American Jewry and Israel*, 250.
479 Ze'ev Jabotinsky was the father of Revisionist Zionism which was adopted in complementary form to protect the political realities.

The Jews are not unique in their desire for autonomy. Their history of persecution would drive any people to seek freedom just as the Pilgrims sought freedom 400 years ago by coming to America. "Zionism is not just a reaction of a people to persecution. It is the quest for self-determination and liberation under the modern conditions of secularization and liberalism."[480] The current Israeli quest is a unique conflict between secular liberalism, derived from the experience in the Diaspora, and Orthodox Judaism with its conservative religious roots. These differences are yet to be worked out.

Avineri suggests one strategic difference with Israel, the idea that Jewish nationalism cannot be separated from its religious connotations. This idea explains in part why Orthodox Judaism has wielded so much influence within Israel today. As a result, the Zionist movement does not recognize pluralism within the borders of Israel as the nation seeks to rediscover its Jewish religious roots while maintaining an open democracy. The two come with conflict, but most Jews tolerate those differences. " It substituted a secular self-identity of the Jews as a nation for the traditional and Orthodox self-identity in religious terms. It changed a passive, quietistic and pious hope of the Return of Zion into an effective social force, moving millions of people to Israel. It transformed a language relegated to mere religious usage into a modern, secular mode of intercourse of a nation-state."[481] The merger of two apparently conflicting ideologies sets Israel up as unique among the nations. Israel today is a secular nation with an extremely deep religious foundation; these cannot help but collide.

Spiritual Zionism

As mentioned earlier, Spiritual Zionism places a higher priority on Arab-Jewish relationships and spiritual Judaism. While Orthodox Judaism tends to be less tolerant and promotes a strong Jewish flavor to the current state of Israel, it is very protective of the Jewish heritage and

---

480 Avineri, *The Making of Modern Zionism*, 13.
481 Avineri, *The Making of Modern Zionism*, 13.

restricts any other claims including all Christians, Messianic Christians, Conservative, and Reformed Jews. Spiritual Zionism places a higher emphasis on cooperation with those living in the land with the emphasis on spiritual renewal rather than possessing the land.

Biblical Zionism predicts the return of the Jews to the Holy Land. It does not fit into any political or secular models that drive current Zionism, but rather reflects more upon the Spiritual Zionism of Ahad-Ha'am. The return of the Jews to their faith, the faith reflected in the prophets as well as the Law, is a heart change where the Jews will again seek God with all their hearts. This Zionism is one that should respect the rights of all men who will accept God as their God, while remaining very protective of its Jewish roots.

Levi Eshkol, former Prime Minister of Israel, said that "he was against separation of the synagogue and the State, and that he believed 'the *status quo* regarding religion in Israel's public life can continue, more or less, for many years'."[482] From this perspective, Judaism in its orthodox form makes claims on the social life of the entire nation of Israel. This will also include Arab Israelites who share little common ground with their Jewish brothers. While Christian Arabs should have some biblical and spiritual connections to the ceremonial aspects of Jewish religious life in Israel. Christian Arabs are in full agreement with Palestinian Arabs in resisting Zionism.

Sand expresses the concern of many Jewish Zionists of their desire for autonomy. "A national consciousness is primarily the wish to live in an independent political entity. It wants its subjects to live and to be educated by a homogeneous national culture. That was the essence of Zionism at its inception, and so it remained for most of its history until recent times. It sought independent sovereignty and achieved it. There have been other Jewish solidarities, but most of them were not national, and some were even expressly antinational."[483] Sand does not specify what those entities were other than what is currently the issue. Nationalism is inclusive, but Zionism tends to move toward

---

482 Moshe Menuhin, *London Jewish Chronicle*, (July 31, 1964): 391.
483 Sand, *Invention of the Jewish people,* 303 .

exclusiveness. Thus it separates or rather differentiates between ethnicity and culture. What is ironic within the Jewish community is that culture tends to be on the most part very secular and Western. Being Jewish does not rest solely on its cultural underpinnings (Kosher Laws, Jewish Festivals, ancestry, and history), but it does reflect a passionate identity that ties the community together in ways that go beyond rationality. Those biblical or spiritual ties are not easily explained and may defy secular theorists an easy explanation.

Zionism as a cause today has in some cases weakened. The constant threat of war, along with conflicts among the Israeli-Arab population, has caused many to question the Zionist ideal. Yoram Hazony notes, "I collided once again with the problem of the "post-Jewish" state."

"Public figures had begun to talk of changing the Israeli national anthem (to remove the words 'Jewish soul') and repealing the Law of Return like overt anti-Zionists of the past."[484] This would appear to be a loss well prompted by the intellectual community. "Israel's intellectuals had long ago abandoned the news that Zionism, while engendering rare acts of injustice, was a fundamentally just cause; instead, they had come to believe that the cause of the Jewish state was wrong in principle, and the result was an entire culture of hatred against the Jewish state."[485] "But a single example was the cultural leaders' habit of identifying the IDF with the Nazis--a trend which had ballooned to include thousands of articles . . . hundreds of poems."[486] This perspective is only a minority but serves as a reminder to changing attitudes within Israel, leaving many wondering about the future of the Zionist state.

Another reason the Zionist dream is in the midst of identity crises in Israel today is that so much press and world opinion has gone against Israel. With the constant threat of war, the reminder of the Arab refugees, and the diligence necessary to keep control, many Israeli's have grown weary. After sixty- plus years, the situation has not gone away. It would seem the Arab community has seen fit to keep these problems before

---

484 Hazony, *The Jewish State the Struggle for Israel's Soul*, 4.
485 Hazony, *The Jewish State the Struggle for Israel's Soul*, 4.
486 Hazony, *The Jewish State the Struggle for Israel's Soul*, 4.

the world press for the purpose of gaining sympathy. Although Israel hoped the situation would be dispersed in time, that did not happen; the conflict continues.

Zionism in Israel Today

Zionism's success brings with it the complexities of maintaining presence and control in Palestine over Arab interests. In order for Israel to maintain a strong hand, it has become necessary for Jewish leadership to operate on a predominant Revisionist philosophy, of a strong military, and a hard line on Arab resistance. Most decisions, both foreign and domestic, must be balanced toward security issues, as well as building a strong economy. Henry Kissinger once remarked, "Israel has no foreign policy, only domestic politics."[487] Israel cannot afford to make mistakes in any of its policies that could result in homeland security risks. With the Oslo Accords and other talks, Israel has demonstrated willingness to talk, demonstrating a strong desire for peace. We have witnessed a softening of Israel's attitude, and desire for peace, with a fleeting peace.

In 1998, "Israeli society was more divided than at any other time since the foundation of the state, and there was no consensus on how to mark the milestone."[488] The conflict between hawks and doves within the Jewish leadership brings in uncertainty. "It is one of the ironies of Zionist history that Benjamin Netanyahu, the proud standard-bearer of Revisionist Zionism, betrayed the legacy of the founder of the movement by spurring the offer of peace with the Palestinians. Ze'ev Jabotinsky's strategy of the iron wall was designed to force the Palestinians to despair of the prospect of driving the Jews out of Palestine and to compel them to negotiate with the Jewish state from a position of weakness."[489] We are witnessing just the opposite as Jews are becoming weary of war. "The Jews of Israel are an exhausted people, confused and without

---

487 Shlaim, *The Iron Wall, Israel and the Arab World*, 597.
488 Shlaim, *The Iron Wall, Israel and the Arab World*, 597.
489 Shlaim, *The Iron Wall, Israel and the Arab World*, 606.

direction."[490] The Arabs, whose lives are very difficult, have a much bigger ax to grind today as they are the ones who seem willing to persevere.

Jewish-Christian Relations and Theology
-- Jewish Christian Thawing

Jewish-Christian relationships take on many facets that will dictate how most Jews, and Christians relate, Zionism being only one factor. The rejection of Jesus Christ as Messiah would be another. "The cross, the holy icons, and the church were all regarded as idolatrous symbols; and the false position assigned to Jesus in Christianity so repelled Jewry that it could not even acknowledge the ethical content of the religion."[491] Understanding of Jewish attitudes toward Jesus of the New Testament is perhaps the biggest factor in understanding Jewish culture for Christians.

For many Jews, Christians worship a false god; Jesus Christ cannot be the Messiah, or the Son of God. "In the view of Jewry the Nazarene was not the son of god, but only an errant son."[492] This attitude is slowly changing for some within the Jewish academic community over the past century as demonstrated by Claude Montefiore and Joseph Klausner. One of the positive factors of emancipation was a more objective view of New Testament Christianity from a Jewish academic perspective. What makes this significant is that a less hostile view of the New Testament Jesus explains in part why many Jews in the Diaspora were not interested in the Zionist movement. For some, the issues of mistrust had become less relevant to the realities of life, and the future; Christianity was viewed in more neutral than hostile terms. Working along with and in relationship with Christians and others helped in thawing negative

---

490 Hazony, Yoram, *The Jewish State: The Struggle for Israel's Soul*, xvii.

491 Avineri, *The Making of Modern Zionism*, 127. Referenced from: Arthur Hertzberg, *The Jewish Problem and the Jewish State*, 333.

492 Avineri, *The Making of Modern Zionism*, 127. Referenced from: Arthur Hertzberg, *The Jewish Problem and the Jewish State*, 333.

stereotypes that often are placed upon those we neither know well nor understand.

As the Zionist dream of a new Israel gained momentum following WWI, and the Balfour Agreement, the relationship between Jews, and Christians must be reexamined in light of assimilation, and academic freedoms granted Jews. Through emancipation, and assimilation, the Jewish community took full advantage of the academic opportunities presented to them, as presented in Chapter Two, making good use of those freedoms to contribute to the greater society.

These prominent scholars of the early twentieth century made significant strides in demonstrating the similarities between Judaism and Christianity. They began to question some Jewish perspective on Jesus of the New Testament. Joseph Klausner and Claude Montefiore were both respected Jewish scholars, who opened the doors a bit wider in Jewish New Testament understanding. It must be noted that this did not result in a conversion to Christianity, only an increased appreciation for the message of one Jew, who had a profound influence on the development of the Christian faith.

What Klausner, Montefiore, and other Jewish scholars did was to remove some of the myth regarding Jesus as a deceiver of Jewish people. To provide information concerning the similarities between Jesus as a deceiver and other Messianic leaders such as the Cabalists of the seventeenth century including Kabocha and Zevi, who misled many people. It was these events that had a profound impact on secular Judaism and led in part to a non-messianic Zionism. Zionism was being led by those more interested in a secular society such as Herzl and Ben-Gurion: a society founded on practical need and where Jews would be in control of their own affairs. Klausner and Montefiore were influenced by the view that Jesus was a product of Jewish education and culture and was not someone that needed to be rejected.

Claude Montefiore was an anti-Zionist who believed in the assimilation of the Jews into secular culture. Montefiore represents Reformed Judaism with a more liberal bent. This may explain in part his openness to the New Testament portrait of Jesus. Montefiore raises several points of value that the Jews rejected, solely to avoid any further contact with Christianity. These scholars demonstrated that the Old and New Testaments work together. "Be this idea too bizarre, it may, nevertheless, be safely asserted that he whose religion is founded upon what has here been presented from Old Testament and New Testament together, will possess a religion which, whatever else may be said of it, is in its fundamental constituents both consistent and Jewish."[493] Montefiore adds, "The solemn nobility and beauty of these words [of Jesus], who can gainsay? Are we not the poorer if we cannot accept them as part of the formative religious literature of the world and of our own religious consciousness?"[494] This reference demonstrates a positive attitude for the New Testament from a Jewish New Testament scholar.

Other Jewish scholars soon realized that Jesus was not anti-Jewish, as they had been led to believe from Jewish folklore. He was indeed a Jewish teacher, that taught for the most part the Mosaic Law. The data of the New Testament about Jesus was either directly or indirectly a result of the Old Testament (Tanakh). The conflicts that exist between Judaism and Christianity were not directly based upon the teachings of Jesus (doctrine), but rather on his Messianic claims.

Joseph Klausner was more pessimistic in his analysis of the person Jesus Christ. Klausner was a professor of Hebrew literature and very devoted to Zionism. He lived a large portion of his life in Israel. He, along with Montefiore was interested in the person of Jesus. For Klausner, Jesus of Nazareth was a Jewish teacher but not Jesus Christ, the Son of God. "To the Jewish nation he can be neither God nor the Son of God, in the sense conveyed by belief in the Trinity . . . . Neither can they regard him as a Prophet; he lacks the Prophet's political perception and the Prophet's spirit of national consolation in the political-national sense . . . neither can they regard him as a law-giver or the founder of a new religion; he did not even desire to be such. Neither is he a 'tanna' or Pharisaic Rabbi: he nearly always realigned himself in opposition to the Pharisee . . . . But Jesus is, for the Jewish nation, a great teacher of

---

493 Montefiore, *The Old Testament and After*, 284-285.
494 Montefiore, *The Old Testament and After*, 239.

morality and an artist in parables."[495] For Klausner, Jesus of Nazareth was a good Jew but not the Christ of the New Testament. "Jewish writers are not concerned with the Second Person of the Holy Trinity but with Jesus of Nazareth, the man and the Jew."[496] The modern development is not necessarily connected with Zionism, but a development as a result of closer ties with modern society and the Christian community in the West.

Klausner appreciated the contributions regarding the influence of Jesus. "With few exceptions, there is a growing desire to appreciate the person of Jesus and to acknowledge his significance for mankind."[497] An increased appreciation for Jesus as a moral influence, removes many barriers to Jewish-Christian relations. This is due to the pluralistic nature inherent in western culture, and implies that different faiths can get along with one another. This does not bridge the gap of trust completely, nor does it remove all suspicions between the Christian Church and the Jewish Synagogue, but it does open doors to dialogue a bit wider.

What makes the Jewish-Christian debate even more conflicted is the role given Jesus within Jewish circles of academia. "The question as to Jesus' significance for the Jews themselves is of recent origin."[498] Jesus takes on a more important role in that he was responsible for bringing the Gentile nations to monotheism, and away from the polytheistic religions of the past. "Once Israelite monotheism became, via Christianity, open to the whole of mankind, a separate and distinct existence of the Jewish people lost its justification."[499] From this point

495 Jakob Jocz, *The Jewish People and Jesus Christ After Auschwitz: A Study in the Controversy Between Church and Synagogue* (Grand Rapids, MI: Baker Book House, 1981), 143.
496 Jocz, *The Jewish People and Jesus Christ After Auschwitz: A Study in the Controversy Between Church and Synagogue,* 142.
497 Joseph Klausner, *Jesus of Nazareth: His Life, Times and Teaching* (London: George Allen & Unwin LTD, Ruskin House 1925, Reprint 1997), 143.
498 Jocz, *The Jewish People and Jesus Christ: The Relationship between Church and Synagogue,* 142.
499 Avineri, *The Making of Modern Zionism,* 18.

of view, the New Testament is a legitimate expression of faith to the Gentiles.

For many within the Jewish community, Christianity has become a legitimate expression of faith from a pluralistic view. "What is unique in Judaism and the core of its witness to other faiths is this concept of religious universality which acknowledges the legitimacy of diverse paths to God, whose ideal is a fellowship of faiths in which they offer each other mutual aid in quest of God."[500] Even though Jocz suggests here a pluralistic approach to faith through Judaism, he begs the question that Christianity is simply another approach and that other faiths are equally valid. Neither Christianity nor Judaism recognizes that fellowship with God is found in any other faith system outside Judaism or Christianity. This may be true for Reformed Judaism as it is lived in the Diaspora and the West, but traditional Judaism saw no equal.

Messianic Judaism and the Rise of the Messianic Church

Though Zionism does not have a direct connection with the increases in Jewish conversions to Christianity, the Messianic movement has made rapid gains within the Christian community following the return of Jerusalem in 1967. It is now estimated, that at least 1% or more of the world Jewish population is Messianic, or Christian.[501] The Jewish Christian communities of Europe, and the United States traditionally were absorbed into the Gentile Churches of the Christian world. From 1967 onward, the Messianic community has grown, establishing Messianic Churches with the emphasis on Jewish traditions, and their connections to the ministry ,and work of Jesus Christ. " . . . And what

500   Jocz, *The Jewish People and Jesus Christ After Auschwitz: A Study in the Controversy Between Church and Synagogue*, 200.

501   There is little consensus on the number of Messianic or Christian Jews in the world. While some Jewish sources will keep the number rather low, Gary Thomas , Christianity Today: September 7,1998, 63. Thomas places the number at over a million or about 8% of the world Jewish population. The 1% figure is relatively conservative.

doth the LORD require of you But to do justice, and to love kindness, And to walk humbly with thy God?"[502]

Menuhin's expressions of inadequacy in being faithful to his faith is most likely consistent with most Jews, and Gentiles who seek to serve God. "If I was a heretic, at least I felt that I was erring in good company. As with ritual, so I felt with creed; the essence of religion, it seemed to me, was not in the words uttered with the lips, but rather in the faith which shows itself in our moral life."[503] Menuhin's reference to what constitutes religion is both an Old and New Testament reflection of faith and obedience. The Jewish connections to Christianity were too stark to remain idle. As Willhelson, Menuhin, and other Jewish scholars testify, "Christianity is Jewish."[504] It is in essence the Christian community following after a Jewish faith, not the other way around. For the Jewish community to remain passive toward the Messianic tradition in the New Testament was unlikely.

Moshe Rosen's "Jews for Jesus" is unique in respect to its philosophy of practicing Judaism as a Christian. To the Orthodox Jew, such a position disqualifies one from being Jewish. This position is based upon the assumption that being Christian is not Jewish and one is automatically disqualified from claiming Jewish heritage. This particular position followed the critique of the early church which was equally selective by demanding Jews to become Gentile. This awkward transition often resulted in dissatisfaction and made more difficult that transition to Christianity by Jews.

It is not only the Jews who have lost touch with their Messianic hope; the Church too lost its foundational roots found in Judaism. Messianic Christianity, has to a degree, brought those two aspects together into a unity of mind. In essence, they have been able to put the majority of parts together into a unity.

---

502   (Micah 6:8)
503   Menuhin, *Decadence of Judaism in Our Time*, 306.
504   Edith Schaeffer, *Christianity is Jewish* (Carol Stream IL: Tyndale Publishers, 1975), 11.

According to Kinzer, a Jewish convert, "Yeshua is the essential link between Judaism and Christianity rather than their fundamental distinguishing factor."[505] For most Jews, regardless of persuasion, "Yeshua becomes the dividing line. Jews often quip that the one thing all branches of Judaism agree upon is that Yeshua was not the Messiah."[506] Reformed Jews would reject Jesus as Messianic on a rational basis, while the Orthodox Jew rejects it based upon a strict adherence to the Law as being sufficient; redemptive grace is not sufficient. The prophetic connections to the Messianic claims are most often ignored.

Jewish-Christian Relations Today

Trust is still a barrier to building closer ties between the Jewish community, and the Church. The Church as a whole, has been less than civil to many within the Jewish community over the course of 2,000 years. Even though the one most responsible for the creation of the Church is a Jew, this makes little difference. The events of the Holocaust were not directly caused by the Church, but for many Jews the Church was instrumental in creating the environment that opened opportunity for the Nazis. In addition, the governments of the so-called Christian Nations of the West did little to assist the Jews of Europe before and during World War II. The perception for Jewish-Christian relations could not have been worse.

For the religious Jew, the person of Jesus Christ is still a divisive issue, separating Jews and Christians. As demonstrated by Montefiore and Klausner, it is only in recent times that "Jesus the Jew" is occupying Jewish scholars. "Increasingly he is admired for his moral courage and his lofty teaching. There is evident pride in the fact that millions worship as their Savior someone who happens to be a Jew. There is a repeated effort made to separate Jesus the Jew from the Christ of the Christian

505 Mark S. Kinzer, *Israel's Messiah and the People of God: A Vision for Messianic Jewish Covenant Fidelity* (Eugene OR: Cascade Books, 2011), preface x.

506 Kinzer, *Israel's Messiah and the People of God: A Vision for Messianic Jewish Covenant Fidelity*, preface x.

Church."[507] The message of Christianity was not new; it may have been a unique form of Judaism, but the essential message remaining was Jewish. "Jesus was not a Christian—he was a Jew. . . . He proclaimed no new faith, only taught the doing of God's will. The will of God for him as for the Jews was in the Law and in the holy Scriptures."[508]

How can the conflicts between Christians and Jews be so stark when the basic message is in all practicality the same? The Christian message has permeated the planet. The message of a Jewish redeemer has been accepted by people from every nation. "The Kingdom for which Christians and Jews pray is still invisible. Yet all these writers, following Rosenzweig's lead, acknowledge the significance of the Church as an act of God. She is the school of the nations and Israel's temptation."[509] Jocz emphasizes the universality of the Jewish-Christian message even at the risk of universalism. "What is unique in Judaism and the core of its witness to other faiths is this concept of religious universality which acknowledges the legitimacy of diverse paths to God, whose ideal is a fellowship of faiths in which they offer each other mutual aid in quest of God."[510] Even though Jocz suggests here a pluralistic approach to faith through Judaism, he begs the question that Christianity is simply another approach and that other faiths are equally valid. Neither Christianity nor Judaism recognizes that fellowship with God is found in any other faith system outside of biblical faith. This may be true for Reformed Judaism as articulated by Montefiore as it is lived in the Diaspora and the West, but Judaism traditions saw no equal. In this sense, Judaism is the prerogative of Jews but not essential to Gentiles.

For the Christian, there is no distinction between Christian and Jew in Christ. "There is neither Jew nor Greek; there is neither slave nor free man, there is neither male nor female; for you are all one in Christ

---

507 Hazony, *The Jewish State the Struggle for Israel's Soul*, 4.
508 Hazony, *The Jewish State the Struggle for Israel's Soul*, 197.
509 Jocz, *The Jewish People and Jesus Christ After Auschwitz: A Study in the Controversy Between Church and Synagogue*, 198.
510 Jocz, *The Jewish People and Jesus Christ After Auschwitz: A Study in the Controversy Between Church and Synagogue*, 200.

Jesus."[511] What makes the division even more profound is the contrast between inclusiveness which describes Christianity or the exclusiveness which characterizes Judaism. Judaism does not discriminate; it only requires conversion and adherence to the Law.

To some extent, Zionism has returned Jews to the ghetto within their own country. They are not isolationists as such, but they are alone in the Middle East, strangers among the Arab nations. "To what extent is Jewish Israeli society willing to discard the deeply embedded image of the 'chosen people,' and to cease isolating itself in the name of a fanciful history or dubious biology and excluding the 'other' from its midst?"[512] That is the question that rests at the center of the Jewish-Christian debate. Separation was the only course for the Jews to maintain their identity. Regardless of hundreds of years of assimilation, Jews have for the most part, succeeded in keeping their identity intact in spite of all efforts by the church and by secular institutions to assimilate the Jews. What makes this matter even more perplexing are the biblical predictions that indicate the continuation of the Jewish race in spite of the interbreeding over 2,000 years; in essence, this separation was biblically necessary. The Church more than any other group possesses the means for understand the necessity of Jewish survival as a biblical mandate. Even questions of ethnicity carry little weight in explaining the fierce independence of Jewish identity over thousands of years by those who identify themselves as Jews.

Christianity still carries with it a negative image with many Jews today in spite of academic progress. "No one can understand the tragic reactions of a people persecuted and martyred for nearly two thousand years in the name of Jesus, and unable therefore to place him in his proper niche in its own history during the long period of persecution."[513] It is the hope of many Jews to rise above political nationalism and religious sectarianism, to put away the bestiality of the past dark ages. Menuhin continues, "we Jews are bound to enroll Joshua of Nazareth in

---

511   (Galatians 3:28)
512   Vernon Williams Jr., *Rethinking Race* (Lexington, KY: University Press of Kentucky, 1996), 312-313.
513   Menuhin, *Decadence of Judaism in Our Time*, 269.

the Hall of Fame of our great prophets who contributed so much to the advancement of humanity."[514] Edith Schaeffer emphasizes, "Christianity is Jewish, the twisted, warped idea that Christians should be anti-Semitic was a horrible travesty on truth. Christianity is meant to be Jewish. That is what it is all about. Christians ought to love Jews."[515] Schaeffer's reference would suggest a strong emphasis on Jewish tradition within Christian worship. The emphasis on confession and repentance for salvation is still a Jewish concept.

Montefiore gives his view on the purpose of Israel in terms of a body of people and thus the Zionist movement in the early 1920's. "Israel is a religious community, and not a nation. No nationalistic predictions have any meaning or value for Liberal Judaism except when transmuted and transferred into terms of religion."[516] It is apparent that these words were written well before the State of Israel came into existence. It is interesting, however, to realize the Balfour agreement had been around for a short period of time. Whether this suggests a pessimistic attitude toward the possibility of the Jewish people gaining a homeland or a straightforward rejection of Zionism is not clear. It must also be remembered that Montefiore was not a witness to the Holocaust and the tragedies of World War II. We can only speculate and look closely at current liberal Judaism from the reformed and conservative view points to determine if those attitudes have remained the same to this day. But, in Montefiore's day, liberal Judaism was anti-Zionist, holding to a strictly religious definition of Israel. "Non-Jewish influences, even these very Jews, in the height of their protest, are greatly affected by the very influences which they deny. And this is true of the Orthodox Jews and of Liberal Jews."[517] The reference to non-Jewish influences can be directed toward Christians or secularists. There can be another influence that we can loosely define as a spiritual connection to the land of Palestine bringing Jews to Israel from every part of the world. This conjecture may not fit exactly with Montefiore's objective, but it does fit

---

514 Menuhin, *Decadence of Judaism in Our Time*, 269.
515 Schaeffer, *Christianity is Jewish*, 11.
516 Montefiore, *The Old Testament and After*, 567.
517 Montefiore, *The Old Testament and After*, 555.

with what many Jews feel when they arrive in Palestine. Daniel Gordis clarifies this attitude common among many Jews who enter Palestine. "This country's gotten under my skin in a way that I've never let happen before, but it doesn't feel new. Instead, it feels like an old relationship restored, and I find myself trying to understand why I feel such a deep attachment to this place."[518] The strong connection to the Land of Palestine gives some impetus to the notion of a spiritual relationship with many Jews to the Holy Land.

Mount Zion and the Land

The attraction for the land of Palestine is a mystery that defies explanation. Zionism is about the land and the connection to the Jewish people that spans history, a history that precedes the nation of Israel itself. It explains why the Uganda affair was so quickly rejected by the persecuted Jews of Eastern Europe. As mentioned before, the Jewish connection to the land of Palestine, is based by many from the Old Testament promises to the Jews, such as the one in Deuteronomy 1:8. It is a land that sees more conflict than any other place on the planet, yet brings out the best and worst among the Jews. It explains why the Jewish people were willing to pay any price, and fight to the death to gain and preserve the opportunity to reclaim the land. "Next year in Jerusalem" has now become a reality for Jews, not only within Palestine but among the Diaspora.

The story of Zionism is still in the process of finding a solution to the Jewish problem. This problem will not be resolved easily from a biblical context. The restoration of the Jewish state and the return of Jerusalem to Jewish control both met biblical expectations as defined by conservative Christians. However, many would still question the role of Justice within the Zionist dreams. Regardless how one wished to interpret the extent of those predictions, Zionism has succeeded in bringing some Christians and Jews together in support of the current state of Israel as a Jewish right.

518   Gordis, *Home to Stay: One American Family's Chronicle of Miracles and Struggles in Contemporary Israel*, 55.

CHAPTER FIVE

THE EFFECTS OF ZIONISM

Predictions Come True

Some schools of theology tend to downplay historic or prophetic connections to the Middle East situation, but the parallels to Biblical predictions are quite stark. How does one explain the destruction of the nation of Israel (70 CE/136 CE), and its reemergence after 2,000 years? "Here was an event that was linked visibly and, as it were, immediately, with something that had happened nineteen centuries earlier!"[519] With the restoration of the Israeli state, we are witnesses to the restoration of the Jewish culture within the nations, having the same traditions, language, and religion, though rabbinic Judaism has taken some modifications, and the absence of the Temple sacrifices. "Where else in the chronicles of the nations do we find past and present brought together with such startling closeness across a span of such magnitude?"[520] In addition, the restoration of the Jewish people within a sovereign state also brought the restoration of enemies that surround them on every side; the nation of Israel was restored along with its conflicts.

Israel and Modern Zionism

The twentieth century brought the first sovereign Jewish state since the Hasmonean Dynasty in the first century BCE. Prior to that period, the Jews wandered among the nations, "The Jew has no Fatherland though he belongs to many lands."[521] This draws a strong connection to Biblical

---

519 Liersi, *Fulfillment, The Epic Story of Zionism*, 7.
520 Liersi, *Fulfillment, The Epic Story of Zionism*, 7.
521 Menuhin, *The Decadence of Judaism in Our Time*, 57.

references in the Tanakh (Old Testament),[522] concerning the scattering of the Jews, a reference that is repeated numerous times throughout the Bible. Eckardt reinforces this idea that the Jews are a nation scattered among the nations. ". . . they are a nation scattered among the nations and thus commit the offense of being "different".[523] Through the Zionist dream, the Jews again have an identity tied to the land, even while most Jews still live among the nations. (Diaspora).

In the face of these facts (scattering and gathering), one is hard pressed to understand how Old Testament writers were able to predict the historical reality of the Jewish people being scattered and gathered unless those same experiences of hostility were encountered throughout Jewish history. Psalm 44 is one example of a Jew's lamentation of the harshness encountered yet endured with faithfulness and hope. Verse 11 amplifies that reality, "You give us as sheep to be eaten and have scattered us among the nations."[524] The reality of that verse comes to life for the Jews of Eastern Europe a century following the French Revolution; Jews were persecuted and pushed out of those countries, having been rejected by the cultures they had adopted for centuries. Scattering has always been present among the Jews through history.

The success of the Zionist movement in bringing about the return of a Jewish State in Palestine brought along with it changes within the Jewish community of Israel and among Diaspora Jews. "Zionism became a source of pride and identity among a persecuted and dispersed people."[525] Though most Jews today are very secular, Zionism has begun to change that attitude, and opened the doors to consider a spiritual reality. Avineri demonstrates how Zionism helped Jews change their perspective, away from a pacifistic, survivalist mentality, to a more assertive, and aggressive movement. "In the process of changing a passive, quietist and pious people that was the Zionist dream prior to

---

522   (Zechariah 7:14)

523   Eckardt, *Christianity and the Children of ISRAEL*, 6. Eckardt credits Reinhold Niebuhr with the phrase while referencing *The Jew in Our Day* by Waldo Frank, 4-5.

524   (Psalm 44:11)

525   Avineri, *The Making of Modern Zionism*, 13.

the twentieth century, into an effective social force, moving millions of people to Israel. It transformed a language relegated to mere religious usage into a modern, secular mode of intercourse of a nation-state."[526] It created in essence a position of equality within whatever culture the Jews lived, as a people again possessing their own nation, language, and identity. The Jews possessed not only a history, but a land and a place.

Jewish identity can now be placed in a nation and a land where before, the Jews had no identity other than their ancestral, ethnic, and religious background. They are a nation again, whether they live in Israel or in the dispersion among the Gentiles. They have a self-determination that gives them a degree of self-respect, opening doors to opportunities to return to their homeland if desired. ". . . the place [Israel] is made for us. It's the difference between being a guest and being home."[527] Though most Jews are successful and at home in many lands, Israel has become a source of security, knowing they have a homeland and an identity.

Zionism has become a two-edged sword, delivering hope to an oppressed people (Jews), while separating peoples (Gentiles: Christians and Arabs) that would harm, or hurt those downtrodden. Much of Jewish identity is wrapped within the Zionist dream and continues to hope for the day that dreams of a safe and secure homeland become a reality. Zionism is not just a reaction of a people to persecution. "It is the quest for self-determination, and liberation, under the modern conditions of secularization and liberalism. As such it is as much a part of the Jewish history of dispersion and return as the universal history of liberation and quest for self-identity."[528] What Avineri suggests is a twofold purpose in the Zionist movement: Zionism, in addition to meeting the need of providing a homeland for a displaced people, many Jews had nowhere to go and were without hope. The primary need was for self-determination, a place of their own where they could live without fear under their own laws. Secularism and liberalism gave them that hope for a period with its emphasis on toleration and equality for all. However,

---

526   Avineri, *The Making of Modern Zionism*, 13.
527   Gordis, *Home to Stay: One American Family's Chronicle of Miracles and Struggles in Contemporary Israel* , 85.
528   Avineri, *The Making of Modern Zionism*, 13.

Secular Israel

As a result of emancipation, the Jewish people have embraced a more secular and liberal philosophy of life. The emphasis on toleration and equality for all within French society, and extending to western secular cultures was a key factor drawing many Jews into the cultural centers of the Western nations, while most Eastern Jews escaping from the Pogroms of Eastern Europe were still wed to the conservative orthodox faith of Judaism. These values conflict in much the same way as liberal philosophies contrast with conservative and fundamentalist Christianity. For most Jews, liberal ideologies were the freeing formula, allowing Jews to participate equally within secular cultures. Gordis articulates this conflict between liberal and orthodoxy within Israel. "Their whole intellectual arsenal has been called to fight the rabbinate, to battle against the stranglehold that they believe Orthodoxy has on private life."[529] This conflict is ongoing within Israel today as these Jews are seeking to understand their unique culture in contrast to secular western ideals. The downside for many emancipated Jews was the surrendering of a liberal ideology for a more strict orthodoxy of their Jewish faith, a paradox between values still being worked out among Israeli Jews.

The expectations between orthodox Jews and emancipated Jews within Israel became a source of conflict between those conservative orthodox beliefs and the liberal secular philosophies of the West. As East met West within the borders of the new Israel, these two philosophies merge, as the majority of Jews embraced their Jewish religious roots, at least in part allowing Orthodox Judaism to take center

---

529 Gordis, *Home to Stay: Family's Chronicle One American of Miracles and Struggles in Contemporary Israel*, 147.

stage in the political arena, while still maintaining a secular society. "Even nonreligious Jews did not oppose the Orthodox drive. For one reason, it seemed peculiarly fitting that Israel, as Jewish state, should follow traditional practices."[530] The emphasis on Orthodoxy brought to Israel and Zionism a greater emphasis on the Jewish religious past. The celebrations of the Sabbath and adherence of Jewish festivals, and holidays brought secular Israel even closer to its religious roots, bringing along with it an increased awareness of Biblical Judaism. "The traditional Jewish holidays, which had originally been based on an agricultural calendar, now made sense once again; there was a definite beauty and satisfaction , for example, in celebrating Shavuot, the feast of the spring harvest, and to see schoolchildren bedecked in garlands of flowers."[531] From this perspective, Jews, even within the secular camp of Israel, have drawn closer in spiritual awareness to their God and to their Jewish faith. A spark of spiritual awareness for many Jews, may lead to a greater Jewish spiritual renewal. The hope of a spiritual awakening would parallel the desires previously stated by Ahad-Ha'am's spiritual Zionism of the early 20th century.

Zionism and the Arab-Jewish Problem

The conflict between secularism and orthodoxy became more heated with the question of how to handle the Arab Palestinians. According to the United Nations mandate, the Jews are to treat Arab Israeli citizens with equality, having the same rights and privileges as all Jews. "Arabs and Jews who, not holding Palestinian citizenship, reside in Palestine outside the City of Jerusalem shall, upon the recognition of independence, become citizens of the State in which they are resident and enjoy full civil and political rights."[532] While this is consistent with secular and liberal ideologies, it runs head-first into conflict with Jewish

---

530   Urofsky, *We are One: American Jewry and Israel*, 250.
531   Urofsky, *We are One: American Jewry and Israel*, 251.
532   United Nations Mandate 181. Chapter 3,1. *UN General Assembly* (Nov. 29, 1947). http://www.mideastweb.org/181.htm. (accessed Sept. 27, 2013).

orthodoxy, which holds Jewish nationalism as priority, and emphasizes exclusivity of Jews over Arabs of any stripe. This conflict creates a paradoxical dilemma for secular Jews, who have shown little will to resist Orthodox Rabbis', allowing restrictions upon others peoples and faiths. " . . . one can be disheartened by the law recently passed in a Knesset reading that permits certain villages to be open only to Jews, allowing people to refuse to sell to Arabs there."[533] These restrictions and others promoted by the Orthodox community continue to dampen the hope of the Zionist dream for peace, as Arab hostilities are fostered.

The responsibility to treat all men with the same dignity and respect, including both Jews and Arabs of all religions is one of the major factors drawing Jews to liberalism. "A secular society should have little trouble recognizing religious freedoms. This should include: Judaism of every stripe, including Messianic Judaism; Palestinian Christians in addition to Palestinian Muslims."[534] Equality is one of the byproducts of emancipation that drew many Jews to secularism and has served to protect Jews living in Western societies. However, the combination of liberalism and nationalism created within the new Jewish state a conflict. "Thus both liberalism and nationalism created in these Jews the beginning of a new self-awareness, no longer determined by any religious terms, but coequal to the emergence of modern, secular nationalism in Europe."[535] What Avineri fails to emphasize in this passage is that nationalism has a strong orthodox root that carries with it the emphasis on Jewish culture, other faiths are restricted, including Christianity.

Zionism has dampened Jewish-Christian relationships within Israel by limiting some freedoms to non-Jews. The Orthodox Jewish community is pressuring legislators to restrict religious freedoms of others: no proselytizing or evangelism within Israel. "A few religious legislators and politicians are trying to make the proclamation of the

---

533 Gordis, *Home to Stay: Family's Chronicle One American of Miracles and Struggles in Contemporary Israel*, 292.
534 Avineri, *The Making of Modern Zionism*, 13.
535 Avineri, *The Making of Modern Zionism*, 13.

gospel illegal in the land and remove Jewish Christians from Israel."[536] Strict laws have been enacted preventing any religious demonstrations other than Jewish festivals and holidays. "All the holidays in this country are either religious holidays from the Jewish calendar, or days associated with Jewish history (Yom Hashoah, etc.), or days linked to Israel's military victories."[537] Even citizenship is restricted to prevent Jewish Christians from becoming Israeli citizens. On December 25,1989 the Israeli Supreme Court disinherited any Christians. In the opinion written by Justice Menachem Elon, he stated that "Messianic Jews cannot make *Aliyah* under the Law of Return."[538] This restriction prevents Jews who became Christians from becoming Israeli citizens. This nationalistic Zionism puts restrictions on both Arabs and Christians.

The refugee problem is given little visibility in Israeli society today among the Jews. Most Jews feel no sense of responsibility for Palestinian refugees even though many were innocent of any wrong committed toward Israel, especially those children who live in those camps today. The conflict caused by Zionism to seek a safe haven on one hand while leaving many homeless on the other creates an inner conflict that exists within the hearts of many Jewish Israelis today. Daniel Gordis, having experienced the difficulty living in Israel today expressed his concern for justice. "Most people here simply don't have the stomach to fight for what's not just, without a sense that justice is on our side. Too many people here have no desire to do battle. A sense of justice for better or worse but probably for better, is too deeply ingrained in the Jewish consciousness to be able to avoid it."[539] While Gordis reflects the conscience of many Jews, others give little thought

---

536 Tilles, Murray. *List of Messiah Ministries News letter*, Volume 16, Issue 6, (June, 2008). www.lightofmessiah.org. (accessed Sept. 27,2013).

537 Gordis, *Home to Stay: Family's Chronicle One American of Miracles and Struggles in Contemporary Israel*, 69.

538 Thomas, Gary, "The Return of the Jewish Church". *Christianity Today*, (September 7, 1998). (accessed Sept. 24, 2013).

539 Gordis, *Home to Stay: Family's Chronicle One American of Miracles and Struggles in Contemporary Israel*, 148.

to the affairs of the Arab refugee and the Palestinian problem. "The Palestinian question (is) distant from the minds of many Israelis."[540] As Israel prospers, little thought is given to the refugee problem.

Spiritual Renewal

For the Christian, the return to Israel by the Jewish people represents God's continued faithfulness to His original promises. ". . . I shall gather you from among the peoples . . . ."[541] Even though we cannot demonstrate why such events took place, we are witnesses to the reconstruction of a nation which was in fact dead, which has come back to life. This can be illustrated in Ezekiel 37, the dry bones have come back to life in a way that brings realism to the prophetic words of the Jewish Bible.

Professor Charles Feinberg, a Jewish Christian scholar, places a strong emphasis on the necessity of the gathering and the establishment of the nation of Israel before a spiritual renewal takes place. As Ahad-Ha'am placed emphasis on the spiritual renewal prior to the establishment of a nation, Feinberg places the emphasis on the reconstruction of a nation prior to its spiritual renewal. "The prophets are one in declaring that the restoration of the people of Israel to their own land will be followed by their conversion to the Lord."[542] This would suggest that Israel's secular culture is moving toward a future spiritual revival. With the rise of a strong Orthodox Judaism, secular Jews may have begun to slowly embrace their historical and cultural faith, at least on the surface as part of their Jewish heritage. Feinberg places the emphasis on this spiritual process after the nation of Israel is brought into existence.

---

540   Vick, Karl. "The Good Life and Its Dangers," *Time Magazine*, (September 13, 2010): 39. (accessed August 10, 2013).

541   (Ezekiel 11:17) Numerous Old Testament passages reference this event.

542   Charles L. Feinberg, *The Minor Prophets* (Chicago, IL: Moody Press, 1951), 324.

Mainline Protestant Christianity and Israel

In this book, the drama between Christian and Jew in the context of the Zionist movement has been played out primarily within the parameters of the Orthodox Protestant Church. Where the Church is used as a universal term, it is understood that there are fundamental differences in interpretations between liberal and evangelical Christianity, regarding Biblical, and current events. This does not exclude all the many mainline Protestant churches that encompass a more liberal, as opposed to a fundamentalist view on the Zionist movement, and the Jews. Remarks made concerning the liberal churches in Chapter Three, are intended to give a general description of the German Church at that time of Nazi control, and may not necessarily reflect on all mainline Protestant churches today. The following portions seek only to recognize some of the differences within liberal theology concerning the Zionist movement, and how that affects Jewish-Christian relations today from that context.

One common point between the liberal and conservative factions of the Church is the recognition of a debt owed the Jews as a result of the Holocaust. For liberal (mainline) Protestants as well as fundamentalists, they believe they have an " . . . ethical debt owed the Jews stemming from Christian indifference during the Holocaust."[543] It is this sense of responsibility that is a factor in the creation of a Jewish state. As previously documented, the creation of Israel would not have happened within the time frame of the early twentieth century, had the Holocaust not occurred.

There is a lessening of support for the Zionist cause as a result of strained relationships with Arab Christians. "The reasons for the lessening of liberal Protestant support are three-fold. First, liberal Protestants are aware of the fact that Christians in the Arab world are offended by pro-Zionist sympathies."[544] The image of Zionism carries with it the horrors of war and the loss of their homeland to make way for Jewish immigrations. Liberal Christianity is less likely

---

543 Epstein, *Zion's Call*, 4-5.
544 Epstein, *Zion's Call*, 4-5.

to give support to the Zionist cause. Second, liberal Protestants have come to view the Palestinian Arabs as having as equal a claim on their humanitarian impulses, as do the Jews of Israel. This conflicts with many evangelical Christians, who maintain a strong support for the Jewish State in Israel. Third, are the contrasting positions between liberal and evangelical theology. "Liberal Protestant theologians, at odds with the fundamentalism espoused by some Evangelicals, . . . are reluctant to support a movement - Zionism - which even has the appearance of confirming a fundamentalist interpretation of Protestantism."[545] This includes the historical and eschatological stance of the Evangelical Church. Most liberal denominations have, to differing degrees, rejected predictive references of the Bible and prefer a less literal message, one of social justice and equality toward both Jews and Arabs.

In summary, the Liberal Church would be somewhat less friendly toward Israel than the Fundamentalist wing. More emphasis would be placed on fairness to the Arabs, along with a strong sense of ethnic and religious tolerance. However, from this view, the liberal church would have stronger relationship with secular Jews. They would contend with fundamentalists on the issues of soteriology in contrast with a more universalistic message of redemption. From this, many liberals would emphasize that the Jews do not need Jesus Christ, and it would be preferable to leave them alone (Universalism). For most within liberal Christianity, Jewish-Christian relationships have become more strained through the continuing Jewish-Arab conflict.

Catholic Christianity and Israel

Catholic tradition has been a barrier to Jewish-Christian relationships since before the Middle Ages. "The Vatican has never established ties with the State of Israel."[546] However, with the success of the Zionist movement and the rejuvenation of the state of Israel, those attitudes are beginning to thaw. "The Israeli government and the Anti-Defamation League and the European Jewish Congress have welcomed

545   Epstein, *Zion's Call*, 5.
546   Epstein, *Zion's Call*, 5.

these overtures [Catholic-Jewish dialogues] and urged [Pope] Benedict to continue his predecessor's [Pope John Paul] work."[547] In spite of these overtures, little movement on the part of the Vatican is expected from the Jewish community. Arthur Hertzberg's assessment is pessimistic, "I am far from certain that a new age in the Jewish-Catholic relationship has dawned."[548] Beyond an improving dialogue, there is little significant recognition of Israel among Catholic leadership.

The Catholic Church has taken a much different approach than the Evangelical Church, in that it gives cautious acknowledgement to Israel while claiming sole possession of religious truth. "The Catholic Church declares that it is in exclusive possession of religious truth. The only real means by which Catholics can give up religious anti-Semitism is that of surrendering their theological claims."[549] One reason given for not recognizing the Israeli state is the absence of recognized borders. The borders have not remained the same and the state of Israel and Arabs are still in a state of conflict. The failure of the Catholic Church to resist recognition also carries another deep theological question: that of official recognition of Judaism as a true faith and means to God. Such recognition would jeopardize the standing of the Catholic Church in light of its treatment of Jews down through the centuries and creates a difficult problem to justify. The barrier between Israel and the Catholic Church will likely remain for a time.

Evangelical Christianity and Israel

Evangelical Christians tend to be pro Zionist holding to a strong biblical necessity for the restoration of the nation of Israel. While

---

547 Hertzberg, Arthur. "The Vatican's Sin of Omission." *The New York Times* (May 14, 2005). www.nytimes.com/2005/05/14/opinion/14hertzberg.html. (accessed Sept. 28, 2013).
548 Hertzberg, Arthur. "The Vatican's Sin of Omission." *The New York Times* (May 14, 2005). www.nytimes.com/2005/05/14/opinion/14hertzberg.html. (accessed Sept. 28, 2013).
549 Eckardt, *Christianity and the Children of ISRAEL*, 141.

many Evangelical Christians have a strong connection to Israel and its security, others take a more sympathetic view of the Palestinian refugee situation. Institutions such as The Moral Majority initiated by Pastor Jerry Farwell have been strong supporters of Israel for many years. Other organizations such as The International Fellowship of Christians and Jews symbolized a comradery focused on biblical history and the legitimacy of prophecy held by most Orthodox Jews and Fundamentalist Christians.[550]

A criticism leveled at the United States in general and the Christian community specifically is for its strong support of Israel. Israeli Jewish leadership depends upon Christian support in Washington to keep strong ties with the United States. Victoria Clark plays on those sympathies in her caricature of fundamentalist Christians. "Likud (Israeli political party) was confident that the vast majority of Christian fundamentalists would not flinch at Israel's poor human rights record."[551] The poor human rights record is a description of the Jewish handling of the Palestinian problem.

While Israel is strongly supported by the Evangelical community, other Evangelical institutions recognize along with mainline protestant Christians the necessity of reaching out to the Palestinian community. Relief organizations such as World Vision do extensive work among Palestinian and Refugee peoples. Evangelical Venture International and Evangelicals for Middle East Understanding are heavily connected to the needs of the Palestinian community.[552] These organizations reflect a Christian obligation to reach out to all people and most particularly those in need, as are many Palestinians.

---

550   International Fellowship of Christians and Jews: www.ifcj.org/site/PageNavigator/eng/USENG_homenew (accessed Oct. 5, 2013).

551   Clark, *Allies for Armageddon,* 190.

552   Evangelical Venture International: http://ventureint.org/irr.html; Evangelicals for Middle East Understanding: http://www.emeu.net/ (accessed Oct. 5, 2013).

For the most part, Evangelical Christians are supportive of Israel at the expense of the Palestinian problem. In contrast, Jewish scholar Claude Montefiore suggests that not all Israel will escape God's wrath: ". . . as Isaiah of old had spoken of a remnant who should escape the judgment, or who should be morally purged by it, so now a distinction was made between the good and the bad: the former should enjoy God's favor; the latter should feel His wrath."[553] The questions faced by Jews and Christians alike is how to treat Palestinian Arabs, Christian and non-Christian. These differing eschatological questions provide some tension between Jewish and Christian theologians as to the future of Israel.

Orthodox versus Secular

The political and social difference between liberal and conservative ideologies has created barriers between Christian fundamentalists and Jews today as mentioned previously. The differences as defined by liberal and conservative terms can also be described as secular versus orthodoxy among Jews. According to Avineri, "Zionism was the most fundamental revolution in Jewish life. It substituted a secular self-identity of the Jews as a nation for the traditional and Orthodox self-identity in religious terms . . . ."[554] Zionism has awakened within many Jews the spark of spirituality that had lain dormant for centuries. In spite of this spiritual renewal, liberalism still thrives. The paradox of secular balancing with orthodoxy would explain in part the realities of modern Zionism in Israel today. This merging of secular and orthodoxy has managed to maintain a degree of harmony among Jews while providing a barrier to Christian influence.

The Zionist movement, at least from the Jewish perspective, comes well after the Enlightenment, Mendelssohn, and the effects of the French Revolution; all carried the Jews well into secularism through emancipation and assimilation. Secularism is more of an offshoot of Emancipation than Zionism. Secularism was carried along within the Zionist movement as a byproduct of assimilation. As previously

[553] Montefiore, *The Old Testament and After*, 62.
[554] Avineri, *The Making of Modern Zionism*, 13.

documented by Avineri, Zionism is, "... the quest for self-determination, and liberation, under the modern conditions of secularization and liberalism."[555] In addition to secularism, Zionism brought Orthodoxy back front and center within Israel as a major religious movement of the country. They, "... substituted the Torah for the Talmud, infused religious holidays with socialist meaning and created a 'holy community' with hidden layers of religious meaning and charisma, Socialist Zionism, with its stress on the Bible, Israel, the Homeland, the Return to Zion from Exile, the Jewish National Fund and the Hebrew language, had sanctified and binding roots in Jewish religion."[556] These strange bedfellows have merged creating a competing ideological mix within modern day Israel. Reformed Judaism still reigned in the Diaspora and among assimilated Jews, yet with a diminished emphasis on the spiritual and historical.

Messianic Judaism

Messianic Judaism is the middle ground between being Jewish, and being Christian, although those in the Messianic community prefer not to be called Christian, due to the negative reflections it carries in the Jewish community. They are often denied their Jewishness by their Jewish cohorts, who would after conversion, refuse to consider them Jews at all. "Rabbinic and secular Jewish authorities who make one exception to this view, that is in the case of a Jew who not only abandons Judaism but actually accepts another religion upon himself. In such a situation, these authorities maintain, the individual forfeits his Jewish identity and membership in the community in favor of his having joined another faith and community."[557] From this, one would be hard pressed

---

555 Avineri, *The Making of Modern Zionism*, 13.
556 Jonathan Adelman, *The Rise of Israel: A History of Revolutionary State* (New York: Routledge, Taylor & Francis Group, 2008), 121.
557 Eckstein, Rabbi Yechiel. "Jewish Christian Relations: How do Jews Define Themselves?/ Part I. I International Fellowship of Christians and Jews. (2013). http://www.jewishvirtuallibrary.org/jsource/anti-semitism/christjew.html. (accessed Sept. 28, 2013).

to equate ethnicity with being Jewish. Perhaps Hart, and Sand were correct; there are no ethnic Jews, while atheistic Jews who deny any knowledge of God, still remain a solid part of the Jewish community. In spite of this inconsistency, most Jews remain loyal to their families.

For the Christian, the test is to be faithful to the great commission: to go into the world and preach the gospel. This commandment is also prioritized to the Jew first. The Christian message would not have come except by the Jews; the entire early Church was composed of practicing Jews. Judaism and Christianity were in harmony, but the Jews are correct in that the Gentiles, have to some degree distorted the message. They demanded that the Jews become Gentiles. While the early Jewish Church had some division between the Judaiziers who demanded that Gentile converts to Christ needed to become Jews; the Jerusalem council (Acts 15:19-20) concluded that Gentiles need not become Jews, but rather keep the basic spirit of God's message. "The professions of faith required by Jewish converts to Christianity in the ancient, and medieval periods indicate the total separation from Judaism required by the church."[558] The following quote from Assermani from the Church in Constantinople demonstrates:

"I do here now renounce every rite and observance of the Jewish religion, detesting all its most solemn ceremonies and tenets that in former days I kept and held." "I altogether deny and reject the error of the Jewish religion." "[I] shun all intercourse with other Jews and have the circle of my friends only among honest Christians." "We will not on any pretext, either ourselves, our children or our descendants, choose wives from our own race; but in the case of both sexes we will always link ourselves in matrimony with Christians."[559]

The early first century church which was universally Jewish had much the same issue with Gentiles seeking to enter fellowship with

---

558 Rausch, *Legacy of Hatred*, 25.
559 Rausch, *Legacy of Hatred*, 25. Source: Church of Constantinople From Assermani, Cod. Lit., 1, p.105. Other resources include: http://www.touchstonemag.com/archives/article.php?id=14-09-049-r (accessed Jan. 26, 2014).

Jewish believers in Jesus; they were upset upon hearing that Gentiles accepted the Christian message. " 'Now when the apostles and brethren that were in Judea heard that Gentiles had believed the word of God, they really were upset'. . . . God had opened the door to other nations, to people of the Gentiles, to come to Him through the Messiah, promised so long ago to the people of Israel."[560] According to the message of the New Testament and the early Jewish believers, becoming Jewish was no longer the only way to God. The second covenant through Jesus provided both Jew and Gentile a direct path to God.

In Messianic Judaism, we are witnesses to the return of the early Church. Those Jews who accept the message of redemption through a Jewish Rabbi, are now free to practice their faith within the context of their Jewish culture. According to Joel Chernoff, "Messianic Judaism is now the fastest growing stream of faith within the Jewish community, by far."[561] The merger of Jewish faith and Jewish culture along with a Redemptive Redeemer is now complete for the Messianic Jew. This movement comes in the aftermath of the success of the Zionist movement, and serves as a possible indicator of the spiritual revival taking place in Israel. The rejection of Messianic Judaism by mainline Judaism, along with the secular Jewish community, has not slowed down the movement.

Even though some indicators give positive movement to this Jewish form of Christian faith, the main body of Judaism, particularly within the Orthodox community, would have nothing to do with such a movement; the Unitarian God of the Torah as perceived by Jews could not allow it. In addition, the secular Jews are reminded of the catastrophe of the Cabalist movements in the seventeenth century that drove many Jews away from their Jewish faith. The barriers to any such rise are still most formidable and leave many Messianic Jews alone and separated from their family and friends. "The personal costs that Messianic Jews

---

560   Schaeffer, *Christianity is Jewish*, 177,178.
561   Gary Thomas, "The Return of the Jewish Church," *Christianity Today*, (September 7, 1998): 66. Statistics by Joel Chernoff, president of the International Messianic Jewish Alliance at the time. (accessed August 10, 2013).

pay for their faith in Yeshua are often severe, from being shunned by their families to being excluded from the local Jewish Community center."[562] Messianic Jews often form their own communities to maintain fellowship and support.

The difference between Messianic and Rabbinic Jews can also be illustrated in the ways that the Old and New Testaments differ in their doctrines. Why is it significant that the Passover was the eating of the Passover lamb? Because according to the New Testament of the Bible, Jesus is the Passover Lamb of God. Communion is a revision of the Passover meal; this represents God's passing over our sins. According to the New Testament, God not only passes over our sins, he removes them completely from us. Edith Schaeffer clarifies the significance of the Passover in regards to its Christian application. "Here is the beautiful ending of the Old Covenant and the clear difference of the New! Why was Christ crucified at Passover, because He is the completed Passover lamb, the symbolism is complete."[563] We are to metaphorically eat Jesus' body just as the Jews were to eat the Passover lamb.

Who would have understood the parallelism and symbolism between the Passover and communion better than the Jews? However for most Jews, this symbolism was offensive because implications were not clear. "Therefore many of His disciples, when they heard this said, 'This is a difficult statement; who can listen to it?'"[564] Many of his Jewish followers left him at this point, however, everything Jesus did was Jewish in its message. The Gentile would not have appreciated or understood much of the symbolism that Passover represented, without the world wide evangelism of the Apostle Paul and the other apostles.

---

562 Gary Thomas, "The Return of the Jewish Church," *Christianity Today*, (September 7, 1998): 65. (accessed August 10, 2013).
563 Schaeffer, *Christianity is Jewish*, 177.
564 (John 6:60)

A Revised Biblical Perspective

One of the positive factors of Jewish emancipation was a more objective view of New Testament Christianity from a Jewish academic perspective. What makes this significant is that a less hostile view of the New Testament Jesus, explained in part, why many Jews in the Diaspora were not interested in the Zionist movement. "The closer contact between Judaism and Christianity necessitated by modern life made it impossible to ignore the Man under whose influence history took shape and whose moral power has endured for centuries."[565] In an age of tolerance, and pluralism, it would be inconsistent to consider someone's faith as misplaced. In addition, the fact that Jesus was a Jew and Christianity has its roots in Judaism can hardly be denied. "The fact that this Man was also a Jew is the most outstanding element in the Jewish discussion."[566] As a result, some tensions between Jews and Christians are relieved. While not significant, it does open opportunities for dialogue. Jews and Christians within the Diaspora were at least talking and working with one another.

Whether one considers Jesus a legend, as do many, others would hold him as a liar or lunatic, fitting closer to earlier Jewish versions of Jesus. How was this Jewish carpenter able to inspire a message that was spread throughout the world and made the impact it has made on western civilization? "Once Israelite monotheism came, via Christianity, open to the whole of mankind, a separate and distinct existence of the Jewish people lost its justification."[567] The idea of Jewish exclusiveness was challenged via Christianity. The Jews were not exclusive in their worship of God and others claimed a share in the Abrahamic Covenant. In this sense, the Jews had competition.

This competition was from a prominent Jew, perhaps the most prominent Jew or individual in the history of mankind. The benefits of

---

565   Jocz, *The Jewish People and Jesus Christ; The Relationship between Church and Synagogue*, 142.
566   Jocz, *The Jewish People and Jesus Christ; The Relationship between Church and Synagogue*, 142.
567   Avineri, *The Making of Modern Israel*, 18.

Christianity to the world cannot be denied. The idea that Jesus may have had some messianic purposes became a realistic idea. "Later, when the spiritual benefits of Christianity became evident, he was given a place in the plan of Divine Providence as a preparer of the way for the King 'Messiah' amongst the Gentiles."[568] Enelow, a Jewish scholar clarifies this point, "No sensible Jew can be indifferent to the fact that a Jew should have had such a tremendous part in the religious education and direction of the human race."[569] For many Jews, the idea of Jesus as the Messiah was too difficult to square with Judaism, but not too difficult to justify through rationalism. Jesus the Jew had a very important function in the history of mankind. "The question as to Jesus' significance for the Jews themselves is of recent origin."[570] This is a change in perspective for many Jews, to consider Jesus in a positive, and not just a neutral light. From this point of view, the New Testament was a new look at the Old Testament Tanakh.

What scholars such as Klausner and Montefiore did, was to remove the myth of Jesus as a deceiver of Jewish people who used sorcery to fool many Jews into believing in a false hope. "The reason for his execution was because he was convicted of sorcery and of enticing Israel into idolatry."[571] Similarities exist between Jesus Christ and other Messianic leaders such as Kabocha and Zevi, who gave many Jews a false hope, resulting in disappointments and deaths. It was these events in part, that had a profound impact on secular Judaism and led to a non-messianic Zionism. Zionism was being led by those more interested in a secular society, one founded on practical need, and where Jews would be in

---

568   Jocz, *The Jewish People and Jesus Christ; The Relationship between Church and Synagogue*, 142.
569   Gerson Enelow, *A Jewish View of Jesus,* (New York: Macmillan, Biblio Life, 1901, Reprint 1912), 9.
570   Jocz, *The Jewish People and Jesus Christ; The Relationship between Church and Synagogue*, 142.
571   Peter Schäfer, *Jesus in the Talmud* (Princeton, NJ: Princeton University Press, 2007), 12. Schafer references from the Babylonian Talmud concerning what most scholars consider Jesus.

control of their own affairs. Herzl, Pinsker, and Hass were all secular Jews who gave little thought to Judaism, at least in the beginning.

From a contemporary Jewish perspective, Jesus is viewed today, not as the Christ, but rather Jesus the Nazarene, the Jewish Rabbi of the first century. Those Jews dismissed as irrelevant the gospel stories written by the early church which cannot be squared with the Unitarian God of the Torah. It is, however, a more realistic view than those written of Jesus prior to the Middle Ages, giving some credence to the historical material as having some validity. The Jews no longer living in the ghetto and living in close proximity to the Christian community needed a more objective view in order to find a more conciliatory working relationship with Gentiles and those in the Church.

For many Jews just as for many Christians, scripture was no longer foundational in its interpretation. Personal interpretations were open to each individual. Montefiore demonstrates, "Only Liberal Judaism can stand above the facts, and examine its own house reverently, tenderly, lovingly, but freely."[572] Montefiore illustrates the higher value Rabbinic Judaism places upon interpretation with a strong emphasis on oral tradition. A Scripture that requires a liberal understanding leaves all other views, orthodox as well as Christian, wanting for misunderstanding. Holding to a strong individual interpretation explains why many can study Christian principles while avoiding any implications from its message.

The question of oral tradition becomes central to the division of Jewish-Christian relationships. "One needs to keep in mind the centrality, in Judaism, of the authority of those who convey the tradition (oral)."[573] Jesus had his greatest conflicts with the Jews of his day on the subject of oral tradition, Klinghoffer clarifies. "As we found in the Gospels, Jesus was dismissive of Torah's oral transmission, which he regarded as a human invention."[574] For many Jews, Scripture is inspired

---

572 Schäfer, *Jesus in the Talmud*, 556.
573 David Klinghoffer, *Why the Jews Rejected Jesus* (New York: Doubleday Random House, 2006), 145.
574 Klinghoffer, *Why the Jews Rejected Jesus*, 145.

but must be interpreted within oral tradition, within Rabbinic Judaism, only Rabbis can adequately interpret scripture, thus oral tradition carries as much or more weight than the written word. "The Torah without its oral tradition is like a divorce: one Torah without the other is like a wife sundered from her husband. When the couple has separated, there is no longer a marriage"[575] Oral tradition is a huge dividing point between Judaism and Christianity.

Concerning Christian's messianic claims, Joseph Klausner in *Jesus of Nazareth* separates the person of Jesus from the Christian Christ, Jesus cannot be the Messiah to the Jews. "To the Jewish nation he can be neither God nor the Son of God, in the sense conveyed by belief in the Trinity .... Neither can they regard him as a Prophet; ... neither can they regard him as a law-giver or the founder of a new religion. He did not even desire to be such. Neither is he a 'tanna' or Pharisaic Rabbi."[576] For many academic Jews along with mainline Judaism, the barriers to a Messianic Jesus are still too high to consider.

For the Jew who accepted Jesus as a moral teacher, there was little room for the Son of God. Therefore, the higher claims attributed to Jesus are considered as inventions by the early Church, and are not worthy to be considered having academic substance. "With few exceptions, there is a growing desire to appreciate the person of Jesus and to acknowledge his significance for mankind." [577] In this case Jesus is no more than a man with a mission, not the son of God.

The divisions between religious Jews and Christians are still formidable, the issues of mistrust between Jews and Gentiles were becoming less relevant to the realities of life and the future for many Diaspora Jews. Assimilation into the culture eased the Jews into a cordial working relationship with Gentiles and Christians, opening

---

575 Klinghoffer, *Why the Jews Rejected Jesus*, 145.
576 Jocz, *The Jewish People and Jesus Christ; The Relationship between Church and Synagogue,* 143 Taken from Joseph Klausner, *Jesus of Nazareth*, 443.
577 Jocz, *The Jewish People and Jesus Christ; The Relationship between Church and Synagogue*, 143.

doors to understanding that previously were not allowed to be opened. An increased appreciation for Jesus as a moral influence removes some barriers to the Jewish-Christian conflict.

One similarity between Old Testament Judaism and Christianity is the central idea of repentance for the forgiveness of sins. The idea comes directly from Old Testament doctrine, according to Montefiore. "The teachers of the Old Testament constantly call the sinner to repentance, and if he repents, if he turns from his evil way, they assure him of the divine forgiveness."[578] According to Montefiore, the Prophets are not in conflict with the New Testament message. Isaiah 30:15 states ". . . In repentance and rest you shall be saved, . . ."[579] The basic tenants of both faiths in regards to repentance is essentially the same.

Jewish Ethnicity

How the Jews have maintained their uniqueness through the millennia is a mystery yet denied by many. The following statement by Alan Hart is indicative of the attitude held by many within secular society. "Most if not all the returning Jews were foreign nationals of many lands who became Jewish by conversion to Judaism . . . ."[580] This denial of Jewish ancestry is used to counter Jewish claims or rights over Palestine, and as a valid reason why many deny Jewish claims to the land (Palestine). Although, ethnicity is still not a proven fact, arguments of a pure ethnic Jew not existing have only limited foundation. There still exists a Jewish ancestry, as many can trace their linage back to one of the tribes of Israel. It is true that many have converted to Judaism through history, yet Jewish blood lines still exist.

As Zionist Jews were advocating their claim on the land (Palestine), they were making an ethnic statement concerning their

---

578 Montefiore, *The Old Testament and After* 252.
579 (Isaiah 30:15) Other Old Testament sources include: (I Kings 8:47) and (Jeremiah 15:7)
580 Hart, *Zionism: The Real Enemy of the Jews, David Become Goliath, Vol. II,* 28.

ancient inheritance. Critics such as Shlomo Sand and Alan Hart contend that Jewish blood is an illusion, that assimilation was completed, and that there are no real pure blooded Jews. This statement might have merit based upon the evidence presented by Sand (references to conversions to Judaism).[581] It could also be stated that Kind David of old would have failed to possess pure Jewish blood in that mothers in his ancestral line were Gentiles including Rahab, who was a Canaanite[582], and Ruth, who was a Moabite.[583] The nation of Israel did not consist of Jews only. The Biblical reference to Israel always included the alien who had adopted the Jewish faith. They became Jewish, just as much as the so-called pure Jew (Hebrew) at the time.

The ethnicity question is relevant to the Old Testament as the survival of the Jews was necessary for the completion of God's purposes in restoring the land. The prophet Jeremiah refers to the offspring of Israel in the same light as the fixed order of stars (ever present) "If this fixed order departs from before Me, declares the LORD, then the offspring of Israel also shall cease from being a nation before Me forever."[584] Jews still exist today; in spite of 2,000-plus years of Diaspora and assimilation. The ghetto played a large part in that survival, separating Jewish communities from Gentiles and Christians. The Jewish faith, along with Kosher laws giving a strong context for separation. Even though ethnicity is blurred and pure Jewish blood is uncertain, Jewish ancestry is still dominant within the Jewish community and among many within the Gentile community as well through assimilation.

The Gentiles in blood were a major part of David's kingdom. The issue for them was faith in God and faithfulness to the covenant (Old Testament Judaism). The New Testament brings out the same question. There is no distinction between Jew and Greek in the New Testament;

---

581   Sand, *The Invention of the Jewish People*, 269; Ernest Renan, *Contemporary Jewish Records,* 6:4 (1943), 444.
582   Rahab was from Jericho of Canaan, (Joshua 2)
583   Ruth was a Moabite woman, (Ruth 1:4); Both Rahab and Ruth were in David's family tree, (Matt.1:5)
584   (Jeremiah 31:36)

"... neither Jew nor Greek ...."[585] comprises the kingdom of God. Christianity consists of all who seek God. Culture in this case is not relevant, only faith. Both Judaism and Christianity are mixtures of Jews and Gentiles who are seeking God. As demonstrated by Claude Montefiore and Klausner, the theological differences between Judaism and Christianity are not great. The most prominent dividing line rests squarely upon the identity of the Jewish Rabbi Jesus.

The question concerning how Zionism has affected Jewish-Christian relationships touches only slightly on the question of ethnicity since the Israeli authorities require that a person possess only 50% Jewish blood. The question of ethnicity takes an even deeper step backwards when we consider the relationship traditional Jews have with Messianic Jews. In the case of Jews who become Christian, the Jewish community no longer regards them as Jews. "Worship of Jesus as the Son of God is considered belief in a foreign god, and the convert would not be considered Jewish."[586] In this case, the question of ethnicity becomes dead; it is no longer an issue with regard to blood, ancestry, or dependency. The irony is broadened even more when one considers that many Israeli Jews today are secularists or atheists. Ethnicity in these cases takes precedence over culture or religious faith. A religious Jew can be either a Jew or Gentile who has converted. "It is a fact that the majority of the Jewish people, both in the Diaspora and in Israel, defines itself in terms that are basically secular—ethnic, national, cultural, and the life style of most Jews in the world today is utterly secularized."[587] The question of who is a Jew is still very much in debate.

Menuhin, a Jewish scholar, places an even heavier weight on the problem of ethnicity. "History, and Jewish history especially, shows that the claim to purity of race on the part of any civilized people is entirely mythical. It is generally put forth by sacerdotal and other

585   (Galatians 3:28a)
586   Persin, Stephanie. "Jews for Jesus: Arguments Against Jews for Jesus." *Washington Post* (August 17, 2004). http://www.jewishvirtuallibrary.org/jsource/anti-semitism/Jews_for_Jesus.html. (accessed Sept. 28, 2013). Reference to (I Kings 18:21)
587   Avineri, *The Making of Modern Israel*, 220.

exploiting groups, and when extensively followed, leads to narrowness and sometimes to degeneracy."[588] Menuhin is perhaps a bit harsh on his own ancestry, but his emphasis on the necessity of diversity of race places a higher value on tolerance and diversity within culture. "No great civilization was ever achieved except by a mixed people freely borrowing from others in religion, language, laws and manners. The Jews were such people when they produced the bulk of Biblical literature, and they certainly increased their contribution to civilization when they left Palestine and mixed with other peoples."[589] Ethnic ties are strong within the Jewish community; scholars cannot remove those completely. While ethnicity has relevance, no one is pure in this regard. The bigger question of ethnicity is more often dependent upon who is defining the terms and why. With regard to religious faith, Judaism and Christianity both consist of ethnic Jews and Gentiles together.

Preservation of the Jews

In spite of blending of Jews within the Gentile population and conversions to Christianity over the history of Jewish-Christian relations, a strong ethnic Jewish community still exists. The Jews have been preserved through the centuries; no other people or nation have had such a history. They have not been completely absorbed into the nations where they have been scattered as contrary to Shlomo Sands claim. They still remain as a distinct "people." According to the Old Testament, they were chosen through Abraham. A promise was given that the Jews will be finally brought together in future times. "The Jew, as Jews, will continue to be a people. It is one of the supernatural proofs of the truth of the Word of God."[590]

The preservation of the Jews also carries with it the preservation of two Covenants. God will abundantly pardon whoever will come to the Lord, as talked about in Isaiah 55:6-7. From this verse we can surmise, the Old Covenant is still in effect. The Jews have always possessed

588 Menuhin, *Decadence of Judaism in Our Time*, 308.
589 Menuhin, *Decadence of Judaism in Our Time*, 309.
590 Schaeffer, *Christianity is Jewish*, 108.

the means to salvation. Does this suggest that Christians should not evangelize Jews? No! Jews and Gentile both are in need of God's grace, whether through the first Covenant or the second. From the context of Covenant Theology, God's redemptive grace is the same for all (For the Christian, the New Testament adds clarity to the redemptive process).

A Revised Biblical Perspective: Old Testament Tanakh Perspective

It is important to reexamine the Biblical context on modern Zionism with the objective to find a parallel to the establishment of Israel and its subsequent treatment of the Arab population. This does not reflect directly upon Jewish-Christian relationships, but it does bring the Zionist Christian community into collaborative agreement with the events of Jewish Independence and the subsequent building up of Israel, including its relationships with the Palestinian Arabs and its Arab neighbors.

Israel was established upon a strong military presence, resulting in war. It was realized from the beginning that the Jews and Arabs would not get along; the UN mandate was given against all rationale that the two cultures and peoples would merge.[591] This did not happen except by force and war; the resulting consequence was the displacement of over 700,000 Arab refugees, many still living in refugee camps today. Though these people fled for the most part of their own free will, they were running from a war that was being fought in their communities. The end result of this was the denial of those Arabs who fled, having the right to return.

The majority of land given to the Jews for a Jewish State in the UN mandate was still owned by Arabs. The question raised by Gary Burge in Chapter Four was based upon the Biblical requirement that

---

591   This reference is to the Peel Commission which recommended in 1937 to abandon the British mandate for two separated Partitions separating Jews from Arabs.

the inhabiting of the land requires a standard of righteousness. "If Israel makes a Biblical claim to the Holy Land, then Israel must adhere to Biblical standards of national righteousness. Land promises are by-products of a covenant with God."[592] The land given to the Jews, from a political agreement among the nations was not actually purchased, but conquered as a result of war. This has been one of the driving points between the Arabs and Jews since the UN mandate. Will Israel be able to maintain control of the land without a spiritual renewal as suggested by Feinberg, or some kind of restitution toward the Palestinian Arabs?

References from the Torah concerning aliens are relevant to the Zionist goal. "So show your love for the alien, for you were aliens in the land of Egypt."[593] Would the Arab population living in Palestine during the War of Independence be considered aliens, or Canaanites? "He executes justice for the orphan and the widow, and shows His love for the alien by giving him food and clothing."[594] God gave victory to the Jews and at least part of the Zionist dream was realized, but not the whole dream; just as the Jews of old, upon conquering the land of Canaan, failed to complete the conquest. "Now these are the nations which the LORD left, to test Israel by them . . . ."[595] The fact that many Arabs remained in Palestine can also challenge the patience of Israeli Jews today.

The question of restitution has been raised numerous times over the past sixty years. Among many Jewish and Christian Zionists little thought is given to the situation of Palestinian refugees. According to many Zionists, Palestinians left on their own cognizance and it was the responsibility of the Arab community to take care of them; this did not happen leaving no resolution to the refugee problem. Israel and its Jewish leaders will not take responsibility for those left without homes. The Christian community cannot walk away from those needing assistance. Christians of all stripes, Zionist and non-Zionists must reach

---

592 Burge, *Whose Land? Whose Promise? What Christians Are Not Being Told about Israel and the Palestinians,* 12.
593 (Deuteronomy 10:19)
594 (Deuteronomy 10:18)
595 (Judges 3:1)

out to the refugee community in a cooperative relationship with Israeli Jews. While Arab countries evicted close to the same number of Jews from Arab lands as Palestinians left Palestine, the refugees still living in and around Israel must be helped.[596]

Accountability carries with it the necessity of regarding the land of Palestine. Abraham gives a good illustration, the father of both Arabs and Jews, sought to buy land from the Canaanite Ephron the Hittite, as a burial plot for Sarah his wife. Though the Canaanites offered to give him the plot, Abraham was not willing to take it without paying. The illustration also applies to King David who wanted to purchase Mount Moriah from the Jebusite, Ornan. David refused to accept, saying, ". . . for I will not take what is yours for the LORD, or offer a burnt offering that cost me nothing."[597] David purchased that ground for the Temple and in doing so, honored God. The question of both Jewish and Christian integrity can be raised by this issue; since both Jews and Christians are to be lights to the nations.[598] From a Biblical perspective, the promise of the land to the Jews as an inheritance would require some restitution for the Jews to remain. "To mistreat the alien by taking his land places Israel's inheritance in jeopardy."[599] From this Biblical perspective, neither God's promises nor his judgments can be taken lightly.

The idea of judgment upon the nation of Israel is the implication made by Burge. This suggests the possibility of Jews being " . . . spewed out of the Land."[600] The other possibility is the one suggested previously by Charles Feinberg who suggested that Israel would not be a spiritual

---

596   Christian Organizations active on behalf of Palestinian refugees: Evangelicals for Middle East Understanding, World Vision International.
597   (I Chronicles 21:24)
598   References to being lights: Old Testament reference (Isaiah 49:6); New Testament reference (Luke 2:32)
599   Burge, *Whose Land? Whose Promise? What Christians Are Not Being Told about Israel and the Palestinians*, 92.
600   (Leviticus 20:22-26)

people when they enter Israel.[601] This can be illustrated by the story of God's promise to bless Jacob and not Esau. Though God promised that the younger Jacob (later called Israel) would receive the birthright, it was through deceit that the inheritance was gained. There was no righteousness in this act; however, Jacob was successful. So too, were the Jews successful in gaining back the land of Palestine through war. Montefiore weighs in on whether Israel is worthy to receive God's blessing. "Israel is not worthy of the divine favors. It does not deserve restoration of prosperity. But Yahweh, in despite of strict justice, will, nevertheless, bring about an era of happiness and national well-being in the ancestral land."[602] Reasons given are not a result of strict justice as suggested by Burge. "For His honor and His glory, which are inseparably bound up with Israel, inasmuch as, through the God of the whole world,"[603] is inseparable. It would appear from the Old Testament text that Israel has a special place in God's program in spite of it failures.

The downside to any injustice is a fitting consequence such as experienced by Jacob. Jacob indeed gained the birthright and the inheritance, however, the outcome in the long term resulted in Jacob being deceived by his Uncle Laban, and later paying restitution to Esau for fear of his life. In like manner, the results of Israel's battle with the Arabs for the land resulted in their conquest, and gaining a portion of the land of Palestine; the down side is the continued unrest and threat of war. Israel has seen little rest in the past sixty plus years of their existence.

Zionism sought independent sovereignty and achieved it. Nationalism is inclusive, bringing some unity and order to Palestine. Zionism, however, tends to move toward exclusiveness; thus it separates and differentiates between ethnicity and culture. What is ironic within the Jewish community, is that culture tends to be, on the most part, very secular and Western. Jewishness does not rest solely on its cultural underpinnings, as mentioned earlier (Kosher Laws, Jewish Festivals, and

---

601 The reference to Israel is compared to Zechariah 14 and God's assembling the nation of Israel.
602 Montefiore, *The Old Testament and After*, 63.
603 Montefiore, *The Old Testament and After*, 63.

history), but it does reflect a passionate identity that ties the community together in ways that go beyond the rational. Those Biblical ties are not easily explained and may defy secular theorists an easy explanation. These ties are exclusive by nature and may explain one reason the Jews resist Christianity with such passion and have maintained their distinctive identities over the millennium.

Issues Today Between Jews and Christians

Putting the economic and scientific benefits of the Jews to the side, the curious conflict between Jews and Christians moved well past a strictly religious or faith arena. The conflict has moved into the social and political arena of moral and ethical ideas. Many of these ideas were founded on the Jewish moral law, the same law many secular Jews have themselves abandoned, or at least failed to support. This does not necessarily mean that all Jews and all Christians are in conflict in modern times. The secularization of religious institutions seems to have brought more harmony than the common ground of religious idealism or Zionism. Never the less, the Zionist cause has been common ground between Orthodox Judaism and Evangelical or Fundamentalist Christianity for centuries. While early Orthodox Judaism resisted Zionism, believing it not necessary for a strictly Messianic redemption, the early Fundamentalist Christians (Puritans) embraced Zionism (Restorationism) as necessary.

Zionism's contribution to Jewish-Christian relationships boils down to the foundational reason for the rise of Zionism within the Jewish community at the end of the nineteenth century; it provided a safe haven for the Jews. Though Christians were a part of the Restorationist (Zionist) movement throughout the history of the Jews, at least since the Puritans, through the Pogroms of Eastern Europe and the events of the Dreyfus Affair, leadership within the Jewish community was pushed to take action on behalf of the Jewish community at large. After more than a century of emancipation and assimilation, it became apparent that the Jews were not being treated as equals at least within Eastern and Central

Europe (including Germany). This was the perspective of many Jewish Zionist leaders.[604]

Little effort was made by Jews prior to the first Zionist Congress in 1897, the Christian community was in some form or fashion working on behalf of the Jews for 300 years. The major problem was the lack of trust that still existed between the Jewish and Christian communities at the end of the nineteenth century. Many Jews still suspected that Christians only wanted to get rid of the Jews rather than seeking their best interests. A second question was the difference in spiritual perspective. Christians carried a more eschatological orientation to the Zionist issue. Jews were much more grounded on a physical earthly kingdom. Little connection was made between the two views. The difference between the physical and the spiritual is extenuated in the Christian message of an eternal spiritual existence as opposed to the Jewish view of earthly success. For many Jews it seems the conflict could not be resolved.

Zionism as a movement stems from the desire to gain some security from the Gentile and Christian communities within both Eastern and Western Europe. Even in the United States, Anti-Semitism existed and gave some credence to the need for a safe homeland for the Jews. This desire for some semblance of security and peace can be traced back to the basic purpose of the Jewish ghettos of the Middle Ages. They separated and protected the Jews from Gentile and Christian influence. Zionism in a sense became a return to the ghetto and a rejection by some of assimilation and emancipation.

Many Christians such as Blackstone, Herzl, Wedgwood, and even Balfour himself gave assistance and encouragement to the Jewish desire for independence and peace. The Christian community was supportive of Zionism not only for spiritual reasons, but for the practical realization of the Biblical predictions for the restoration of Jews to the ancient land of Israel (today's Palestine). According to conservative Christians, these can be attributed only to the hand of God, demonstrating the reliability of the Biblical account and giving credibility to its historical roots. In this sense, Zionism was self-serving in that it provides the fundamentalist

---

604 These Zionist leaders include Moses Hess and Theodor Herzl.

Christian community with a prophetic apology concerning the return of the Jews to the Holy Land.

Jewish Success

Jews have contributed well beyond their numbers to science, literature, entertainment and business helping Western civilization benefit in extraordinary ways. Any list of Nobel Prize winners will demonstrate an unusually high proportion of Jewish winners; Rabbi Levi Brackman states: "Thirty percent of Nobel Prize winners in science are Jewish, ..."[605] Jewish contribution can be documented in many fields. Much of our economic strength and success in the West was the output of Jewish enterprises. The Jews have contributed enormously toward Industrial growth in the United States over the past century. One case in point was the contributions made by Albert Einstein.

The Biblical account gives us a hint to the possibilities of future hope; that through Abraham's seed the Jews, ". . . all nations of the earth will be blessed."[606] From a Christian perspective this is often interpreted to reference Jesus, the Christian Jewish Messiah. It is true that through the Christian message, the God of Israel has become the God of the nations as the message has traversed the entire world. Even many within the Jewish community have accepted Him. The other side of that blessing can be seen through Jewish contributions to civilization that have had profound effects on the development of mankind. Though Jewish-Christian relationships have suffered under the guise of Jewish rebellion against a Jewish Messiah, the problem can also be attributed to the failure of the Gentile community to recognize the blessing potential of the Jews who have succeeded in every venue of life. Even the most

---

605 Brackman, Rabbi Levi. "Why Jew are disproportionally successful." *Jewish World*, (Sept. 5, 2008). http://www.ynetnews.com/articles/0,7340,L-3592566,00.(accessed Oct. 5, 2013); www.jewcy.com/category/arts-and-culture/page/265?page=7 (accessed Oct. 5, 2013).

606 (Genesis 18:18)

effective witnesses to the Christian faith are often time Jews.[607] Theodor Herzl recognized the status of Jewish entrepreneurship over 100 years ago. "The world is provoked somehow by our prosperity, because it has for many centuries been accustomed to consider us as the most contemptible among the poverty-stricken."[608] The Christian community would benefit by being more understanding in their treatment of Jews. Eckardt stresses the importance of kindness exhibited between Christians and Jews. "Christians are to behave toward Jews in a good neighborly way—with friendliness, helpfulness, and tolerance."[609] All people deserve consideration.

Jewish Successes and Intolerance

Class envy could be described as one of the motives for anti-Semitism, at least in the past. Using the famous businessman's Henry Ford's letter, ". . . the Jews are a very successful people. They are gifted with the ability to overcome, to find a way to success in the midst of any obstacle."[610] Ford's statement gives some insight on Jewish perseverance and entrepreneurship. In addition to any commercial or political pressures placed against Jewish successes, the Church resisted the Jews, because they were unwilling to conform to Gentile culture. The light of both Judaism and Christianity had grown dim as a result, leading to, "The revival of anti-Semitism, which brought the Jew moral expulsion from Europe, gave new meaning and purpose to an ancient hope. . . . The world will be freed by our liberty. . . . enriched by our wealth, and magnified by our greatness."[611] "This reawakened spirit of

---

607   "Jews for Jesus," a present day mission group, has a worldwide outreach ministry not only to Jews but Gentiles as well.
608   Herzl, *The Jewish State*, 27.
609   Arthur Roy Eckardt, *Elder and Younger Brothers: The Encounter of Jews and Christians* (New York: Schocken Books, 1967), 33.
610   The Ford International Weekly, *The Dearborn Independent*, May 22, 1920. (accessed Sept 24, 2013).
611   Herzl, *The Jewish State*, 79.

nationalism, firing the most vigorous elements in Jewish life, gave birth to modern Zionism, one of the miracles of modern history."[612] Herzl's statement is indicative of Jewish entrepreneurship that has made the Jewish people an example of success in whatever enterprise they have invested. Zionism is an offshoot of the Jewish will to survive in spite of any obstacles.

The Jews have had to battle for their place in society within nearly every culture in which they have lived. They tried hard to be optimistic within their adopted countries. Through emancipation, they most often identified themselves with liberal and radical parties to fight against injustices, hoping always that history would not repeat itself. Sachar summarizes the reality of Jewish influence. "Yet in every political and economic crisis a whole nation lost its equilibrium, and the most elementary rights of the Jews, rights taken for granted by every self-respecting person, became woefully insecure."[613] Throughout most of history, the Jews found little peace among the nations, even as the nations struggled to find a place for the Jews. It is these factors that contributed to the rise of Zionism and clarifies the purpose of the Zionist zeal within Israel today.

Jewish-Christian Relationships Today

Several questions arise when speaking of Jewish-Christian relationships today. Roy Eckerdt brings some insights to light, when he suggests that Jewish-Christian relationships are the products of a contrasting paradox. "Jesus of Nazareth called the Christ embodies the paradox of uniting Jews with Christians and of separating Jews from Christians. Any discussion of the Jewish-Christian relationship must presuppose both elements in this ultimate tension."[614]

Eckerdt suggests that both the merging and the separation of Jews, and Christians are part of the larger purpose. To maintain that, it is not

---

612 Sachar, *A History of the Jews*, 349.
613 Sachar, *A History of the Jews*, 344.
614 Eckerdt, *Elder and Younger Brothers*, 142.

possible at this time for Jews and Christians to completely reunite as the product of Old and New Testament theology. The return of the nation Israel is also a product of that division. Israel must remain a separate entity consisting of Jews, and Gentiles (Arabs). Israel has never been solely Jewish, and it is doubtful it ever will be. The history of Israel has always maintained a mixture of Jews and Gentiles in its population.

Jewish-Christian relationships in our culture today have many factors that go well beyond the Zionist question. Zionism has served as one vehicle over the centuries that brought Christians and Jews together into a common cause. The land of Israel is precious to both Christians and Jews, being the land of promise and future hope, in both Christianity, and Judaism. Other commonalities are the religious heritage of the Old Testament which serves as foundational for both faiths. The Biblical foundations serve to give Jews and Christians a purpose and a goal. Both groups claim to be the children of God and set apart for a higher purpose.[615] Though each claim gravitates toward exclusivity, it does not totally exclude the possibility that God has a distinct purpose for both Jews and Christians. As for ethnicity, both Judaism and Christianity are comprised of both Jews and Gentiles, neither is exclusive.

Jewish-Christian relationships are both strengthened and hindered by the Zionist cause. Israel has come to depend heavily upon the support of Evangelical Christians today. Many organizations such as Christian Coalition of America, CFOIC, IFCJ,[616] and others having Jewish-Christian ties exist with the express purpose of funneling money to Israel. Christian Zionists are perhaps the most ardent supporters of Israel today and give nearly unconditional support to the Nation of Israel and its Jewish enterprise.

The other side of the Zionist coin brings a much deeper conflict between the Christian and Jewish communities that did not exist before.

---

615   To both Jew and Gentile who receive Jesus Christ. (John 1:12). Israel as the people of God, (Judges 20:2). A reference to both Jews and Gentiles, (Hebrews 4:9).
616   CFOIC: Christian Friends of Israel Communities; IFCJ: International Fellowship of Christians and Jews.

The Ultra-Orthodox community of Jews within Israel sprang up from the remnants of traditional Judaism gaining a strong foothold within modern day Israel. Though Israel today is very secular with nearly 70% of the population being predominantly secular, Orthodox Judaism has become the national religion exerting a strong influence in the Knesset today. This influence gives very little room for religious diversity, giving preference to Jews and Judaism within Israeli society in conflict with liberal ideologies.

Zionism is connected to the Jewish-Christian debate intrinsically through the events of Israel's development from a prophetic thought until today. The existence of Israel came in part through the Christian community. The realization of a Jewish homeland came through political means in the form of the Balfour Agreement. Though weak in its structure, giving equal concern for the indigenous Arab community, it provided a framework for the further development of the Zionist dream from within Palestine. Without Balfour and the other Christian contributors to this agreement, the door may not have been opened, or at least not until much later.

Throughout the history of Israel, the Christian community, at least within the evangelical ranks has been perhaps the strongest ally of the continuation of the Zionist state, with its strong eschatological foundation. This perspective, however, gives little encouragement to many Jews within Israel, suggesting an ending that many Jews do not like to consider - Judgment. For the Christian and Jew, the ending would result in the restoration of Israel not only as a nation, but the head of all the nations as suggested by Jeremiah 3:17. The idea of Christianity still does not resonate with the average Jew, even though the hostility is not what it once was. Though the doors of dialogue are opened more to the Christian community, the idea of evangelism is resisted and denounced within the Jewish community in general.

Jewish-Christian Relationships and Zionism

Christian Zionists today are in sync with many of the current ideological goals of Israel to hold the land while keeping the Arab Palestinian community in check. However, the bitterness created by Jewish & Christian opposition of Palestinian Arabs to keep the land defies a Biblical mandate to, " Go therefore and make disciples of all the nations baptizing them in the name of the Father and the Son and the Holy Spirit, . . ."[617] From a New Testament perspective as well as the Old Testament, the God of the Bible seeks and desires ". . . all men to be saved and to come to the knowledge of the truth."[618] not just the Jews. For the Christian, their concern cannot be just for Israel and the Jews. From this context, the Christian must also be responsible for the well being of the Arab community as well as the Jewish community in Israel.

While many Jews and Christians are in agreement concerning Jewish rights to Palestine as an eternal inheritance, the extent of Jewish Christian harmony is limited to the support for the state of Israel and little more. Most Jews still do not trust Christians; this goes for both religious and secular Jews. Though Zionism is one of the limited areas where both communities agree. That connection is tied almost exclusively to the continued need for economic and political support of the Christian community for Israel. Secular Jews still resist Christian influences in the culture that would break down separation of Church and State. Fears of Christian discrimination are still too strong a memory for many secular Jews.

Zionism succeeds to a large extent in bringing the Jewish community together. The primary concern for many Jews is economic support along with survival of the predominantly Jewish state of Israel. As previously discussed, the Christian community is more divided on the issue of Zionism. Though many Christians are unconditional in their support for Zionism, many conservative Christians are interested in the safety and well being of Israel for the eschatological support it gives

---

617 (Matthew 28:19)
618 (I Timothy 2:3-4) In the Old Testament: (Ezekiel 18:23); The entire book of (Jonah)

biblical Christianity. For other Christians, Zionism creates a human rights problem yet to be resolved concerning the Palestinian Arab refugee problem. The Palestinian-Christian community is in agreement with the Muslim Palestinians that Zionism was a Nikba (catastrophe). The events leading to the establishment of the nation of Israel through the Zionist venture has brought economic prosperity to the Middle East at least for the Jewish population but has done little to bring peaceful relations between Palestinian Christians, Palestinian Muslims, Arabs in general, and the Jews.

CONCLUSION

The initial premise upon which this book was intended, anticipated that Zionism contributed to closer ties between Jews and Christians. As a result of this research, that postulate has been revised. Zionism or the Zionist movement has had little effect on Jewish-Christian relationships. In a sense, Zionism is a movement away from closer Jewish-Christian ties as Israel seeks to distance itself from Christian influence other than those that provide for economic benefits. Meanwhile deep-seated suspicions between Christians and Jews have softened over the past 300 years due to several other factors such as emancipation, assimilation, education, and participation within the greater secular societies of the West and East. The failure of emancipation to grant European Jews the security they sought opened the doors wide for a Zionist solution. Christian contributions to the eventual success of the Zionist movement in gaining a homeland in Palestine have been offset by the failures of the church during the harshest periods of Jewish persecution.

For some (Jews), nothing will bridge the gap of mistrust of Christians. "The Jews have nothing to apologize for to the Christians, since nothing that we can do will ever expiate their sins."[619] As a result of this mistrust of Christians in the aftermath of the Holocaust, and European Pogroms, the Jewish community within Israel has become less open to Christian influences, most prominently Messianic Jews who threaten the concept that Jews could be both Christian and Jewish. At the same time, Christians carry a lingering mistrust of Jews who deny the tenants of the Christian faith.

The history of the Jewish-Christian relationship has been a rocky road over the past two thousand years. Jews have demonized the Christian Church and the person of Jesus Christ since the first century while the Church has tried to convert the Jews without much success, even to the point of forced conversions (Spanish Marranos). Though

---

619 Urofsky, *We are One: American Jewry and Israel*, 150.

hostilities became great, one of the few points in which both groups agreed was that one could not be both a Jew and a Christian; this concept translated into a total separation between Judaism and Christianity. That position is being challenged today by Messianic Jews who adopted New Testament Christianity while following Jewish law, a reflection of the first century Jewish church.

The Zionist movement, instigated early on by Christians, was not accepted by most Jews until after Theodor Herzl initiated the Zionist congress in 1897. Jews, however, were still slow in adopting any Zionist philosophy. Events of the nineteenth century, East European Pogroms, and twentieth century Nazi persecution of the Jews awoke many Jews to the need for a Jewish homeland. "Americas five million Jews had been indifferent to Zionism until the late 1930's."[620] The Holocaust inadvertently salvaged Jewish support for the Zionist movement.

The Jews sought to enter Palestine by legal market participation, but were restricted by Ottoman, British, and Arab resistance. Wealthy Jewish investors such as Montefiore and Rothschild along with others purchased some land prior to World War I, but laws were enacted preventing or limiting Jewish land purchases keeping the Palestinian Arabs in firm control of 75% of Palestine up to Jewish Independence in 1948. Except for some wealthy Palestinian Arabs, the indigenous population of Palestinians had little interest in opening their land to Jewish immigration. The thirty years between the two wars demonstrated the depth of hostility that developed between the Arabs and Jews. The UN mandate was given against all rationale that the two cultures and peoples would merge or live peacefully side by side.[621] A unified country

---

620   Urofsky, *We are One: American Jewry and Israel*, 3.

621   This reference is to the Peel Commission which recommended in 1937 to abandon the British mandate for two separated Partitions separating Jews from Arabs. Google Site "Palestine Royal Commission Report pdf.", (July 1937). www.unispal.un.org/UNISPAL.NSF/0/88A6BF6F1BD82405852574CD006C457F

seemed impossible; even in partition there seemed little likely success to completely divide the people of Palestine. For the Zionist Jews as well as Arabs, war was inevitable.

Israel was established upon a strong military presence from near the beginning of the British Mandate (1917). Ze'ev Jabotinsky raised the stakes through revisionist Zionism, moving Palestinian Jews toward a stronger defensive posture and closer to armed conflict instigated through numerous Arab riots. Jewish terrorist organizations, such as Lehi and Ingram, were coordinated with the Haganah, contending with both Arabs and the British even as Britain was entering World War II. Zionist leaders were conscious of world opinion regarding terrorist connections and sought to distance themselves from events such as Deir Yassin and the growing refugee problem prior to Independence. Both groups (Lehi and Ingram), were pardoned after Independence and each of their leaders eventually became prime ministers of Israel.

The objective as stated by Herzl for the Zionist movement and an independent state was to secure a safe haven for the persecuted Jews of Eastern Europe. Even though the land (Palestine), was eventually secured from the Arabs through war, and security measures taken, the safe haven has yet to be completely realized. Mistrust remains between Jews and Arabs. Palestinian Arabs continue to resent Jews for taking their land, while causing a mass exodus of Palestinian refugees out of Palestine. The Arab community became united upon the issue of solving the Palestinian refugee problem, while doing little to bring the issue to a close among the Arab peoples. "That is why the Palestinians today are almost entirely dependent on American, European and Japanese money for survival."[622] The backlash of war, intifadas and terrorist attacks reflect those attitudes while the Arab Palestinian refugee problem remains.

---

622 Toameh, Khaled Abu. "What Do Wealthy Arab Really Care About." *Gatestone Institute International Policy Council,* (July 29, 2011). www.gatestoneinstitute.org/2303/23ql5y-arabs. (accessed Oct. 6, 2013).

In spite of early Jewish disinterest, Christian contributions to the Zionist movement were critical to its success in bringing about the nation of Israel. Major events, such as the Balfour Declaration, the British Mandate, and President Harry Truman's influence on the UN mandate to partition the land of Palestine, can be attributed to Christian values that carried significant political weight. President Truman was driven by personal conviction to support Israeli partition in 1947, and was first to recognize the state of Israel. "He agreed with his whole heart . . ."[623] the necessity of partition and recognition of the Israeli state. Support of the Christian community from Blackstone, Hechler, and Westcott contributed to the advancement of the Zionist cause leading to the eventual success of an Independent Jewish state. However, it was not until the Jews took the reins of the Zionist cause for themselves in the form of political secular Zionism, that it began to move progressively forward, culminating in the eventual war for Independence, and the establishment of a national Jewish homeland (Israel) in Palestine.

In contrast, the West gave little support to Jews during the growing Nazi persecution. This trend continued during the Holocaust and the early struggle for Jewish Independence. Those nations in the West which confessed at least a form of Christian faith, such as Britain, Canada, and the United States maintained harsh restrictions on immigration preventing Jews in Central and Eastern Europe from immigrating to the West contributing to the severity of the Holocaust. Britain maintained blockades to Palestine, in the effort to prevent Jews from being smuggled into Palestine, in accordance to the Peel commission limitations. "This high level (immigration) should be fixed for the next five years at 12,000 per annum."[624] The Jews needed to evacuate hundreds of thousands from Europe. Christians took much of the blame for these events (indicated through the Biltmore Hotel conference May 1942).

---

623 McCullough, *Truman*, 612.
624 Peel Commission Report, Chapter X, Immigration. "Palestine Royal Commission Report pdf.", (July 1937). www.unispal. un.org/UNISPAL.NSF/0/88A6BF6F1BD82405852574CD006C457F

Britain, in the beginning of the mandate, supported the idea of a Jewish state (Balfour Declaration), and did little to restrain conflict as the British Mandate came to a close, allowing atrocities by both Jews and Gentiles within Palestine. The promise, made under the Balfour Declaration, was but a promise that the British were never able to completely uphold. Christian influences were cast aside in preference to political necessity and reality, as the management of Palestine became unmanageable for the British.

Following the tragedy of the Holocaust, and the failure of the Christian community to support the Jews in their darkest hour, the United Nations with influence from the United States under Truman's support, took stock of the Jewish condition in Europe accepting partition and the concept of a Jewish state in Palestine. Through the new UN mandate, Zionism became a call for restitution for many Christians, but the beginning of a nightmare, for the Palestinian Arab community. The Palestinian Arabs did little to help their cause, as they contributed little to the War effort for Britain. In addition, Palestinian Arab leadership sided with the Nazis pushing Palestinian Arab interest out of favor among the Alliances.

Jews, who were able to immigrate into Palestine, during the British Mandate, brought their education and skills, which brought prosperity and productivity to the region. Arab leadership along with Arab labor/workers were fearful of Jewish development, even though it brought economic benefits. Among the Palestinian Arabs, there were few competitive enterprises; in addition, there was no comparable Arab developmental plan among the Arab nations, which were themselves in the infancy of their national development. The Jews represented a threat to their way of life and livelihood, in spite of the economic benefits to the Palestinian people. In addition, the British, who were more interested in protecting their interests in the region, were fearful of disrupting Arab interests, and displayed little confidence in Jewish development, which thus resulted in the response of the various White Papers (White Papers generally restricted Jewish immigration and land purchases).

During the course of history, the Gentile community fought Jewish exclusiveness tied into Judaism, and Jewish entrepreneur successes. This course of action by religious, political, and private entities both within and outside the Church created hardships for the Jews. In spite of Arab riots and British restrictions, Jewish entrepreneurship thrived in Palestine, proving both the British and Arabs wrong in their assessments of potential Jewish development. Learsi gives an example of Jewish productivity. "In the first three years of the War (WWII) the value of the industrial products manufactured by the Yishuv (Jewish community in Israel) for the military increased twelvefold."[625] As it stood, Jewish business sense provided thousands of jobs for the Arabs as well as opportunities for Jewish immigrants who brought many of the skills necessary for industrial expansion. Besides the many hardships experienced by the Jews, by the 21st century, Israel became an economic power in the Middle East. As stated in Time Magazine, Israel is, " . . . second only to the U.S. in companies listed on the NASDAQ exchange."[626] Israel is in the process of becoming a world economic power through innovation and business success.

Jewish successes in business and science give some support to the Biblical account of a future hope; " . . . all nations of the earth will be blessed."[627] From a Christian perspective, this is a reference to Jesus as the Jewish Messiah. Though many Jews have resisted this reference to Jesus; the God of Israel has become the God of all nations, as the message has traversed the entire world. Even many within the Jewish community have accepted the New Testament account. The other side of that blessing can be seen through Jewish contributions to civilization that have had profound effects on the development of mankind. As previously stated, the innovative ability of Jewish entrepreneurs far exceeds the typical numbers of any particular people group.

For Israeli Jews today, maintaining political control is vital to the continued success of the Zionist enterprise. Palestinian Arabs continue

---

625 Learsi, *Fulfillment, The Epic Story of Zionist*, 321.
626 Vick, Karl. "The Good Life and Its Dangers," *Time Magazine*, (September 13, 2010): 39. (accessed August 10, 2013).
627 (Genesis 18:18)

to be a threat, as increasing birthrates by far favor Palestinian Arabs. The contrast between Arab and Jewish birth rates puts Israeli Jews in a defensive position, to maintain a strong majority and political control. For Israeli leadership, marginalizing and removing Palestinian Arabs in Palestine is necessary in maintaining a strong Jewish majority. As a result of these fears, Palestinian Arabs are now in the process of being evicted from their homes in various places of Israel. Laws exist that prevent Arabs from purchasing land owned by Jews. This condition is a direct result of Israeli fears that Palestinian Arabs will eventually gain a majority within Israel. For Jewish Israeli leadership, this cannot be allowed to happen. The historical equivalent would be the rapid birthrates that characterized the Jewish population in Egypt prior to the biblical Exodus. Egypt was fearful of Jewish population growth. "But the sons of Israel were fruitful and increased greatly, and multiplied, . . ."[628] Those tables are now turned, in modern day Palestine.

Zionism sought independent sovereignty and achieved it, raising nationalism and a pride in Israel as a Jewish state. It is inclusive to Jews but not Palestinian Arabs, bringing some unity and order to Palestine. Zionism tends to move toward exclusiveness, thus separating and differentiating between ethnicity and culture even among Jews. Being Jewish in Israel does not rest solely on its ethnic or cultural underpinnings. Even Gentiles who convert to Judaism carry almost a second class citizenship. Within the Jewish community, culture tends to be on the most part, secular and Western. In spite of it predominant secular flavor, Orthodox Judaism along with Kosher Laws, Jewish Festivals and Jewish history have taken a prominent place in society, leaving Israeli Arabs without any recognized history in Palestine. Zionism reflects a passionate identity that ties the community together in ways that go beyond the rational. Biblical ties to Sinai carry significant weight, are not easily explained, and may defy secular theorists an easy explanation. These ties are exclusive by nature and may explain one reason the Jews resist Christianity with such passion, and have maintained their distinctive identities over the millennium.

---

628   (Exodus 1:7)

Catholics, Orthodox, Protestants, and Evangelicals have all contributed to the mistrust between Christians and Jews. Most Jews will not make the distinction between factions within Christianity. In many cases, Jews make little distinction between Gentiles and Christians. Jewish fears of Gentiles in general and Christians specifically have had a strong effect on Zionist motives to reestablish Palestine as a national homeland. In a sense, the Jews have returned to the ghetto of their own making. Even the construction of the "Apartheid" Barrier Wall "fence", around the West Bank of Israel, is used to separate the Israelites from the Arab Palestinian Gentiles. In retrospect, but because of differing circumstances, this wall is similar to the Nazi built walls that separated Jews from Gentiles prior to and during World War II.

Stereotypes creep into Jewish-Christian relationships from both communities. As Jews condemn the Christian community for their failures from the Crusades on through the Holocaust, thousands of Christians reached out to rescue Jews during both these times in history, with little recognition by the Jewish community. In the same way, many Christians have stereotyped Jews with deceptive business practices, when in reality success in any venture requires a diligence to work and detail that typifies any success in life. In many cases, political and economic persecutions have been committed by individuals having little or no real Christian commitment. Perceptions from both communities may need some corrective lenses.

The Zionist dream has drawn Jews and Christians together in the common goal of establishing a Jewish homeland; it has also served to separate and divide. How Israeli Jews treat Palestinian Arabs is a key factor in that division. The Jews gained their homeland in Palestine during a time of universal goodwill following the events of the Holocaust, much of that good will has been spent as a result of the continuing Jewish-Arab conflict.

Messianic Judaism presents a conflict within Israel as do Christians in general. Unless they possess a marketable skill, Christians are welcome to Israel as volunteers and as tourists but not as welcome members of society. Freedom of religion is limited to Judaism, proselytizing is discouraged. In contrast, Messianic Judaism presents a challenge to the notion that Christians cannot be both Jewish and Christian. The rapid growth of the Messianic Church in the Diaspora and Israel presents a threat to many Jews wishing to maintain separation between Christians and Jews. Messianic Jews tend to be passionate in their faith and like any indigenous people, they communicate most effectively to their own community as the most effective witnesses to the Christian faith among Jews are Jews.[629] While many secular Jews have become more open to issues of their ancestral faith, Orthodox and Ultra-Orthodox Judaism have become a powerful force pushing for legislation limiting access of other faiths.

While Israel is pushing for stronger Jewish ties to Jewish culture and its historic faith, Diaspora Jews are facing a more challenging fate. The Jewish community in America is in the midst of major change as assimilation is increasing rapidly." Overall, the intermarriage rate is at 58 percent, up from 43 percent in 1990 and 17 percent in 1970. Among non-Orthodox Jews, the intermarriage rate is 71 percent.[630] The relevance of Jewish faith is being continually diminished and replaced by secularism. The successes of the Jewish community within the Diaspora contributed to its slide away from Judaism and into secularism and materialism.

The Jews possess the foundations of the Christian faith; all the connections that explain the Messianic hope are found in Judaism, along with the celebrations that refer to the promise of a redeemer. The Messianic hope is yet to be realized among the Jews, yet for the Christian

---

[629] *Jews for Jesus* Volume 10:5772 (June 2012) http://www.jewsforjesus.org (accessed Oct. 1, 2013). This magazine has a worldwide outreach ministry not only to Jews but Gentiles as well. Each of their magazine's speak to this issue. Jews for Jesus International Headquarters, San Francisco, CA.

[630] Heilman, Uriel. "Pew Survey of U.S. Jews: Soaring Intermarriage, Assimilation Rates*." JTA: The Global Jewish New Source*. (October 1, 2013). http://www.jta.org/2013/10/01/news-opinion/united-states/pew-survey-u-s-jewish-intermarriage-rate-rises-to-58-percent. (accessed Oct. 5, 2013).

community, that piece of the puzzle has taken shape. According to the New Covenant (New Testament) God's provision for man (Jew and Gentile) was covered on the Cross by a Jew.

" . . . for salvation is from the Jews."[631] The Christian gospel carries the message of redemption to the world. Judaism remains more exclusive, the expectation being that Gentiles must become Jews. The first century church was Jewish while Gentiles were able to participate without becoming Jewish. Though years of struggle and persecution have existed for the Jews, maintaining a Jewish group of people has been a critical mandate.

Zionism carries with it the promise of the land. The Holy Land is essential to all the world monotheistic faiths. It is based on the promise of the restoration of the land, which is yet incomplete according to many Jews. The land is in the midst of trials as Zionism has yet to obtain the goal of peace. Zionists will continue to battle for that precious commodity, as that goal seems ever elusive. For Christians, Zionism is a divisive issue; for most Catholics, Zionism is a neutral issue with the primary concern for the Arab Catholic community. For mainline Protestants, as well as a growing number of Evangelical Christians, justice for Arabs is important The more conservative Christians generally contend along with most Zionist Jews that all Palestine belongs to the Jews as an eternal birthright. This ever changing landscape gives no guarantee for a peaceful future for land of Israel.

The hope that Jews and Christians could come together in a common goal is still in doubt. It would seem that secularism, first through emancipation and then through assimilation has done more to bring Jews and Gentiles closer together than either religion or Zionism. Zionism, hopes for the peace of Jerusalem and the restoration of the people of God; both Jews and Christians are still in the process of seeking a common solution to this hope. The Arab Palestinian community both Christian and non-Christian is dealing with the bitter realities of losing their land and their hope. The Biblical promises as seen in Isaiah present a hope that all nations will come together in (Zion) Jerusalem. According

---

631 (John 4:22)

to biblical promises, Jews and Christians will eventually be in unity as one people of God. Both Judaism and Christianity hold to a Messianic promise. With that hope, the final piece of the puzzle (the Messianic hope) would be realized by all, and the restoration of the land would be complete. The goal of peace in the Middle East would be accomplished and God firmly established on the throne of all those who put their trust in God. On this point both Jews and Christians can agree, " Pray for the peace of Jerusalem (Zion): May they prosper who love you. May peace be within your walls, And prosperity within your palaces."[632]

---

[632] (Psalms 122:6,7)

BIBLIOGRAPHY

Adelman, Jonathan. *The Rise of Israel: A History of Revolutionary State*. New York: Routledge Taylor & Francis Group, 2008.

Armstrong, Karen. *Holy War: The Crusades and Their Impact on Today's World*. New York: Anchor Books, Random House, 2001.

Avineri, Shlomo. *The Making of Modern Zionism The Intellectual Origins of the Jewish State*. New York: Basic Books Inc., 1981.

Avishai, Bernard. *The Tragedy of Zionism How Its Revolutionary Past Haunts Israeli Democracy*, New York: Helios Press, 2002.

Begin, Menachem. *The Revolt*. Plainview, New York: Nash Publishing Corporation, 1978.

Ben-Gurion, David. *Israel: A Personal History*. New York: Funk & Wagnalls Inc. 1st ed. June 1971.

Ben-Gurion, David. *Israel: Years of Challenge*, New York: Henry Holt & Company Inc. 1st ed. June 1963.

Bible, Ryrie, Charles. *New American Standard Edition*, Chicago: Moody Press. 1995 Update.

Burge, Gary. *Whose Land? Whose Promise? What Christians Are Not Being told about Israel and the Palestinians*. Cleveland, OH: Pilgrims Press, 2004.

Chazan, Roberts. *In the Year 1096 . . . The First Crusade & the Jews*. Philadelphia, PA: The Jewish Publication Society, 1996.

Clark, Victoria, *Allies for Armageddon: The Rise of Christian Zionism*. New Haven, CN: Yale University Press, 2007.

Cohen, Israel. *A Short History of Zionism*. London: Frederick Muller Ltd., 1951.

Cohen, Richard. *Vision and Conflict in the Holy Land*. Jerusalem: Yac Ben-Zvi and St. Martin's Press, 1985.

Congdon, Jim, ed. *Jews and the Gospel at the End of History*. Grand Rapids, MI: Kregel Pub., 2009.

Conway, John S. *The Nazi Persecution of Churches, 1933-45*. Vancouver BC.: Regent College Publishing 1997.

(The) Dearborn Independent, (The Ford International Weekly). "International Jew, the World's Foremost Problem." Series of news articles by Henry Ford, published from May 22 to October 2, 1920. Dearborn, Michigan: Dearborn Pub. Co., 1920. General Collections (135).

Durant, Will and Ariel. *Heroes of History: A Brief History of Civilization from Ancient Times to the Dawn of the Modern Age*. New York: Simon Schuster Publishing, 2001.

Durant, Will and Ariel. *The Story of Civilization*; *The Age of Reason Begins*. New York: Simon Schuster Publishing, 1961.

Eckardt, Arthur Roy. *Christianity and The Children of ISRAEL*. Morningside Heights, N.Y: King's Crown Press, 1948.

____. *Elder and Younger Brothers, The Encounter of Jews and Christians*. New York: Schocken Books, 1967.

Einstein, Albert. *Out of My Later Years*. Estate of Albert Einstein, 1956. New York: Edition by Open Road Integrated Media, 2011.

Enelow, Gerson. *A Jewish View of Jesus*. Biblio Life, 1901, New York: Macmillan, Reprint 1912.

Epp, Theodore H. *Portraits of Christ in the Tabernacle*. Lincoln, NE: Back to the Bible Publishers, 1976.

Epstein, Lawrence J. *Zion's Call*. Lanham, MD: University Press of America, Inc., 1984.

Feinberg, Charles L. *The Minor Prophets*. Chicago, IL: Moody Press, 1951.

Friedman, Saul S. *No Haven for the Oppressed; United States Policy Toward Jewish Refugees, 1938-1945*. Detroit, MI: Wayne State University Press, 1973.

Goldberg, Michelle. *Jews and the Christian Right: Is the honeymoon over?* Salon online magazine, www.salon.com. Tuesday, November 29, 2005, 6:00AM, CST.

Gordis, Daniel. *Home to Stay: One American Family's Chronicle of Miracles and Struggles in Contemporary Israel*. New York: Three Rivers Press, 2003.

Gordis, Robert. "The Rabbi", *National Jewish Monthly*, (July-August, 1957).

Halpern, Ben. *The Idea of the Jewish State*. Cambridge, MA: Harvard University Press,1969. (Harvard Middle Eastern Studies 2nd ed. 1969).

Hart, Alan. *Zionism: The Real Enemy of the Jews, Vol.1, The False Messiah*. Atlanta, GA: Clarity Press, 2009.

____. *Zionism: The Real Enemy of the Jews, Vol.2, David Becomes Goliath*. Atlanta, GA: Clarity Press. 2009.

Hazony, Yoram. *The Jewish State: The Struggle for Israel's Soul*. New York: Basic Books, 2000.

Hertzberg, Arthur, ed. *The Zionist Idea: A Historical Analysis and Reader*. New York: Doubleday & Co. Inc. Herzl Press, Garden City, 1959.

Herzl, Theodor. *Complete diaries of Theodor Herzl*. New York: Scopus Publishing, 1941.

____. *The Jewish State.* Original 1896. Adapted from edition published in 1946 by The American Zionist Emergency Council. PDF e book by http://www.MidEastweb.org.

Jacobs, Joseph. *Jewish Contributions to Civilization.* Philadelphia: Jewish Publication Society of America,1919. http://books.google.com/books/about/Jewish_contributions_to_civilization.html?id=4dopAAAAYAAJ

Jocz, Jakob. *The Jewish People and Jesus Christ After Auschwitz: A Study in the Controversy Between Church and Synagogue.* Grand Rapids, MI: Baker Book House, 1981.

____. *The Jewish People and Jesus Christ: The Relationship between Church and Synagogue.* Grand Rapids, MI: Baker Book House, 1979.

Juster, Dan. *Jewish Roots A Foundation of Biblical Theology.* Shippensburg, PA: Destiny Image. Pub., Inc., 1995, 1st ed. 1986.

Kenny, Anthony J. *Catholics, Jews and the State of Israel.* Mahwah, NJ: Stimulus Books, 1993.

Kinzer, Mark S. *Israel's Messiah and the People of God: A Vision for Messianic Jewish Covenant Fidelity.* Eugene, OR: Cascade Books, 2011.

Klausner, Joseph. *Jesus of Nazareth: His Life, Times and Teaching.* London: George Allen & Unwin LTD, Ruskin House, 1925. Reprint 1997.

Koehn, Ile. *Mischling Second Degree My Childhood in Nazi Germany.* New York: Greenwillow Books, 1977.

Klinghoffer, David. *Why the Jews Rejected Jesus.* New York: Doubleday Random House, 2006.

Kohn, Hans. "Zion and the Jewish National Idea." New York: Menorah Association, *The Menorah Journal*, Autumn-Winter 1958.

Laqueur, Walter. *A History of, Zionism: From the French Revolution to the Establishment of the State of Israel* New York: Schocken Books Inc.,1972 reprint 2003.

Learsi, Rufus. *Fulfillment, The Epic Story of Zionist.* New York: World Publishing, 1951.

Lewis, Geoffrey. *Balfour and Weizmann: The Zionist, the Zealot and the Emergence of Israel.* London: Continuum Books, 2009.

Lipis, Joan R. *Celebrate Passover, Haggadah, A Christian Presentation of the Traditional Jewish Festival.* San Francisco, CA: Purple Pomegranate Productions, 2000.

Lowdermilk, Walter Clay. *Palestine, Land of Promise.* New York: Harper & bros. 2nd ed., 1944.

Luther, Martin. *The Jews and Their Lies (1543).* Edited and copywriter Coleman Rydie. www. lulu.com, cdrydie@ hotmail.com, 2009. ID 6147320. ISBN 978-0-557-05023-9.

May, Melanie A. *Jerusalem Testament: Palestinian Christians Speak, 1988-2008.* Grand Rapids, MI: Eerdmans Pub. Co., 2010.

McCullough, David. *Truman.* New York: Simon & Schuster, 1992.

McDowell, Josh. *More Evidence that Demands a Verdict.* San Bernadino, CA: Campus Crusade for Christ International, 1977 Fourteenth printing.

Menuhin, Moshe. *Decadence of Judaism in Our Time.* Lebanon, Beirut: Institute for Palestinian Studies, 1969.

Metaxas, Eric. *Bonhoeffer Pastor, Martyr, Prophet, Spy.* Nashville, TN: Thomas Nelson Pub., 2010.

Montefiore, Claude. *The Old Testament and After.* London: Macmillan & Co., 1923.

Morris, Benny. *1948: A History of the First Arab Israeli War.* New Haven, CN: Yale University Press, 2008.

____. *Righteous Victims A History of the Zionist-Arab Conflict 1881-2001.* New York: Vintage Books, (rev. ed. 2001).

Moshe Menuhin, *London Jewish Chronicle,* (July 31, 1964).

Neumann, Michael. *The Case Against Israel.* California: CounterPunch & AK: Press, 2005.

(The) New Bible Commentary: Revised, Ed. D. Guthrie, J.A. Motyer, A.M. Stibbs, D.J. Wiseman, Leicester, England: Inter-Varsity Press, 1986.

Pappé, Ilan. *The Ethnic Cleansing of Palestine.* Oxford, England: Oneworld Publications, 2006.

Palumbo, Michael "The Palestinian Catastrophe", *Al HaMishmar,* (April 5, 1985).

Pinsker, Leo. *Auto-Emancipation.* London: 1932 translated by D.S. Blondheim, ed. A.S. Super. New York: Maccabaean Pub. Co.1906.

Radosh, Allis and Ronald. *A Safe Haven Harry S. Truman and the Founding of Israel.* New York: Harper Collins Pub., 2009.

Raheb, Mitri. *I am a Palestinian Christian.* Translated by Ruth C. Gritsch. Minneapolis, MN: Fortress Press, 1995.

Rausch, David A. *Legacy of Hatred: Why Christians Must Not Forget the Holocaust.* Grand Rapids, MI: Baker Publishing Group, 1990.

Resnik, Rabbi Russell. *Gateways to Torah: Joining the Ancient Conversation on the Weekly Portion.* Clarksville, MD: Lederer Books, Messianic Jewish Publishers, 2000.

Rosen, Moishe. *Y'shua: The Jewish Way to Say Jesus.* Chicago, IL: Moody Bible Press, 1982.

Rosenblum, Mort. *As tensions rise, violence increases, Jews fear 'new' anti-Semitism.* Des Moines, IA: Associated Press, Des Moines Register, Dec. 7, 2003.

Rosenthal, Marvin J. *Not Without Design.* West Collingswood, NJ: The Friends of Israel, Gospel Ministry, Inc., 1980.

Ruether, Rosemary. *Faith and Fratricide: The Theological Roots to Anti-Semitism.* New York: Seabury Press, 1974.

Sachar, Abram Leon. *A History of the Jews.* New York: Alfred A. Knopf Pub., 1967.

Sachar, Howard M. *A History of Israel from the Rise of Zionism to Our Time.* New York: Alfred A. Knoff Inc. Pub. Distributed: Random House, 1979.

Sand, Shlomo. *The Invention of the Jewish People.* Translated by Yael Lotan. New York: Verso Books, 2009.

Schaeffer, Edith. *Christianity is Jewish.* Carol Stream, IL: Tyndale Pub. 1975.

Schäfer, Peter. *Jesus in the Talmud.* Princeton, NJ: Princeton University Press, 2007.

Shalom, Zaki. *David Ben-Gurio, The State of Israel, and the Arab World, 1949-1956.* Brighton and Portland: Sussex Academic Press, 2002.

Sharfman, Glenn. "Jewish Emancipation." http://www.ohio.edu/chastain/ip/jewemanc.htm, November 4, 2005.

Shlaim, Avi. *The Iron Wall: Israel and the Arab World.* New York: W.W. Norton & Company, 2001.

Snaith, Norman H. *The Jews from Cyrus to Herod.* Nashville TN: Abindon Press, 1956.

Snyder, Louis. *The Making of Modern Man: From the Renaissance to the Present.* New York: Van Nostrand Co., 1967.

Stein, Joshua B. *Our Great Solicitor: Josiah C. Wedgwood and the Jews.* Selinsgrove, PA: Susquehanna University Press, 1992.

Stern, David H. *Restoring the Jewishness of the Gospel.* Jerusalem: Jewish New Testament Pub., 1988.

Stifan, Naim. *A Palestinian Christian Cry for Reconciliation.* Maryknoll, New York: Orbis Books, 2008.

Studd, C.T. Poem by missionary C.T. Studd lived 1860-1931. "Only One Life, Twill Soon be Past." Multiple web sites can be used to find this, one of which is www.susanskitt.com.

Telchin, Stan. *Betrayed.* Grand Rapids, MI: Baker Publishing Group, Chosen Books, 2004.

_____. *Messianic Judaism Is Not Christianity: A Loving Call to Unity.* Grand Rapids, MI: Baker Publishing Group, Chosen Books, 2004.

Time Magazine, New York, NY: September 13, 2010.

Thomas, Gary. *The Return of the Jewish Church.* Carol Stream, IL: Christianity Today (Magazine), April, 1998.

Truman, Harry S. *Memoirs of Harry S. Truman Volume Two: Years of Trial and Hope.* New York: Smithmark Publishers Inc., 1996.

Tucker, Ruth. *Not Ashamed: The Story of Jews for Jesus.* New York: Random House, 2011.

Urofsky, Melvin. *We Are One: American Jewry and Israel,* Norwell, MA: Anchor Press Inc., 1978.

Vital, David. *Global Politics Essays in Honor of David Vital.* London: Frank Cass, 2001.

———. *The Origins of Zionism.* Oxford: Claredon Press, 1980.

———. *Zionism: The Crucial Phase.* New York, NY: Commentary Magazine, August, 1988.

———. *Zionism: The Crucial Phase.* Oxford: Claredon Press, 1987.

———. *Zionism: The Formative Years.* Oxford: Claredon Press, 1982.

Weizmann, Chaim. *Trial and Error.* New York: Harper and Brothers, 1949, reproduced 1972.

Williams, Vernon J. *Rethinking Race.* Lexington, KY: University Press of Kentucky, 1996.

Youssef, Michael. Radio broadcast: Program "Leading the Way." (via American Family Radio) June 13, 2011.

Zuck, Roy B. *A Biblical Theology of the Old Testament.* Electronic ed. Chicago, IL: Moody Press, 1991; Published in electronic form by Logos Research Systems, 1996, S. 343.

SOURCES CONSULTED

DISSERTATIONS:

Ajken-Klar, Emma Jo. *Remembering Zion: Jewish Diasporic Identify on a Canadian University Campus,* Diss., Canada: University of Toronto, 2008.

Sadeh, Eligar. *Militarization and State Power in the Arab-Israeli Conflict: Case study of Israel, 1948-1982.* Diss., Jerusalem: Hebrew University, 1994.

Silsby, Susan P. *Antonius: Palestine, Zionism, and British Imperialism, 1929-1939.* Diss., Washington D.C.: Georgetown University, 1986.

Umoren, Gerald Emen, Romae, apud Pont. *The Salvation of the Remnant in Isaiah 11:11-12: An Exegesis of a Prophecy of Hope and Its Relevance Today.* Diss., Universitatem s. Thomae, 2006.

ONLINE RESOURCES:

http://www.aish.com

http://www.amnesty.org

http://www.answers.com

http://www.commentarymagazine.com

http://www.defencejournal.com/2001/october/roots.html.

http://www.emeu.net   Online source for Evangelical Venture International Organization.

http://endtimesmadness.com/CZandMJ.html

http://www.gatestoneinstitute.org

http://www.haaretzdaily.com/ Daily news for World financial and business news. Information of events throughout Israel and the Middle East.

http://www.ifcj.org

http://www.jewishmag.com

http://www.jewishvirtuallibrary.org

http://www.jewishvirtuallibrary.org/jsource/History/balfour.html

http://www.jewsforjesus.org

http://www.jpost.com/ChristianInIsrael/Features/Article.aspx?id=185477

http://www.jta.org

http://www.leadingtheway.org

http://www.lightofmessiah.org

http://www.mideastweb.org/181.html

http://www.NYTimes.com, New York Times (newspaper).

http://www.ohio.edu/chastain/ip/jewemanc.html Glenn Sharfman, *Jewish Emancipation*.

http://www.ourjerusalem.com/history/story/history20020124.html Arnold Fine, Jewish Press January 18, 2002.

http://www.palestinefacts.org/of-mandate-whitepaper-1922.php.

http://www.plato.stanford,edu/entries/scholem Gershom Scholem, Stanford Encyclopedia of Philosophy, April, 10.2008.

http://www.princeton.edu/research/cases/campdavid/pdf.

http://www.religionfacts.com/judaism/denominations/reform

http://www.search.archives.jdc.org/multimedia/documents/ny_ar_45-54.pdf.

http://www.unispal.un.org

http://www.unrwa.org

http://urj.org/about/union/leadership/rabbijacobs/?syspage=article&item_id=90580

http://ventureint.org/irr.html

http://wiki.answers.com/Q/FAQ/7415-6

http://www.wordiq.com/definition/List_of_Jews_by_country Columnist Sultan Ahmed, The roots of terrorism (Arab perspective).

http://www.ynetnews.com

http://www.zionism-israel.com/bio/kalischer_biography.html

MARK ALAN ANDERSON

PERSONAL
Birthplace
Oakland, Nebraska, USA

EDUCATION
Bachelor of Arts in Education
Wayne State College,
Nebraska 1976

Masters of Science
Fort Hays State University,
Kansas 1982

Masters of Arts in Religion
Trinity Evangelical Divinity
School, Illinois 1988
(Trinity International
University)

CERTIFICATES AND LICENSURE
Certificate in Biblical Studies
Trinity Evangelical Divinity School, Illinois 1982

French Language Certificate
Bethel Bible College Sherbrooke Quebec 1989

Certificate of Commission
Evangelical Free Church Mission 1989

Master Educator License
State of Iowa - Active in 2013

EMPLOYMENT
Ottumwa High School Technology Teacher
1991 to Present

Missionary to Africa, Bible & Technology Institutes Zaire Africa
1987 to 1992

High School Technology Teacher - several schools
in Nebraska & Kansas
1976 to 1989

MEMBERSHIPS
Evangelical Free Church

Evangelical Free Church Overseas Mission

Christian and Missionary Alliance

Christian Education Association

Iowa Industrial Technology Association

Youth For Christ Board

CPSIA information can be obtained
at www.ICGtesting.com
Printed in the USA
FFOW01n2108200814
6984FF